MINORITY SERVING INSTITUTIONS

America's Underutilized Resource for
Strengthening the STEM Workforce

Lorelle L. Espinosa, Kent McGuire, and Leigh Miles Jackson, *Editors*

Committee on Closing the Equity Gap: Securing Our STEM
Education and Workforce Readiness Infrastructure
in the Nation's Minority Serving Institutions

Board on Higher Education and Workforce
Policy and Global Affairs

A Consensus Study Report of

The National Academies of
SCIENCES · ENGINEERING · MEDICINE

THE NATIONAL ACADEMIES PRESS
Washington, DC
www.nap.edu

THE NATIONAL ACADEMIES PRESS   500 Fifth Street, NW   Washington, DC 20001

This activity was supported by contracts between the National Academy of Sciences and the ECMC Foundation (unnumbered award), the Helmsley Charitable Trust (Award # 2016PG-EDU026), the Alfred P. Sloan Foundation (Award # G-2016-7134), the W.K. Kellogg Foundation (unnumbered award), and the Wallace Foundation (unnumbered award). Any opinions, findings, conclusions, or recommendations expressed in this publication do not necessarily reflect the views of any organization or agency that provided support for the project.

International Standard Book Number-13: 978-0-309-48441-1
International Standard Book Number-10: 0-309-48441-3
Digital Object Identifier: https://doi.org/10.17226/25257

Additional copies of this publication are available for sale from the National Academies Press, 500 Fifth Street, NW, Keck 360, Washington, DC 20001; (800) 624-6242 or (202) 334-3313; http://www.nap.edu.

Printed in the United States of America

Suggested citation: National Academies of Sciences, Engineering, and Medicine. 2019. *Minority Serving Institutions: America's Underutilized Resource for Strengthening the STEM Workforce*. Washington, DC: The National Academies Press. doi: https://doi.org/10.17226/25257.

The National Academies of
SCIENCES · ENGINEERING · MEDICINE

The **National Academy of Sciences** was established in 1863 by an Act of Congress, signed by President Lincoln, as a private, nongovernmental institution to advise the nation on issues related to science and technology. Members are elected by their peers for outstanding contributions to research. Dr. Marcia McNutt is president.

The **National Academy of Engineering** was established in 1964 under the charter of the National Academy of Sciences to bring the practices of engineering to advising the nation. Members are elected by their peers for extraordinary contributions to engineering. Dr. C. D. Mote, Jr., is president.

The **National Academy of Medicine** (formerly the Institute of Medicine) was established in 1970 under the charter of the National Academy of Sciences to advise the nation on medical and health issues. Members are elected by their peers for distinguished contributions to medicine and health. Dr. Victor J. Dzau is president.

The three Academies work together as the **National Academies of Sciences, Engineering, and Medicine** to provide independent, objective analysis and advice to the nation and conduct other activities to solve complex problems and inform public policy decisions. The National Academies also encourage education and research, recognize outstanding contributions to knowledge, and increase public understanding in matters of science, engineering, and medicine.

Learn more about the National Academies of Sciences, Engineering, and Medicine at **www.nationalacademies.org**.

The National Academies of
SCIENCES · ENGINEERING · MEDICINE

Consensus Study Reports published by the National Academies of Sciences, Engineering, and Medicine document the evidence-based consensus on the study's statement of task by an authoring committee of experts. Reports typically include findings, conclusions, and recommendations based on information gathered by the committee and the committee's deliberations. Each report has been subjected to a rigorous and independent peer-review process and it represents the position of the National Academies on the statement of task.

Proceedings published by the National Academies of Sciences, Engineering, and Medicine chronicle the presentations and discussions at a workshop, symposium, or other event convened by the National Academies. The statements and opinions contained in proceedings are those of the participants and are not endorsed by other participants, the planning committee, or the National Academies.

For information about other products and activities of the National Academies, please visit www.nationalacademies.org/about/whatwedo.

COMMITTEE ON CLOSING THE EQUITY GAP: SECURING OUR STEM EDUCATION AND WORKFORCE READINESS INFRASTRUCTURE IN THE NATION'S MINORITY SERVING INSTITUTIONS

Members

LORELLE L. ESPINOSA (*Co-Chair*), Vice President for Research, American Council on Education

KENT MCGUIRE (*Co-Chair*), Program Director of Education, William and Flora Hewlett Foundation

JIM BERTIN, Math Instructor, Chief Dull Knife College

ANTHONY CARPI, Dean of Research, Professor, Environmental Toxicology John Jay College, CUNY

APRILLE J. ERICSSON, New Business Lead, Instrument Systems and Technology Division and Aerospace Engineer, Technologist, Project and Program Manager, National Aeronautics and Space Administration Goddard Space Flight Center

LAMONT HAMES, President and CEO, LMH Strategies, Inc.

WESLEY L. HARRIS, Charles Stark Draper Professor of Aeronautics and Astronautics, Massachusetts Institute of Technology

EVE HIGGINBOTHAM, Vice Dean, Office of Inclusion and Diversity, Penn Medicine and Senior Fellow, Leonard Davis Institute for Health Economics and Professor of Ophthalmology, Perelman School of Medicine, University of Pennsylvania

SPERO M. MANSON, Distinguished Professor of Public Health and Psychiatry, Director, Centers for American Indian and Alaska Native Health, Colorado School of Public Health at the University of Colorado Denver and The Colorado Trust Chair in American Indian Health, Colorado School of Public Health, Anschutz Medical Center

JAMES T. MINOR, Assistant Vice Chancellor and Senior Strategist for Academic Success and Inclusive Excellence, California State University

LEO MORALES, Professor and Chief Diversity Officer, School of Medicine and Adjunct Professor, Health Services, School of Public Health, University of Washington

ANNE-MARIE NÚÑEZ, Associate Professor, Department of Educational Studies, The Ohio State University

CLIFTON POODRY, Senior Science Education Fellow, Howard Hughes Medical Institute

WILLIAM SPRIGGS, Chief Economist, American Federation of Labor— Congress of Industrial Organizations, Professor, Department of Economics Howard University

VICTOR TAM, Dean, Science, Technology, Engineering, and Mathematics, Santa Rosa Junior College

CRISTINA VILLALOBOS, Myles and Sylvia Aaronson Professor, School of Mathematical and Statistical Sciences, University of Texas Rio Grande Valley

DOROTHY C. YANCY, President Emerita of Johnson C. Smith University and Shaw University

LANCE SHIPMAN YOUNG, Associate Professor and Chair, Department of Chemistry, Morehouse College

Study Staff

LEIGH MILES JACKSON, Study Director
BARBARA NATALIZIO, Program Officer (*September 2017–June 2018*)
IRENE NGUN, Research Associate (*until June 2017*)
AUSTEN APPLEGATE, Senior Program Assistant
ADRIANA COUREMBIS, Financial Officer
THOMAS RUDIN, Board Director, Board on Higher Education and Workforce

Consultants

ANDRÉS CASTRO SAMAYOA, Lynch School of Education, Boston College
MARYBETH GASMAN, University of Pennsylvania, Center for Minority Serving Institutions
DESHAWN PRESTON, Morehouse School of Medicine
MATTHEW SOLDNER, Commissioner, National Center for Education Evaluation and Regional Assistance
MORGAN TAYLOR, Senior Policy Research Analyst, American Council on Education
PAULA WHITACRE, Full Circle Communications

Preface

Research suggests that the cultural diversity of a nation's workforce is a key factor in its ability to innovate and compete in a global economy. This report on the role of Minority Serving Institutions (MSIs) in creating a diverse science, technology, engineering, and mathematics (STEM) workforce is motivated by the realization that the United States is unlikely to maintain its competitive advantage in STEM without the contributions that these institutions are uniquely positioned to make. As such, the purpose of this committee's work was to better understand contributing factors to the success and challenges that MSIs face in recruiting, retaining, and graduating students of color who are prepared to enter the STEM workforce. We further sought to identify the actions that those in the public and private sectors need to take to ensure the success and sustainability of the more than 700 MSIs that exist today, with the understanding that many more will emerge in the coming decades given our country's demographic changes.

More specifically, our charge was three-fold, to (1) identify model programs with demonstrated evidence of success; (2) examine the challenges MSIs face in preparing scientists, engineers, and other STEM professionals; and (3) surface the institutional components for scaling and sustaining effective policies and practices in STEM education. In response, we analyzed and synthesized the available evidence and highlight in the report effective and promising practices on how MSIs are bolstering success (e.g., through enrollment, persistence, retention, degree attainment, and employment) for students seeking STEM degrees and credentials.

Through visits to a sample of MSIs, the committee explored with administrators, faculty, and students, the strategies they pursue in preparing STEM professionals. The committee examined the prevailing evidence on federal, state, and institutional policies that support such strategies, and collected data on institutional profiles of select MSI sectors and their contributions to their communities. Based on this evidence, the committee offers a series of findings, conclusions, and recommendations that aim to support the expansion of effective practices, and the study of promising ones, such that both can be scaled and thus reach more institutions and their students.

In the body of this report are actions we think will focus, and increase, financial and other investments in MSIs in ways that produce strong *returns*, thus benefiting students, MSIs, their communities, the national workforce, and the overall economy. It is our hope that these recommendations will be taken on their merits and used as guideposts in efforts to improve STEM education and workforce pathways for MSI students, whatever the stakeholder vantage point— institutional leader, faculty member, business and industry partner, public official, philanthropic contributor, advocate, or student.

As with any study, there are limitations, and we had our share. Chief among them is the very limited, rigorous research available on MSIs generally, but especially knowledge that sheds light on how these institutions organize, deliver, and support learning opportunities for students of color in STEM. The committee reviewed all of what is available but acknowledged the fact that the strength of the evidence, especially regarding program effectiveness, varies widely. The breadth of MSI institution types and contexts is a strength of the MSI community, but proved a challenge given the committee's charge. Available time and resources limited the committee's ability to explore fully the rich diversity of institutional forms, missions, and socio-historical contexts that make up this set of institutions.

One of the ways we sought to overcome these limitations was to invite comment and testimony from a broad range of MSI constituencies, advocates, and beneficiaries, and to visit a diverse set of MSIs for on-the-ground observations and information gathering. We learned a great deal from the public forums, and these insights have found their way into various chapters of this report, including our recommendations; we thank all who engaged the committee for their contributions. The time we spent in the field, learning about the intentionality with which MSIs work to prepare and graduate STEM professionals, was singularly important to completing our charge. We cannot thank enough the leadership, faculty, staff, students, and alumni of the colleges and universities we visited. Committee members were warmly received and the visits well organized. We recognize how much time and effort is involved in preparing for curious visitors with many questions about what you do and how you do it. The context and perspective the institutions provided was nothing short of invaluable.

This has been a collective effort, and thanks go to the very hard work of our committee. It has been a joy and a great privilege to work with such a knowledgeable and committed group of individuals. You have contributed in immeasurable ways to this important effort, and we cannot thank you enough for your time and attention. We next appreciate greatly the support of the sponsors of this study, which include the Alfred P. Sloan Foundation, ECMC Foundation, Helmsley Charitable Trust, Wallace Foundation, and W.K. Kellogg Foundation. This work would not have been possible without the broad philanthropic support we received, and we hope our recommendations will be useful as ways to advance interests in STEM education are considered.

Finally, we cannot say enough about the dedication and hard work of the National Academies leadership and committee staff. It is through a combination of delicate pressure and strong support that we have emerged with this report. We are all indebted to Board on Higher Education and Workforce Director Tom Rudin for taking on the important charge of examining the role of MSIs in preparing a diverse STEM workforce. To Senior Program Officer and Study Director, Leigh Miles Jackson, thank you for seeing us through the arduous and rigorous process through which all study committees go. We could not have done this without you. Additional thanks to Program Officer Barbara Natalizio and Senior Program Assistant Austen Applegate for their contributions.

In the end, we feel confident that this report adds to the much-needed conversation about how this country strengthens its STEM workforce and clarifies the central role of MSIs in meeting this challenge. The available data presented here make clear that this conversation is in need of more voices and subsequent action. It also illustrates the central role of MSIs in meeting our nation's education and workforce goals. To restate the obvious, we will not meet these goals without them.

> Drs. Lorelle L. Espinosa and Kent McGuire,
> *Co-Chairs,* Committee on Closing the Equity Gap:
> Securing Our STEM Education and Workforce
> Readiness Infrastructure in the Nation's Minority
> Serving Institutions

Acknowledgments

This report reflects contributions from a number of individuals and groups. The committee takes this opportunity to recognize those who so generously gave their time and expertise to inform its deliberations.

To begin, the committee would like to thank the sponsors of this study for their guidance and support. Support for the committee's work was generously provided by the Alfred P. Sloan Foundation, ECMC Foundation, Helmsley Charitable Trust, Wallace Foundation, and W.K. Kellogg Foundation.

The committee greatly benefited from the opportunity for discussion with individuals who attended and presented at the open session meetings (see Appendix B), as well as with the leadership, faculty, staff, students, and alumni at the nine MSIs it visited (see Appendix C). The committee is thankful for the many contributions of these individuals.

The committee could not have done its work without the support and guidance provided by the National Academies project staff: Leigh Miles Jackson, study director; Barbara Natalizio, program officer; and Austen Applegate, senior program assistant.

We appreciate Adriana Courembis for her financial assistance on this project, and gratefully acknowledge Tom Rudin of the Board on Higher Education and Workforce for the guidance he provided throughout this important study.

Many other staff within the National Academies provided support to this project in various ways. The committee would like to thank the executive office staff of Policy and Global Affairs, as well as Marilyn Baker, Karen Autrey, and Rita Johnson for the management of the report review and publication process. We would like to thank Jorge Mendoza-Torres and the National Academies

Research Center staff for their assistance in the committee's research efforts, and the National Academies Press staff.

This committee is grateful to the research and writing consultants that generously contributed to this body of work. We thank the committee's consultants Marybeth Gasman (University of Pennsylvania's Center on Minority Serving Institutions) and Andrés Castro Samayoa (Boston College), Matthew Soldner (American Institutes of Research), and DeShawn Preston (Morehouse School of Medicine) for their invested time and support of this study. We thank Katherine Hale, Darius Singpurwalla, and Daniel Foley (National Science Foundation), Lance Selfa and colleagues (NORC at the University of Chicago), and Katherine Cardell (American Indian Education Consortium) for their generous assistance with data collection and analyses. We are particularly grateful to Morgan Taylor (American Council on Education) for her expertise, assistance, and support throughout the study process. And to the leadership, faculty, staff, students, and alumni of the colleges and universities we visited, we thank them for their gracious hospitably and for the context and perspective they provided.

Finally, the committee is indebted to Paula Whitacre (Full Circle Communications) for her valuable commissioned work, Jay Labov for his expertise and advice, and Heather Phillips for her editorial assistance in preparing this report.

Acknowledgment of Reviewers

This Consensus Study Report was reviewed in draft form by individuals chosen for their diverse perspectives and technical expertise. The purpose of this independent review is to provide candid and critical comments that will assist the National Academies of Sciences, Engineering, and Medicine in making each published report as sound as possible and to ensure that it meets the institutional standards for quality, objectivity, evidence, and responsiveness to the study charge. The review comments and draft manuscript remain confidential to protect the integrity of the deliberative process.

We thank the following individuals for their review of this report: Carlos Castillo-Chavez, Arizona State University; Kevin Christian, American Association of Community Colleges; James Dalton, U.S. Army Corps of Engineers; Timothy Fong, California State University, Sacramento; Noël Harmon, Asian and Pacific Islander American Scholarship Fund; Tatiana Melguizo, University of Southern California; John Moder, Hispanic Association of Colleges and Universities; Christine Nelson, University of Denver; Ivory Toldson, Howard University; Hannah Valantine, National Institutes of Health; Lydia Villa-Komaroff, Intersections SBD; and Darrell Warner, The Boeing Company.

Although the reviewers listed above provided many constructive comments and suggestions, they were not asked to endorse the conclusions or recommendations of this report nor did they see the final draft before its release. The review of this report was overseen by Marigold Linton, University of Kansas and Alan Leshner, American Association for the Advancement of Science. They were responsible for making certain that an independent examination of this report was carried out in accordance with the standards of the National Academies and that all review comments were carefully considered. Responsibility for the final content rests entirely with the authoring committee and the National Academies.

Contents

Appendixes

Boxes, Figures, and Tables

BOXES

FIGURES

TABLES

Summary

Twenty-first century advances require the United States to expand its science, technology, engineering, and mathematics (STEM)-capable workforce, both in terms of the quantity and diversity of the individuals who enter these fields and in the quality of their contributions. In fact, evidence suggests that the nation will need 1 million *more* STEM professionals than it is on track to produce in the coming decade.

Fortunately, the United States has two valuable and underutilized resources to help ensure its global preeminence in STEM productivity and innovation. The *first* national resource is the more than 20 million young people of color[1] in the United States whose representation in STEM education pathways and in the STEM workforce is still far below their proportions of the general population. The impact of this underrepresentation is critical to understand, given the imminent transition toward a non-White majority in the United States. **A clear takeaway from the projected demographic profile of the nation is that the educational outcomes and STEM readiness of students of color will have direct implications on America's economic growth, national security, and global prosperity.** Accordingly, there is an urgent national need to develop strategies to *substantially* increase the postsecondary and STEM degree attainment rates of Hispanic, African American, American Indian, Alaska Native, and underrepresented Asian American students.

---

[1] This number represents 15- to 24- year olds and includes residents of Hispanic and non-Hispanic origin, excluding non-Hispanic Whites, U.S. Census Bureau, Population Division, Annual Estimates of the Resident Population by Sex, Age, Race, and Hispanic Origin for the United States and States: April 1, 2010 to July 1, 2017.

Efforts to boost the number of students of color in the STEM workforce are not new. Previous studies conducted by the National Academies and other organizations have underscored this urgency. This new study builds on and extends that work by recognizing the educational and economic contributions of a *second* national resource, the nation's more than 700 Minority Serving Institutions (MSIs) and their collective potential to help strengthen, expand, and diversify the rapidly evolving STEM workforce.

Two- and four-year MSIs enroll almost 5 million students, or nearly 30 percent of all undergraduates enrolled in U.S. higher education. Although these institutions have long provided pathways to educational success and workforce readiness for millions of nontraditional students and students of color (e.g., African American, American Indian, Alaska Native, Hispanic, and underrepresented Asian American students), their contributions to STEM education and the workforce are often overlooked. In fact, more undergraduate students (from all backgrounds) are enrolled in STEM fields at four-year MSIs than at four-year non-MSIs, and when taken together, Historically Black Colleges and Universities, Hispanic Serving Institutions, and Asian American and Native American Pacific Islander-Serving Institutions produce one-fifth of the nation's STEM bachelor's degrees.[2] Moreover, the individual contributions of these institutions to STEM degree completions (measured as a proportion of all completions) are on par with non-MSIs. In terms of student outcomes, a growing body of literature demonstrates that students who matriculate at MSIs do as well, or even better, than those who attended non-MSIs, particularly when it comes to individual income mobility. **This evidence suggests that MSIs are valuable resources for producing talent to fulfill the needs of the nation's current and future STEM workforce.** See Box S-1 for an overview of MSIs and their students.

STUDY CHARGE

In response to the nation's need to strengthen, expand, and diversify its STEM-capable workforce, the National Academies of Sciences, Engineering, and Medicine have undertaken a series of efforts, including creation of the Committee on Closing the Equity Gap, to focus on securing the nation's STEM education and workforce readiness infrastructure in MSIs. The sponsors of this study, the Alfred P. Sloan Foundation, the ECMC Foundation, the Helmsley Charitable Trust, the Wallace Foundation, and the W.K. Kellogg Foundation, charged the committee to review the goals, successes, and challenges of MSIs and to identify the most promising programs and effective strategies that they use to increase the quantity and quality of their STEM graduates. In accordance with the statement of task, this report provides an overview of the seven federally recognized types of MSIs,

---

[2] Based on most recently available data from 2016.

BOX S-1
An Overview of Minority Serving
Institutions and Their Students

Minority Serving Institutions (MSIs) are ubiquitous in America's higher education landscape, while at the same time representing a diverse set of institutions with as many similarities as differences. MSIs encompass two-year and four-year, public and private, rural, urban, and suburban institutions, enrolling from a few hundred to tens of thousands of students, and representing a range from highly selective to open-access institutions. MSI students are also not a monolithic group—varying in terms of race and ethnic origin, but also age, economic backgrounds, and enrollment intensity (i.e., attending school as full- or part-time status). MSI students are more likely than those at non-MSIs to be the first in their family to attend college, and are more likely to come from low-income backgrounds than are students who attend Predominantly White Institutions, both private and public.

Two types of MSIs bear a historical designation to serve a specific groups of students: Historically Black Colleges and Universities and Tribal Colleges and Universities. Other MSIs qualify for designation by the U.S. Department of Education through their enrollment and expenditure thresholds—meaning they serve a defined number of students of color and often do so with limited resources. Enrollment-designated MSIs include Hispanic-Serving Institutions, Asian American and Native American Pacific Islander-Serving Institutions, Predominantly Black Institutions, Alaska Native-Serving Institutions or Native Hawaiian-Serving Institutions, and Native American-Serving Nontribal Institutions. The number of enrollment-designated MSIs—and thus the number of students served by them—has grown significantly in the past 20 years. As the country's demographics continue to change, many more MSIs can be expected to emerge in the coming decades, reflecting their increasingly diverse surrounding communities.

MSIs with a mission-driven, intentional focus to support the success of their STEM students strive to maintain an effective *balance* by employing diverse faculty and staff, providing environments that customize student learning and cultivate leadership skills, and offering role models of various ethnic backgrounds, while also ensuring that the institution, faculty, and students are equipped to meet the high standards and expectations for quality in STEM teaching, learning, and research.

describes MSIs' student populations, reviews the nation's current investments in MSIs, and examines *what works* at MSIs, particularly the under-resourced MSIs, to overcome long-standing challenges and expand educational opportunities for their students. Much has been written about the nation's MSIs in the past three decades, including numerous reports on the challenges that these institutions face. In contrast, this committee also examined the evidence base behind effective strategies and practices used by many MSIs to overcome those challenges and, by doing so, expand educational opportunities for their students.

PROMISING PRACTICES AND STRATEGIES TO
SUPPORT THE SUCCESS OF MSI STUDENTS

In its review of MSIs' most promising programs, policies, and practices
to support their students, the committee identified a common thread that distinguishes the most successful efforts from other initiatives: *intentionality*. For
purposes of this report, the committee defines intentionality as *a calculated and
coordinated method of engagement by institutions, agencies, organizations, and
private investors to effectively meet the needs of a designated population within
a given higher education institution*. Intentionality in this context translates to the
creation of tailored initiatives, policies, and practices that meet students where
they are in their college careers academically, financially, and socially, while
doing so with cultural mindfulness that moves students toward higher levels of
academic achievement and self-confidence.

With intentionality as an overarching principle, and with a deliberate focus
on what works at MSIs, the committee explored how this principle manifests
itself in programs currently implemented at these institutions. These selected
programmatic, institutional, and/or national initiatives are highlighted throughout
the report, with particular emphasis on six programs that serve as illustrative examples: (1) Achieving the Dream, (2) the Alaska Native Science and Engineering
Program, (3) A Student-Centered ENtrepreneurship Development (ASCEND)
program, (4) the Building Infrastructure Leading to Diversity initiative, (5) the
Louis Stokes Alliances for Minority Participation program, and (6) Math Engineering Science Achievement.

The diversity of the programs reviewed, in terms of structure, scale, goals,
and funding, demonstrates that there is no one-size-fits-all formula to foster
success. In reviewing the strategies and programs in this report, established
MSIs may find new ideas for initiatives that complement their efforts to recruit and retain students, while newly emerging MSIs can become aware of the
most effective strategies to support the success of their rapidly changing student
demographic.

The sources of evidence reviewed by the committee included results from
a commissioned literature search, conducted by the study's consultants at the
University of Pennsylvania's Center for Minority Serving Institutions; findings
resulting from discussions at nine MSI site visits; expert testimony and presentations of data and information at two open session meetings; and committee
members' own research expertise and experiences working with and on MSI
campuses. These varied sources notwithstanding, one of the most challenging
aspects of this study was to contend with the limited available evidence on the
effectiveness of programs to bolster student success at MSIs. MSIs, like other
institutions, implement an eclectic mix of evidence-based and promising (albeit
not fully evaluated) programs, practices, and strategies. They range from large,
established, federally funded initiatives to small, newly launched, faculty-piloted
efforts. The majority of them, however, lack clear, quantifiable evaluations, often

because of limited financial resources and institutional capacity for assessment, data collection, analysis, and communication. The lack of designated grant funding and the overall challenge to evaluate programs as a collective contributes to the inadequacy of the data.

In spite of these limitations, the committee was able to compile available quantitative, qualitative, and anecdotal evidence to identify seven broad promising practices and strategies that hold the greatest promise for strengthening the quality of STEM education, research and workforce preparation for MSI students—if implemented with intentionality and fidelity and if sustained over time. **Bold ideas and new, targeted investments guided by these practices and strategies promise to tap the still unrealized potential of MSIs and yield substantial returns for continuing the nation's historic prominence in STEM-related fields**. These practices and strategies are as follows:

(1) Dynamic, multilevel, mission-driven leadership

All institutions of higher education need strong, effective leaders. MSIs in particular are best served by forward-looking, mission-driven presidents and other senior leadership (i.e., governing boards) who have a well-articulated vision and willingness to hold themselves accountable for committing the necessary capital, educational resources, and services to the particular characteristics and needs of their student body.

(2) Institutional responsiveness to meet students where they are

Because student populations of MSIs include a high percentage of students of color and low-income students, these institutions have a particular need to design and implement policies and practices that intentionally support nontraditional student bodies, particularly those in STEM fields, who may need additional academic, financial, and social support and flexibility given the unique demands and rigor of these fields.

(3) Supportive campus environments

While true at all institutions of higher education, organizational cultures play an especially significant role in promoting student success at MSIs. A welcoming and nurturing campus climate—one that supports a fundamental sense of community and an equity-oriented culture—contributes to academic attainment and professional commitment at MSIs.

(4) Tailored academic and social supports

Intentional policies and practices, and holistic, student-centered supports, such as Summer Bridge programs and supplemental instruction, help guide students through higher education and make an important difference in persistence and success.

(5) Mentorship and sponsorship

Strong mentorship is frequently cited in the literature as key to student success at MSIs. This is an experience valued by students and alumni alike, who credit meaningful, accessible relationships with faculty and other meaningful adults as critical to their success in STEM education, and whose advocacy and support helped to advance their careers.

(6) Availability of undergraduate research experiences

Entry into graduate and professional fields increasingly demands high-quality research experience as an undergraduate—an opportunity that non-research-intensive institutions may find challenging to provide. Increasing numbers of MSIs are pioneering creative ways to extend such opportunities to more students at their institutions through course-based research experiences and external partnerships with research-intensive colleges and universities, government agencies, and private companies.

(7) Mutually beneficial public- and private-sector partnerships

Local and national partnerships between MSIs and business, industry, and state and federal governments, as well as with other MSIs and non-MSIs, have the potential to provide alternative funding mechanisms and educational and research opportunities for students, while also encouraging collaboration among academic faculty and business and industry scientists, engineers, and health professionals.

A CALL TO STAKEHOLDERS OF EDUCATION, INNOVATION, AND ADVANCEMENT

Identifying *what works* at MSIs is only half the battle. Through its review of the evidence base, the committee concluded that **substantial resources are needed to help promote, sustain, and advance the success of MSIs and their students.** Meeting this charge is not without consequence or effort on the part of these institutions, or on the part of their stakeholders.

Commitment from external stakeholders of all kinds—including federal and state governments, tribal nations (particularly in the case of Tribal Colleges and Universities), and the philanthropic and private sectors—along with a shared commitment from MSIs themselves is needed. Such investments include support that enables MSIs to recruit and retain high-quality faculty, to procure and maintain state-of-the-art laboratories and facilities, to offer extraordinary academic and social support services to students, and to compete effectively for access to the federal grants and contracts that fuel important research discoveries, innovation, and scientific advancement for our nation. Business and industry should also be motivated to invest in MSIs, largely because they are the primary beneficiaries of a highly educated, skilled workforce that increases their success and enhances the U.S. economic prosperity and national security. Stakeholders should expect a return on investment when they provide sufficient resources to MSIs to ensure that they are equipped to meet the high standards and expectations for quality in STEM teaching, learning and research.

At the same time, a significant portion of responsibility for elevating the role of MSIs in the nation's educational and economic infrastructure lies with MSIs themselves. For MSIs to be competitive in the educational marketplace and to contribute to the nation's overall economic competitiveness, they will require bold leadership and a purposeful commitment to innovate, especially in an era where neither federal nor private funding is plentiful. This is especially important for non-research-intensive MSIs.

More hard choices lie ahead. MSIs may need to take a critical, holistic look at their current resources and academic offerings to prioritize those that contribute most directly to students' workforce readiness in high-demand fields, as well as to their sociocultural development and preparation for active citizenship in their communities, on a national and global stage. This does not always mean a move toward a "STEM for all" focus, for the committee firmly believes in a *balanced set of experiences* for students at MSIs that give them rich exposure to the humanities, arts, business, and classical education—along with experience in science, engineering, and medicine.[3] But MSIs may need to conduct internal analyses of their departmental and disciplinary strengths and capabilities, invest more heavily in campus research support systems that will enable them to attract external grant and contract dollars, conduct outreach to new partners and funders, and identify the unique value add of their institutions in ways that highlight a competitive advantage to potential funders. It may mean that the leaders of MSIs—including trustees, presidents, and provosts—become more "STEM savvy" regardless of their own disciplinary specialties, so that their investment decisions are based on a deeper understanding of the relationships between investments in STEM education and research and the capacity of their graduates to thrive in the 21st-century workforce.

The committee calls on federal and state policy makers, MSI leaders and faculty, and other key stakeholders to help implement the promising practices and effectives strategies identified in this report, but to also take bold, innovative steps to enhance and enrich the education, student development, training, and research capabilities of MSIs. As we call on governments and the business community to invest more public and private dollars in MSIs, we also ask MSIs to

---

[3] The committee was inspired by the recent National Academies report, *The Integration of the Humanities and Arts with Sciences, Engineering, and Medicine in Higher Education: Branches from the Same Tree* (National Academies of Sciences, Engineering, and Medicine. 2018. The Integration of the Humanities and Arts with Sciences, Engineering, and Medicine in Higher Education. Branches from the Same Tree. Washington, DC: National Academies Press. https://doi.org/10.17226/24988), which urged colleges and universities to give their students experiences in a wide range of fields and disciplines—regardless of their "major"—to prepare them as citizens for life, work, and civic participation.

continue to use those dollars wisely, strategically, and with an eye toward being more accountable for their use. Finally, we ask all partners involved in this shared enterprise to approach these responsibilities with a commitment to excellence and with a heightened sense of urgency, both for the benefit of students and for the well-being of the nation.

COMMITTEE RECOMMENDATIONS

To support the advancement of MSI students in postsecondary STEM education, and the capacity of MSIs to educate an increasingly diverse student body, the committee makes the following 10 recommendations in the broad areas of *Leadership, Public and Private Partnerships, Financial Investments, Institutional Research Capacity, and Performance Measures*. See Chapter 6 in the full report for a detailed description of each recommendation and a larger explanation of the committee's intent.

Leadership

MSIs are best served when presidents and other senior leaders (i.e., governing boards) foster connections with key stakeholders and demonstrate an understanding of the need for intentionality to serve as a driving factor in shaping academic and social support systems on campus. Such leaders set high expectations, meet students where they are when they enroll on campus, and deploy innovative academic and social support systems to ensure that their students achieve at high academic levels and are prepared for careers in the 21st-century economy. Advancement in leadership training and succession planning is critical for the development and implementation of sustainable programs and policies that support STEM education that bolster student success at MSIs.

Summary of Recommendation 1: Leadership of MSIs, including governing boards, presidents, deans, and provosts, should develop appropriate policies, infrastructure, and practices that together create a culture of intentionality upon which evidence-based, outcomes-driven programs and strategies to support student success are created and sustained. This is especially important for emerging and newly established MSIs.

Summary of Recommendation 2: To cultivate the next generation of forward-looking, mission-driven MSI leaders, MSIs and their stakeholders, including professional associations and university-based leadership programs, should prioritize and invest in succession planning and professional development training programs for current and future leaders of these institutions.

Public- and Private-Sector Partnerships

MSI partnerships with the public and private sectors have the potential to provide additional funding mechanisms, educational, research, and workforce opportunities for students, and collaborations among faculty and staff, all of which would benefit the involved parties and strengthen STEM teaching and learning, programmatic efforts, and student outcomes. A focus on *mutual benefit* (e.g., sharing responsibilities for governance of the partnership, sharing of human capital as well as financial and other resources, and equal voices for policy and decision making within the partnership) will distinguish a meaningful, sustaining partnership for all parties involved.

Summary of Recommendation 3: Leadership from within MSIs, non-MSIs, government agencies, tribal nations, state agencies, private and corporate foundations, and professional, higher education, and scientific associations should prioritize efforts to establish new or expand current mutually beneficial and sustainable partnerships that support education, research, and workforce training for the nation's current and future STEM workforce.

New and Expanded Financial Investments

Capital and human resources matter in promoting STEM student success and achieving positive student outcomes. At a time when MSIs are uniquely positioned to serve an increasingly diverse student population and increase U.S. STEM degree production, they have markedly fewer financial resources, as compared to non-MSIs. This disparity reduces their capacity for innovation, experimentation, quantifiable evaluation, and replication of evidence-based programs to support the nation's future workforce. As the number of MSIs continues to grow, funding must keep pace with educational and workforce demands of the nation. The recommendations below are directed to funding agencies and higher education stakeholders (Recommendations 4-7) and Congress (Recommendations 8 and 9).

Summary of Recommendation 4: Public and private funding agencies should continue to develop and expand grant competition programs that serve the nation's MSIs. Such agencies include but are not limited to the Department of Education, Department of Energy, Department of Defense, National Aeronautics and Space Administration, National Science Foundation, National Institutes of Health, tribal nations, state agencies, private and corporate foundations, and local, regional, and national businesses.

Summary of Recommendation 5: Given the institutional resources required to effectively compete for large grants and contracts, public and private funding agencies should reconsider the practicality of current competitive

funding models for under-resourced MSIs. Such agencies include but are not limited to the Department of Education, Department of Energy, Department of Defense, National Aeronautics and Space Administration, National Science Foundation, National Institutes of Health, state agencies, private and corporate foundations, and local, regional, and national businesses.

Summary of Recommendation 6: MSI presidents and senior leadership should take aggressive, proactive steps to better position themselves to compete for public and private STEM research grants and contracts, either independently or in collaboration with local, regional, and national partners.

Summary of Recommendation 7: Public and private funding agencies should issue new and expand current grant opportunities to support evidence-based research on MSIs, their students, and the sociobehavioral and sociocultural factors and conditions that impact the efficacy of programmatic interventions at these institutions. Such agencies include but are not limited to the Department of Education, National Science Foundation, National Institutes of Health, tribal nations, state agencies, private and corporate foundations, and local, regional, and national businesses.

Summary of Recommendation 8: To more effectively measure MSIs' returns on investments, and to inform current and future public-private partnership initiatives, Congress should prioritize actions to enhance the clarity, transparency, and accountability for all federal investments in STEM education and research at MSIs, including the production of an annual MSI STEM Research and Procurement report.

Summary of Recommendation 9: As it considers regular adjustments to federal higher education policies and programs—including, but not limited to, its reauthorization of the Higher Education Act—Congress should use the legislative process to incent greater investments in MSIs and the strategies outlined in this report.

MSI Performance and Accountability

Given the complex concept of student success in higher education, particularly for MSI student bodies, the committee challenges the applicability of traditional metrics to ascertain institutional and student performance. Metrics such as retention rate, graduation rate, and postgraduate income are used to compare the quality and success of academic institutions, yet they do not readily apply to MSIs because these metrics fail to consider a number of contextual factors, including students' financial circumstances, life stage, competing commitments to work and family, academic preparation, enrollment intensity, and, importantly, the resources available at each institution. We caution policy makers against taking a broad-brush approach when it comes to accountability measures for institutions of higher education, recognizing an uneven playing field in terms of institutional resources, and the work that MSIs must undertake when serving the nation's most diverse communities.

Summary of Recommendation 10: Federal and state educational agencies, state legislators, and other entities that utilize indicators of institutional success, including for accountability purposes, should reassess and refine methods of measuring student outcomes to take into consideration institutional missions, faculty investment, student populations, student needs, and institutional resource constraints.

IN CONCLUSION

MSIs have great potential to serve as a larger part of the solution to broaden the participation of underrepresented groups in STEM and to promote the diversity of perspectives that drive innovation and discovery and advance the nation's global impact. The recommendations of this report are offered as guideposts for Congress, federal agencies, state leaders, business and industry leaders, association and nongovernmental organization leaders, and higher education faculty and administrators across the nation. It is our hope that this study will incentivize the adoption of evidence-based approaches to support and advance STEM education and workforce outcomes for the tens of millions of students enrolled at two- and four-year MSIs.

1

Introduction

Once the unchallenged leader in the fast-paced, complex global economy, the United States now faces steadily increasing competition, and its position as the global leader in innovation in science, technology, engineering, and mathematics (STEM) is at risk. The nation's diminished role in producing new technologies is seen, for example, in the decreased number of U.S. patent grants issued for technologies developed within the United States compared to those of international origin (USPTO 2018). The nation's decreased standing became apparent in the early 2000s, when China surpassed the United States as the world's top high-technology exporter; by 2010, Germany followed, and today, Singapore and South Korea are not far behind (World Bank 2018). To support faster economic growth and advance the nation's global standing, the U.S. economy will need to rely increasingly on higher levels of productivity, which will come, in part, from increased investments in research and technological advances (Bloom et al. 2017). These gains will also require a strategic effort to expand the labor force—increasing the number of well-educated and highly skilled STEM-capable professionals to maintain the pace of producing meaningful technological breakthroughs.

The enhancement of the U.S. STEM workforce entails more than simply increasing the number and expertise of its future professionals. New discoveries in STEM are fast becoming characterized by interdisciplinary collaboration—by "team science" that capitalizes on diverse perspectives, knowledge, and skills (NRC 2015). **To address national priorities related to progress and innovation, and to facilitate advances in the grand domestic and international challenges in STEM, the diversity of the U.S. workforce matters** (European Commision 2003; NAS, NAE, and IOM 2011; page 2017).

Although America's STEM workforce has grown more diverse over time, its numbers are still far below the level of diversity represented in the general population (Pew Reserch Center 2018). The impact of this underrepresentation is critical to understand, given the imminent transition toward a non-White majority in the United States. In 2016, nearly 50 percent of the nation's population 0-17 years of age was non-White; based on current projections, by year 2060, two-thirds of the nation's youth will be of color (U.S. Census Bureau 2015, 2018). **A clear takeaway from these population estimates is that the educational outcomes and STEM readiness of students of color will have direct implications on the nation's economic growth, national security, and global prosperity.** This takeaway leads to an important question: What *specific* and *strategic* actions can the nation take to ensure high-quality STEM education and impactful workforce preparation experiences for the growing population of students of color, in the hope to secure a larger, well-trained, STEM-capable workforce? One solution is to identify the most effective initiatives currently used to support the postsecondary STEM education and workforce preparation for students of color.

Fortunately, the nation has a major asset in achieving this goal: the more than 700 Minority Serving Institutions (MSIs) that enroll nearly 30 percent of all undergraduates in the U.S. higher education system, the vast majority of whom are students of color (Espinosa et al. 2017; Gasman and Conrad 2013). As detailed later in this report, MSIs vary substantially in their origins, missions, student demographics, and levels of institutional selectivity, but, in general, these institutions provide a gateway to higher education, particularly for students of color and those with low-income backgrounds. Although many are long established, their accomplishments and contributions to the educational success and workforce readiness for STEM students are often overlooked. This report examines the role of MSIs in the nation's higher education system, identifies their most promising programs and effective strategies to increase the quantity and quality of STEM graduates, and reviews their contributions to advance America's capacity for STEM research, innovation, and advancements.

STUDY CHARGE

In response to an urgent need to strengthen STEM education and research opportunities for students from underrepresented minority groups, over the past decade, the National Academies of Sciences, Engineering, and Medicine (the National Academies) have undertaken a series of efforts to inspire and encourage improvements in the academic experiences of underrepresented students (Box 1-1). This study extends the National Academies' commitment to these issues by focusing on the nation's MSIs and examining their position to contribute to national priorities related to economic growth, scientific discovery, national security, infrastructure, public health, and social well-being.

Box 1-1
Previous National Academies Efforts
Relevant to the Study Charge

- Workshops:
  - *Partnerships for Emerging Research Institutions: Report of a Workshop* (2009)
  - *Colloquy on Minority Males in Science, Technology, Engineering, and Mathematics* (2012)
  - *Advancing Diversity in the US Industrial Science and Engineering Workforce* (2014)
  - *Surmounting the Barriers: Ethnic Diversity in Engineering Education* (2014)
- Reports:
  - *Enhancing the Community College Pathway to Engineering Careers* (2005)
  - *Rising Above the Gathering Storm: Energizing and Employing America for a Brighter Economic Future* (2007)
  - *Expanding Underrepresented Minority Participation: America's Science and Technology Talent at the Crossroads* (2011)
  - *Assuring the U.S. Department of Defense a Strong Science, Technology, Engineering, and Mathematics (STEM) Workforce* (2012)
  - *Review of Army Research Laboratory Programs for Historically Black Colleges and Universities and Minority Institutions* (2014)
  - *Barriers and Opportunities for 2-Year and 4-Year STEM Degrees: Systemic Change to Support Students' Diverse Pathways* (2016)
  - *Promising Practices for Strengthening the Regional STEM Workforce Development Ecosystem* (2016)
  - *Supporting Students' College Success: The Role of Assessment of Intrapersonal and Interpersonal Competencies* (2017)

Sponsors of this study include the Alfred P. Sloan Foundation, Helmsley Charitable Trust, Wallace Foundation, W.K. Kellogg Foundation, and ECMC Foundation. The study's full Statement of Task is presented in Box 1-2.

In response to the Statement of Task, the study committee examined research evidence to identify the most promising programs and effective strategies to bolster outcomes of success for MSI students (e.g., enrollment, persistence, retention, degree attainment, and employment)—with a particular focus on students in STEM fields. The committee also examined the role of federal and state policies in supporting these initiatives.

Unlike many previous reports on MSIs, which tend to highlight the limitations of these institutions, this report provides a fuller picture of MSIs, offering important context for the missions of these institutions and examples of their return on investment for students, as well as for federal, state, and local economies. By focusing this report on *what works*, rather than on *what's wrong*, the committee calls attention to (1) the achievements of MSIs and the opportunities

BOX 1-2
Committee Statement of Task

An ad hoc committee under the oversight of the Board on Higher Educa-tion and Workforce, in collaboration with the Board on Science Education, will undertake a study to examine the goals, aspirations, challenges, and successes of postsecondary institutions that enroll and serve a significant portion of our na-tion's African American, Hispanic, Asian American and Native American STEM graduates—often collectively referred to as Minority Serving Institutions (MSIs).

This study will address the following questions:

1. What are examples of model programs on MSI campuses that have dem-onstrated strong evidence of success in producing quality STEM graduates, including those models that involve partnerships with other local institutions of higher education, the private sector, or government agencies, and those that model exemplary curricula and laboratory experiences?

2. What are the key challenges, obstacles, and opportunities facing MSIs as they continue to produce scientists, engineers and health care providers who are prepared for success in the 21st-century workplace? In particular, what challenges are unique to MSIs (e.g., as a consequence of the demographics of the students they serve, and their history of support and funding), and how are these institutions working to address those challenges?

3. What are the key institutional components for scalability and sustainability of model programs, which may include invested leadership, durable infrastruc-ture, or secure partnerships, and how are they promoting student success?

4. What public policy interventions are needed to support and sustain efforts on MSI campuses? Which public policy interventions may inhibit these efforts?

The resulting report will provide findings and recommendations to help create the conditions, systems, policies, and practices on MSI campuses that propel more students toward degree attainment in STEM fields and toward strong preparation for success in STEM careers.

for other institutions (MSIs and non-MSIs) to replicate and/or adapt specific initiatives, and (2) the multifaceted returns that could accrue from investing both financial and human capital in MSIs and the educational experiences that they provide to millions of students.

Based on an assortment of evidence, the committee offers a series of key findings and recommendations to study stakeholders—administrators and faculty at MSIs and non-MSIs, Congress, federal agencies, state and local legislatures, tribal nations, governors, higher education researchers, the business community, and professional and nonprofit organizations. If implemented, these recommendations could support the scale-up and/or expansion of effective practices for students, and create clearer, more efficient pathways and policies for two- and four-year MSIs to thrive in the nation's postsecondary education system.

STUDY APPROACH

In spring 2017, the National Academies appointed an 18-member committee of experts to address the objectives outlined in the Statement of Task. The resulting Committee on Closing the Equity Gap: Securing Our STEM Education and Workforce Readiness Infrastructure in the Nation's Minority Serving Institutions includes scientists and engineers, current and former MSI and non-MSI administrators and faculty, business and industry leaders, current and former policy makers, and economists. In addition, most committee members have direct expertise in STEM-related disciplines. (See Appendix A for the biographical sketches of committee members.)

In conducting its work, the committee convened eight times from April 2017 through August 2018, including four in-person and four virtual meetings. In conjunction with two of the in-person meetings, the committee held public information-gathering sessions to gather background information, data, and general input from the study sponsors; the White House; content experts; representatives from MSI; relevant professional organizations; business, industry, and government agencies; and other stakeholders. In addition to public discussions, the committee's own expertise and the conclusions from other relevant National Academies studies (see Box 1-1) were also used to inform the committee's deliberations.

To assist in efforts to collect and evaluate published, evidence-based findings, the committee commissioned a literature review from the Center for Minority Serving Institutions at the University of Pennsylvania (the Penn Center), a private research organization that serves as a repository for research and data, on and within MSIs.[1] The committee soon discovered substantial limitations to the data on the effective strategies to support STEM students at MSIs, in terms of the limited number of publications and the low level of rigor used to produce conclusions of "student success." As such, the committee commissioned the Penn Center to conduct a broader review that encompassed three areas of focus: (1) STEM education for students of color across higher education (MSIs and non-MSIs), (2) student success at MSIs (STEM and non-STEM), and (3) student success in STEM at MSIs. Using committee-directed criteria and casting a wide net of search terms, the Penn Center identified and analyzed more than 170 studies[2] for common themes or lessons learned. Importantly, given the search strategy,

---

[1] Additional information is available at https://cmsi.gse.upenn.edu/.

[2] The commissioned review included peer-reviewed articles, case studies, dissertations, and research reports from academic researchers, government agencies, nonprofit research centers, and professional organizations.

much of the evidence for success discussed throughout this report, particularly in Chapter 5, can be applied to more widespread demographics (i.e., underrepresented minority students in STEM and general education in both MSI and non-MSI settings) than originally anticipated. This implies that targeted support for one population does not have to come at the expense of another. (Chapter 5 and Appendix E further describe the literature search and its limitations.)

Although the committee considered diverse forms of research evidence as appropriate and usable for analyses, wherever possible—particularly in Chapters 3 and 4—the committee members made an intentional effort to prioritize peer-reviewed publications and research articles with the greatest level of scientific rigor and internal validity. In addition, because the set of issues on which this study focuses is underresearched, the committee submitted a number of specific data requests to higher education research organizations. These organizations included the American Council on Education, the American Institutes for Research, the American Indian Higher Education Consortium, the NORC at the University of Chicago, and the National Science Foundation.

Finally, serving as a significant component of the committee's information-gathering efforts, from September through November 2017, a subset of committee members conducted informational site visits at nine MSIs known to have implemented effective or promising programs, policies, practices, and/or strategies to help propel more students toward degree attainment in STEM fields and toward strong preparation for success in STEM careers. Participating MSIs were selected from a list of nominated institutions culled from discussions with key stakeholders of the study's report. Nominations also were accepted from the Penn Center and MSI advocacy and association groups (e.g., the United Negro College Fund, the Hispanic Association of Colleges and Universities, the American Indian Higher Education Consortium, and the Asian & Pacific Islander American Scholarship Fund). In the selection of sites, the committee made a conscious effort to include a diversity of perspectives represented across the different classifications of MSIs, size and type of institution, setting (rural, urban, etc.), and region. The MSIs selected were Morgan State University (Maryland), West Los Angeles College (California), San Diego State University (California), Dillard University (Louisiana), Xavier University (Louisiana), University of Texas Rio Grande Valley (Texas), North Carolina A&T State University (North Carolina), Mission College (California), and Salish Kootenai College (Montana). (See Appendix C for site visit agendas.)

As a result of the open and candid discussions held during these site visits, the committee was able to collect unique, mostly unpublished, qualitative and quantitative data. These data provided illustrative examples of long-standing models and approaches to support students of color in STEM, as well as examples of promising and innovative efforts to address the changing STEM education and research landscapes and future workforce needs in these disciplines. These data helped to inform several of the research conclusions and recommendations within this report.

STUDY SCOPE AND KEY DEFINITIONS

The committee first determined how to define and limit the scope of its work, as articulated in the Statement of Task. Decisions on key words and concepts are presented in the following chapters, but it is important to note that the committee recognizes that alternative definitions of the terms can be found in the research literature (Box 1-3). In addition, illustrative examples of effective strategies to support students of color in STEM are presented throughout the report; however, the committee recognizes that these examples are inadequate to cover the range of possible types of promising or innovative programs or strategies implemented in MSIs across the nation.

Throughout the report, the committee focused its research efforts on four of the seven types of MSIs listed in Box 1-3: Historically Black Colleges and Universities (HBCUs), Tribal Colleges and Universities (TCUs), Hispanic-Serving Institutions (HSIs), and Asian American and Native American Pacific Islander-Serving Institutions (AANAPISIs). It did so because these four types of MSIs have a more robust evidence base and/or overall serve a larger proportion of students of color as compared to the other three types: Alaska Native-Serving and Hawaiian-Serving (ANNHIs), Predominately Black Institutions (PBIs), and Native American-Serving Nontribal Institutions (NASNTIs). It is important that future efforts invest in research that can lead to a more thorough examination of all MSI types.

REPORT ORGANIZATION

The remainder of this report provides a more thorough discussion on MSIs, the students they serve, and their role in advancing the STEM workforce and national, regional, and local economies. The report provides both quantitative and qualitative evidence and, where relevant, distinguishes where the evidence is used to support findings for students of color in STEM at MSIs, students of color at MSIs in all fields, and students of color at higher education institutions, more broadly.

Chapter 2 provides an overview of the nation's STEM workforce, its needs, and the role that cultural diversity plays in promoting its success.

Chapter 3 provides an overview of federally recognized types of MSIs; presents a short review of the MSI community, including the diversity among its students, faculty, and presidents; describes challenges with current assessment metrics; and considers what it means to "serve" students of color.

Chapter 4 describes the current federal, state, and local funding landscape for MSIs and presents select examples of the various kinds of returns on invest-

---

BOX 1-3
Key Definitions

Community College: For purposes of this report, two-year, public or private, nonprofit institutions.

Intentionality: As defined by the committee, a calculated and coordinated method of engagement for institutions, agencies, organizations, and private investors to use to effectively meet the needs of a designated population within a given higher education institution.

Minority Serving Institution (MSI): Based on federal designations:

Historically Defined MSIs
Established with the expressed purpose of providing access to higher education for a specific racial minority group:
• Historically Black Colleges and Universities (HBCUs)
• Tribal Colleges and Universities (TCUs)

Enrollment-Designated MSIs
Federally recognized as MSIs based on student enrollment thresholds:
• Hispanic-Serving Institutions (HSIs)
• Alaska Native-Serving and Native Hawaiian-Serving Institutions (ANNHIs)
• Asian American and Native American Pacific Islander-Serving Institutions (AANAPISIs)
• Predominantly Black Institutions (PBIs)
• Native American-Serving Nontribal Institutions (NASNTIs)

Non-Minority Serving Institutions (non-MSIs): Also referred to throughout the report as majority institutions or Predominately White Institutions (PWIs).

---

ment for MSI students, the STEM workforce, and MSIs' local and regional communities.

Chapter 5 describes seven evidence-based strategies that have demonstrated or show unique promise in cultivating success for students of color. It also presents illustrative examples of programs, policies, and practices that have successfully implemented these strategies.

Chapter 6 revisits the key messages conveyed in Chapters 2 through 5 and offers targeted recommendations to multisector stakeholders who hold the power to create, adapt, and scale up specific policies and practices that can advance the STEM education and workforce outcomes for tens of millions of Americans—the nation's current and future workforce. With prompt and intentional support, MSIs can bolster the nation's international impact in the STEM fields.

Nontraditional Students: Are generally defined as students with one of the following characteristics: independent, having one or more dependents, being a single caregiver, not having received a standard high school diploma, having delayed enrollment in postsecondary education by a year or more after high school, working full time while enrolled, and/or attending school part time.

Open-Access Institutions: Institutions that have no selectivity-based admissions policies and are open to all students. These institutions commonly devote resources to academic and nonacademic programming that cater to students from all preparation levels, such as developmental education and academic support services such as tutoring and supplemental instruction.

STEM: For the purposes of this report, the committee considered science, technology, engineering, and mathematics, or STEM, programs of study to include those that culminate in a certificate or an associate's, bachelor's, master's, or doctorate degree, or in a professional designation, including technician, registered nurse, allied health professional, or physician.

Student Success: For the purposes of this report, the committee applied a comprehensive use of the term to allow *student success* to include academic success (e.g., increase in grades or grade point average), STEM pathway success (e.g., positive impact on measures of enrollment, persistence, retention, and completion of a degree in STEM-related fields), postbaccalaureate STEM education (e.g., graduate school), and/or securing employment in a STEM-related field.

Students of Color: For the purposes of this report, this group includes Hispanic, African American, Native American Indian/Alaska Native, Native Hawaiian/Pacific Islander, and Asian American students. This term is also used to replace similar terms, such as minorities, underrepresented minorities, and non-Whites.

REFERENCES

Bloom, Nicholas, Charles I. Jones, John Van Reenen, and Michael Webb. 2017. Are Ideas Getting Harder to Find?: National Bureau of Economic Research. Available at: https://www.nber.org/papers/w23782. Accessed October 2018.

Espinosa, Lorelle L., Jonathan M. Turk, Morgan Taylor. 2017. Pulling Back the Curtain: Enrollment and Outcomes at Minority Serving Institutions. Washington, DC: American Council on Education.

European Commission (European Commission Centre for Strategy and Evaluation Services). 2003. The Costs and Benefits of Diversity: A Study on Methods and Indicators to Measure the Cost Effectiveness of Diversity Policies in Enterprises. Executive summary. Kent, UK: Centre for Strategy and Evaluation Service.

Gasman, Marybeth and Clifton F. Conrad. 2013. Minority Serving Institutions: Educating All Students. Philadelphia, PA: Penn Center for Minority Serving Institutions, Graduate School of Education, University of Pennsylvania.

NAS, NAE, and IOM (National Academy of Science, National Academy of Engineering, and Institute of Medicine). 2011. Expanding Underrepresented Minority Participation: America's Science and Technology Talent at the Crossroads. Washington, DC: The National Academies Press. Available at: https://doi.org/10.17226/12984.

NRC (National Research Council). 2015. Enhancing the Effectiveness of Team Science. Washington, DC: The National Academies Press. Available at: https://doi.org/10.17226/19007.

Page, Scott E. 2017. The diversity bonus: How great teams pay off in the knowledge economy. Vol. 2. Princeton, NJ: Princeton University Press.

Pew Research Center. 2018. "Women and Men in STEM Often at Odds Over Workplace Equity." Chapter 1: Diversity in the STEM workforce varies widely across jobs. Available at: http://assets.pewresearch.org/wpcontent/uploads/sites/3/2018/01/09142305/PS_2018.01.09_STEM_FINAL.pdf. Accessed September 2018.

U.S. Census Bureau. 2015. Projections of the Size and Composition of the U.S. Population: 2014 to 2060. Population Estimates and Projections. Current Population Reports. P25-1143. U.S. Census Bureau. Available at: https://www.census.gov/content/dam/Census/library/publications/2015/demo/p25-1143.pdf. Accessed October 2018.

U.S. Census Bureau. 2018. Demographic Turning Points for the United States: Population Projections for 2020 to 2060. Figure 3, p. 8. Washington, DC: United States Census Bureau. Available at: https://www.census.gov/content/dam/Census/library/publications/2018/demo/P25_1144.pdf. Accessed October 2018.

USPTO (U.S. Patent and Trademark Office). 2018. "U.S. Patent and Statistics Chart: Calendar Years 1963-2015." Patent Technology Monitoring Team. Available at: https://www.uspto.gov/web/offices/ac/ido/oeip/taf/us_stat.htm. Accessed August 2018.

The World Bank, World Development Indicators. 2018. High-technology exports (current US$). http://databank.worldbank.org/data/High-technology-exports-(current-US$)/id/3d5f6af5. Accessed August 2018.

2

Closing the Gap and Advancing the Nation's STEM Workforce

"America cannot afford to fail to develop the talents of young people from low-income and minority families. It's not good for our economy. And it's not good for our democracy."
– Kati Haycock, Founding President, The Education Trust
(*Charting a Necessary Path, 2009*)

"Supporting MSI students is about building the scientific infrastructure of America."
– Alumnus and Community Partner of Dillard University

KEY FINDINGS

- In a rapidly evolving labor market, the demand for a domestic, STEM-capable workforce continues to grow.

- Common metrics are needed to approximate the true size of the U.S. STEM workforce, to improve the accuracy of estimates for future needs, and to assess progress in reaching a shared national goal of a larger, STEM-capable workforce.

- Communities of color are a vital resource to grow and advance the nation's future STEM workforce.

- Two- and four-year Minority Serving Institutions are poised to address the nation's STEM workforce supply problem.

Demands of the science, technology, engineering, and mathematics (STEM) workforce, both domestic and abroad, continue to grow more complex with each passing year, as noted in Chapter 1. To remain competitive on a global playing field, the United States will need to cultivate a larger, more agile and diverse STEM workforce. In this chapter, the committee considers these workforce needs within the context of an ever-evolving and changing nation.

THE STEM WORKFORCE

The STEM workforce is a generalized term used to describe professionals within fields under the broad categories of science, technology, engineering, mathematics, and, in some cases, health-related professions. Researchers tend to use different parameters to define similar STEM occupations, and some may categorize certain positions as STEM focused, while others do not (e.g., technicians, health care professionals, social scientists, and educators). As a result, reported data on STEM often provide different workforce totals, conclusions, and projections. For example, the National Science Foundation (NSF) provides estimates for the science and engineering (S&E) workforce that range from 6 million to more than 23 million professionals (NSF 2018).[1] A Brookings analysis reported that in 2011, 26 million jobs (20 percent of total jobs) required a high level of STEM knowledge (Rothwell 2013). In contrast to both the NSF and Brookings reports, based on 2015 data, government agencies estimated the STEM workforce at roughly 9 million jobs[2] (BLS 2017; U.S. Department of Commerce 2017). The variation in these workforce estimates suggests that common metrics are needed to approximate the true size of the U.S. STEM workforce and to increase the accuracy of analytics used to predict future workforce needs.

Despite the inconsistent categorization of STEM positions, job growth has increased across the STEM workforce, more broadly (U.S. Department of Commerce 2017). As the needs of modern business and industry become more complex, more jobs require at least some STEM competency and literacy, and fields not traditionally defined as STEM occupations (e.g., sales, marketing, and management) have begun to shift into new STEM-related categories (BLS 2017; NSB 2018). As a reflection of these changes, workforce projections anticipate that opportunities in STEM and STEM-related fields will continue to be in demand, particularly in the fields of research and development, and will outpace the

---

[1] NSF refers to S&E occupations and S&E-related occupations as components of the S&E workforce. S&E occupations encompass life scientists, computer and mathematical scientists, physical scientists, social scientists, and engineers, as well as postsecondary educators in these disciplines. The S&E-related occupations category is broader and includes health-related occupations, managers, technicians and technologists, architects, actuaries, and precollege educators.

[2] The STEM occupation list used for these estimates primarily included core occupations in the hard sciences, engineering, and mathematics. They did not include allied health or medical professions.

growth of non-STEM positions over the next several years (Langdon et al. 2011; NASEM 2017a; U.S. Department of Commerce 2017).

In considering these workforce projections, **there is evidence that the current domestic supply of STEM workers is not sufficient to meet the nation's future workforce needs** (NAS, NAE, and IOM 2011; NSB 2015). In fact, some estimate that the United States will need *1 million* more STEM professionals than it is on track to produce in the coming decade (PCAST 2012). Others have raised concerns that this deficit is not a "personnel shortage," but rather a "skills shortage" (Cappelli 2015; NAE and NRC 2012; PCAST 2012; PCAST 2014). Either way, these arguments advocate for a closer examination of the nation's efforts to bolster postsecondary STEM education and workforce training to support its future workforce (NAS, NAE, and IOM 2007; Pew Research Center 2017).

STEM provides a unique level of critical thinking and technical skills, and workers who can master these competencies are in greater demand and earn more than their counterparts without these competencies (Carnevale et al. 2011). In terms of economic impact, STEM occupations generally offer higher wages and additional opportunities for advancement, as compared to non-STEM occupations (Rothwell 2013; U.S. Department of Commerce 2017). For example, the national average wage for all STEM jobs in 2015 was $87,570, which was nearly double the national average wage for non-STEM jobs ($45,700) (BLS 2017). This suggests that individuals who pursue STEM careers have the potential for greater upward mobility and a lasting impact on family wealth.

BUILDING A STEM WORKFORCE IN THE CONTEXT OF A CHANGING NATION

The Loss of the "Majority" and "Minority"

In efforts to expand the domestic STEM workforce, it is important to consider the current demographic profile of the nation. Understanding the changing demographics of the nation will help to identify the population best primed to fill open STEM positions.

Today, the face of the nation looks very different than it did 50 years ago. With the substantial increase in the nation's minority population, perhaps the most salient change is that referring to people of color as "minorities" is no longer accurate (U.S. Census Bureau 2018). In 1965, people of color, including African Americans, Hispanics, Asian Americans, and Native Americans, represented approximately 18 percent of the U.S. population, with non-Hispanic Whites making up the difference (Pew Research Center 2016). By 2020, people of color are projected to constitute 45 percent of the population, and by 2065, 54 percent of the population (Pew Research Center 2016) (Figure 2-1). Thus, within 50 years, no single racial or ethnic group will comprise the "majority" population group in the United States. Recognizing the realities of the changing nation is critical

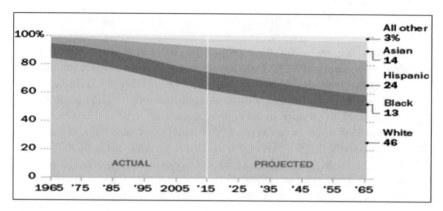

FIGURE 2-1 Changing U.S. demographics from 1965 to 2065, percentage of the total population.
NOTE: Whites, Blacks, and Asians include only single-race non-Hispanics; Asians include Pacific Islanders. Other races include Native American/Alaska Native, and multiple-race non-Hispanics. Hispanics can be of any race.
SOURCE: Pew Research Center (2016) Data from Pew Research Center (2015).

in targeting efforts to bolster STEM education and workforce training for the future workforce.

The Changing Demographics of Youth in the United States

The transition toward a non-White majority in the United States is all the more obvious when considering the demographic makeup of younger generations. For example, among the population 0-17 years of age, nearly 50 percent was non-White in 2016 (U.S. Census Bureau 2018). By 2060, roughly two-thirds of the nation's youth will be of color (U.S. Census Bureau 2018). See Figure 2-2.

As expected, these demographic changes are also reflected in the nation's education system. The enrollment of students of color, particularly Hispanic populations, is rising. Correspondingly, the percentages, as well as the total number of non-Hispanic White students, are on the decline (BLS 2017; National Center for Education Statistics 2018; U.S. Census Bureau 2018), as shown in Figure 2-3.

Based on this evidence, it becomes critical to understand that as the nation's demographic profile changes, so should its public policies and practices. With a sense of urgency, the nation has a responsibility to redirect the necessary funding, training, and attention to the strategies that best support its next generation. (See Box 2-1 for a discussion on the research methods in a changing nation.)

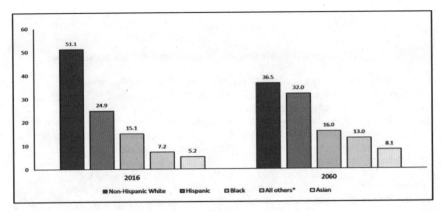

FIGURE 2-2 The racial and ethnic composition of U.S. children under age 18 (in percent). NOTE: The "all others" race group includes children who identify as American Indian, Alaska Native, Native Hawaiian, and Other Pacific Islander, and two or more races. The U.S. Census considers Hispanic as an ethnicity, not a race. Given that Hispanics may be of any race, the percentages in the graph do not add to 100.
SOURCE: Adapted from U.S. Census Bureau (2018).

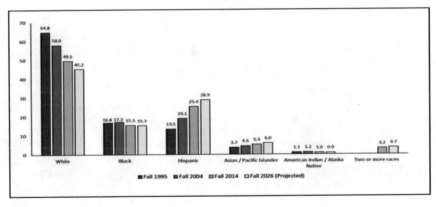

FIGURE 2-3 Percentage distribution of students enrolled in public elementary and secondary schools, by race/ethnicity, fall 1995 through fall 2026.
NOTE: Due to rounding, the percentage totals may not equal 100. Race categories exclude students with Hispanic ethnicity. Data on students of two or more races were not collected prior to 2008.
SOURCE: Adapted from National Center for Education Statistics (2018).

BOX 2-1
Demographic Research in a Changing Nation

While it is generally known that the population of people of color in the United States will continue to grow in the foreseeable future (U.S. Census Bureau 2017), many critical aspects of this trend are overlooked.

As reflected in the data presented in this chapter, some populations of color have poor visibility in national datasets. Evidence suggests that certain populations of color (e.g., Native American, Alaska Native, and multiple-race populations) are more commonly excluded from reports or in having secondary analyses conducted, as compared to other populations, in part due to small sample sizes, language barriers, cultural differences, or variability in self-identified race. Data from these populations are commonly compiled into one group, referred to in a footnote or with an asterisk in reports. For example, in several reports reviewed by the committee, the only education and workforce data available for Native American, Alaska Native, and multiple-race populations were collapsed into a single demographic category labeled as "other races."

Another area for review is the failure of certain datasets to disaggregate diverse populations by ethnicity. For example, Asian populations (e.g., Chinese, Filipino, Japanese, and Korean) are commonly examined as a single subgroup and, as a result, research conclusions are made and policies are developed based on potentially inaccurate data. Similarly, Pacific Islanders are often collapsed into the same category as Asians, while the category "two or more races" potentially oversimplifies a far more complex picture.

In addition to the potentially missed opportunities to advance evidence-based policies for the U.S. education system and workforce, these methods may also unintentionally convey a devaluation of these populations. It is important that research practices are culturally mindful and intentional in their efforts, and use best practices to promote equity among the populations researched in order to address each group's unique attributes and challenges.

In response to the changing face of the nation, there is a national responsibility to continue to reassess and revise the research methods used to collect, analyze, evaluate, communicate, and disseminate demographic data, particularly as it relates to describing the profiles of the education system and the landscape of the STEM workforce. In recent years, efforts have begun to address this concern (e.g., data initiatives in Oregon, Minnesota, and Washington state), but standardized, nationwide practices are needed.

SOURCES: Chang et al. (2015), Holland and Palaniappan (2012), Ramakrishnan and Wong (2018), Springer et al. (2013), U.S. Department of Health and Human Services (2007), White House (2016).

THE NATION'S STEM WORKFORCE NEEDS

An Urgent Need to Expand the Nation's Domestic STEM Workforce

To support the needs of the STEM workforce, the prevailing strategy of the nation has been to rely heavily on immigration (Hanson and Slaughter 2016; Jaimovich and Siu 2017; NAS, NAE, and IOM 2011). Highly skilled talent, whether domestic or from international sources, is critical for innovation; however, dependence on immigration, rather than cultivating domestic talent, is not a viable, *long-term* strategy to grow our capacity for advancements in STEM (NAS, NAE, and IOM 2011).

Many foreign-born workers travel to the United States to earn advanced STEM degrees and, using a green card or H-1B visas, often stay in the country to work (Alphonse 2013; Atkinson 2013; Hanson and Slaughter 2016; Hunt 2011; Jaimovich and Siu 2017). These workers, many of whom are counted as underrepresented minorities, help to fill open gaps in the STEM workforce but do not serve to increase domestic "minority" representation in STEM[3] (Tapia 2007). As foreign nations continue to advance their own STEM workforce and economies, fewer individuals may need or be able to seek out educational and employment opportunities in America. In fact, over the past 15 years, the number of S&E degrees earned in India and China has risen much faster than in the United States (NSB 2018). Furthermore, given that the rate of immigration to the United States ebbs and flows with national policies and the demographic and economic forces of source countries, relying on immigration as a reliable, long-term strategy may not sufficiently address the U.S. workforce needs. (See Box 2-2 for additional discussion.)

Recent national reports, including *Before It's Too Late* (U.S. Department of Education 2000) and *Rising Above the Gathering Storm* (NAS, NAE, and IOM 2007), among many others, have emphasized a sense of urgency to fill the STEM gap with domestic talent. These reports have focused on the severe repercussions of failing to improve STEM education at all levels of the educational spectrum. Similar expressions of urgency have been issued by the National Summit on Competitiveness (2005) and in investigations by the Congressional Research Service (Kuenzi 2008). As a consequence of these and other warnings, Congress, through the America Competes Act of 2007,[4] authorized several government agencies to establish more STEM programs within the U.S. education system. While these congressional actions are necessary, they are just a begin-

---

[3] Considering international students who earn advanced degrees in the United States and then fulfill such vital roles in the nation's STEM workforce, a National Academies committee recommended that all master's and Ph.D. recipients in STEM should also automatically receive a green card to eliminate barriers to their being able to remain and move toward citizenship (NAS, NAE, and IOM 2007, pp. 457, 470).

[4] H.R.2272, 110th Congress (2007-2008): America Creating Opportunities to Meaningfully Promote Excellence in Technology, Education, and Science Act.

BOX 2-2
A Reflection: Relying on Foreign-Born Talent
to Support Domestic Workforce Needs

Immigration to the United States is influenced by national policies that are sub-ject to political trends, legal challenges, public support, and the available number of employment-based visas. Rates of immigration are also influenced by the de-mographic forces within home countries. When countries of origin have incomes and levels of education and equality that are comparable to that in the United States, there is less pressure or motivation to emigrate. However, countries with a rapidly growing, young workforce and that are low income and have high levels of inequality are hard pressed to make the necessary investments to produce large numbers of highly educated and skilled workers. These factors result in a young workforce with fewer skills having higher motivation and need to emigrate. For these reasons, policies that promote a skill-based immigration system make it difficult to find enough skilled workers to meet domestic needs. Rather, with the income advantages, and superior educational infrastructure of the United States, the comparative advantage lies in the United States producing its own workers with fewer relative costs.

SOURCES: Clark et al. (2002), Guillermina et al. (2000), Hatton and Williamson (2005, 2009).

---

ning. **There is substantial value in all segments of society aligning with the singular goal of achieving a progressive makeup of domestic talent in the STEM workforce.**

An Urgent Need to Increase Diversity in the STEM Workforce

Advancement of the STEM workforce will require more than simply increas-ing the number and expertise of its future professionals. It will also require a marked increase in the cultural diversity of its talent (Kochan 2002; NAS, NAE, and IOM 2011; Page 2008). In recognition of this point, the America Com-petes Reauthorization Act of 2010[5] directed attention to increasing the number of underrepresented minorities in STEM fields. The successor to the America Competes Act, the American Innovation and Competitive Act[6] that was signed into law in 2017, focuses on broader participation in STEM studies and careers. These initiatives are supported by cross-disciplinary research that concludes that the long-term social and economic benefits to increasing the number of people of color in the workforce far outweigh any potential challenges that have been raised

---

[5] H.R.5116, 111th Congress (2009-2010): America Creating Opportunities to Meaningfully Promote Excellence in Technology, Education, and Science Reauthorization Act of 2010.

[6] S.3084, 114th Congress (2015-2016): American Innovation and Competitiveness Act.

in the scholarly literature (e.g., triggering short-term changes to social networks) (NAS, NAE, and IOM 2011; Putnam 2007).

As an asset, diversity in the workplace not only expands the available talent pool, but also increases the range of perspectives and expertise available to solve grand challenges in STEM (NAS, NAE, and IOM 2011). Diversity in the workplace, particularly the STEM workforce, also improves work performance and engagement, enhances the quality of research and provision of health care, and promotes innovation and growth (Cohen et al. 2002; Federal Glass Ceiling Commission 1995; Florida 2014). Box 2-3 provides a few cross-sector examples on the impacts of diversity in the workplace.

Despite the demonstrated advantages to diversity in the workforce, it remains an unfortunate truth that the current composition of the STEM workforce does not reflect the current or future demographic realities of the United States. In 2017, the Government Accountability Office (GAO) concluded that Hispanics, African Americans, and other racial and ethnic minorities (e.g., American Indian/Alaska Native), remain underrepresented in the science and technology workforce compared to their presence in the workforce more generally (GAO 2017). Similarly, other studies determined that the STEM workforce compromises only 9 percent African Americans and 7 percent Hispanics, even though the total U.S. workforce is made up of 11 percent African Americans and 16 percent Hispanics (Pew Research Center 2018). Furthermore, among employed adults with a bachelor's degree or higher, African Americans make up only 7 percent and Hispanics 6 percent of the STEM workforce (Pew Research Center 2018).[7] As it looks to the future, the United States can help to address the underrepresentation in the STEM workforce, by turning to one of its most underutilized resources: the more than 20 million young people of color[8] who have the capacity to enter the STEM fields and close these current gaps.

Recent projection data estimate that by 2030, the number of White public school graduates will decrease by 14 percent, compared to 2013 data (Bransberger and Michelau 2016). Correspondingly, between 2018 and 2028, the projected growth in the number of non-White public high school graduates will increase and replace the numerical decrease in White graduates (in public and private schools) nearly one-to-one (Bransberger and Michelau 2016). **Based on these findings, the committee suggests that the most efficient way to advance the STEM workforce is to capitalize on the nation's changing demographics, and**

---

[7] Additional estimates suggest that Asians are overrepresented across all STEM occupational clusters (Pew Research Center 2018); however, these analyses do not disaggregate the data by ethnicity and miss an opportunity to expose potential disparities among this diverse group. In addition, these analyses did not include data on American Indian/Alaska Native's underrepresentation in STEM.

[8] Category includes 15- to 24-year olds, including residents of Hispanic and non-Hispanic origin and excluding non-Hispanic Whites. U.S. Census Bureau, Population Division; Annual Estimates of the Resident Population by Sex, Age, Race, and Hispanic Origin for the United States and States: April 1, 2010 to July 1, 2017.

BOX 2-3
Diversity in the Workforce

Benefits to Ensuring Diversity in Business, Industry, and Local Communities

Corporate America has long acknowledged the value of achieving diversity and inclusion in the workforce. Corporations with a commitment to diversity have access to a wider pool of talent and a broader mix of leadership skills than corporations that lack such a commitment. Research has shown that corporations with intentional efforts to recruit and promote minorities and women are more profitable. And scientific research groups that are more heterogeneous, based on gender, produce research that is more likely to be published in high-impact journals.

The Intel Corporation provides an illustrative example of an organization that has realized the potential in increasing diversity and inclusion within its workplace. In 2015, the company launched a $500 million initiative to achieve full representation of women and underrepresented minorities in its workforce by 2020. In a 2017 midyear progress report, Intel noted an 84 percent improvement in its diversity from 2014 to 2017. As part of its strategy to increase diversity in the future STEM workforce, Intel has also invested in select Historically Black Colleges and Universities to support scholarships, research experiences, and professional development workshops for faculty and students.

The Role of Diversity in America's Health Care System

A lack of racial and ethnic diversity within the medical field has significant implications for the biomedical sciences and the U.S. health care system, in terms of both scientific research and effectiveness of health care delivery. Research shows that engaging a more diverse team of investigators translates into more impactful research, particularly when working across disciplines. Diversity also improves the delivery of health care by helping to bridge cultural gaps and improve access, quality, and patient safety.

From a health finance perspective, discussions about inclusion and diversity have become more important than ever before. For example, between 2003 and 2006, the cost of health inequities and inadequate care was an estimated $1.24 trillion. Reports reviewing those same years suggest that eliminating health disparities for minorities would have reduced direct medical care expenditures by almost $230 billion. The pivotal Margaret Heckler Report on Black and Minority Health documented health disparities in care more than 30 years ago, and yet, despite the longevity of this report, little progress appears to have been made.

Given the current and projected changes to the demographics of the United States, the physical, mental, and emotional health of the nation is dependent upon a collective ability to optimize the health of communities. Lack of diversity in the nation's health systems, particularly among the leadership within these systems, can result in policies that do not adequately address the needs of diverse populations and subsequently result in loss of revenue, directly impacting the bottom line—of life and of dollars.

SOURCES: Betancourt et al. (2003), Campbell et al. (2013), Cohen et al. (2002), European Commission (2003), Evans (1999), Florida (2014), Heckler (1985), Hunt et al. (2018), LaVeist et al. (2009), Murray et al. (2006), NASEM (2017b), Sullivan (2004), U.S. Department of Health and Human Services (2014), Valantine and Collins (2015).

invest, support, and expand efforts to bolster success in STEM education and workforce training among the plurality of college-age students of color.

Diversity in Higher Education

The current demographic profile of students enrolling in college today is very different from the profile 25 years ago. There has been a rapid rise in the number of students of color graduating from U.S. high schools (Bransberger and Michelau 2016). In addition, students identified as nontraditional[9] are a rapidly growing percentage of the total enrollment in higher education and are in line to outpace traditional undergraduates in the near future (National Center for Education Statistics 2002, 2017). These findings should worry stakeholders of the STEM workforce, in that the nation's fastest-growing population group, with the greatest employment potential, is also the most underrepresented across the entire STEM workforce (Carnevale et al. 2011; Huang et al. 2000).

And while the challenges tied to the new profile of students in higher education are complex, including the need to reexamine every institution's current social, financial, educational, and cultural support systems, one solution is to **invest in institutions that already have an established and intentional focus to educate and train this particular population of students.** Following this logic, it can be argued that turning the nation's attention to the underutilized resource of Minority Serving Institutions (MSIs) is a strategy that holds great promise for growing the size and diversity of a STEM-capable workforce.

MINORITY SERVING INSTITUTIONS: AN UNDERUTILITIZED RESOURCE

Attempts to increase both the total number of students of color and their representation within the STEM workforce are not new propositions. Previous studies conducted by the National Academies and other organizations have underscored this urgency (e.g., NAS, NAE, and IOM 2011; NSF 2017; Palmer et al. 2015; Rodriguez et al. 2012). However, an underappreciated strategy to accomplish this goal is to turn the nation's attention and resources to the schools that are most intentional in their efforts to provide pathways to educational success and workforce readiness for today's student body: the nation's more than 700 two- and four-year MSIs can serve in this capacity.

Chapter 3 begins a fuller discussion of MSIs and the students they serve. For now, we will note that MSIs vary substantially in their origins, missions, student

---

[9] Nontraditional students are generally defined as students with one of the following characteristics: independent, having one or more dependents, being a single caregiver, not having received a standard high school diploma, having delayed enrollment in postsecondary education by a year or more after high school, working full time while enrolled, and/or attending school part time (Brock 2010; Choy 2002; Horn and Carroll 1996; Kim 2002, Taniguchi and Kaufman 2005).

demographics, and levels of institutional selectivity. But in general, their service to the nation provides a gateway to higher education and the workforce, particularly for underrepresented students of color and those from low-income and first-generation-to-college backgrounds. Taken together, two- and four-year MSIs enroll nearly 30 percent of all undergraduates in the U.S. higher education system (Espinosa et al. 2017). **Given the nation's urgent need for a well-trained, domestic STEM-capable workforce, and the strong value proposition for inclusion and diversity, MSIs are perhaps the most poised of any sector within American postsecondary education to solve an unaddressed STEM workforce supply problem.** In the interest of bolstering national achievements in STEM and remaining competitive in a global economy, determining the most effective strategies to support student success at MSIs becomes all the more urgent.

REFERENCES

Alphonse, Lylah. 2013. Are we misinterpreting the STEM crisis? *US News & World Report*. Available at www.usnews.com/news.com/stem-solutions/articles/2013/09/09. Accessed October 2018.

Atkinson, Robert. 2013. A short and long-term solution to America's STEM crisis. *The Hill*. https://thehill.com/blogs/congress-blog/technology/287435-a-short-and-long-term-solution-to-americas-stem-crisis. Accessed January 2019.

Betancourt, Joseph R., Alexander R. Green, J. Emilio Carrillo, and I. I. Owusu Ananeh-Firempong. 2003. "Defining cultural competence: a practical framework for addressing racial/ethnic disparities in health and health care." *Public Health Reports* 118 (4):293-302.

BLS (U.S. Bureau of Labor Statistics). 2017. STEM Occupations: Past, Present, and Future. Available at: https://www.bls.gov/spotlight/2017/science-technology-engineering-and-mathematics-stem-occupations-past-present-and-future/pdf/science-technology-engineering-and-mathematics-stem-occupations-past-present-and-future.pdf. Accessed August 2018.

Bransberger, Peace and Demarée K. Michelau. 2016. Knocking at the College Door: Projections of High School Graduates, 9th Edition. Boulder, CO: Western Interstate Commission for Higher Education. Available at: https://knocking.wiche.edu/reports/2017/3/22/the-west-a-decade-of-rapid increase-of-hispanic-graduates-before-a-sudden-reversal. Accessed October 2018.

Brock, Thomas. 2010. "Young adults and higher education: Barriers and breakthroughs to success." *The Future of Children* 20 (1):109-132.

Campbell, Lesley, G., Siya Mehtani, Mary E. Dozier, and Janice Rinehart. 2013."Gender-heterogeneous working groups produce higher quality science." *PLOS ONE* 8 (10).

Cappelli, Peter H. 2015. "Skill gaps, skill shortages, and skill mismatches: Evidence and arguments for the United States." *ILR Review* 68 (2):251-290.

Carnevale, Anthony P, Nicole Smith, and Michelle Melton. 2011. STEM, Science, Technology, Engineering, Mathematics. Washington, DC: Georgetown University, Center on Education and the Workforce.

Chang, Mitchell, Mike Hoa Nguyen, and Kapua L. Chandler. 2015."Can data disaggregation resolve blind spots in policy making? Examining a case for Native Hawaiians." *AAPI Nexus: Policy, Practice and Community* 13 (1-2):295-320. doi: 10.17953/1545-0317.13.1.295.

Choy, Susan P. 2002. Access and Persistence: Findings from 10 Years of Longitudinal Research on Students. Washington, DC: American Council on Education, Center for Policy Analysis.

Clark, Ximena, Timothy J. Hatton, and Jeffrey G. Williamson. 2002. Where Do U.S. Immigrants Come from and Why? Cambridge, MA: National Bureau of Economic Research.

Cohen, Jordan J., Barbara A. Gabriel, and Charles Terrell. 2002. "The case for diversity in the health care workforce" *Health Affairs (Project Hope)* 21 (5).

Espinosa, Lorelle L. Jonathan M. Turk, and Morgan Taylor. 2017. Pulling Back the Curtain: Enrollment and Outcomes at Minority Serving Institutions. Washington, DC: American Council on Education. Available at: https://www.acenet.edu/news-room/Documents/Pulling-Back-the-Curtain-Enrollment-and-Outcomes-at-MSIs.pdf. Accessed October 2018.

European Commission (European Commission Centre for Strategy and Evaluation Services). 2003. The Costs and Benefits of Diversity: A Study on Methods and Indicators to Measure the Cost Effectiveness of Diversity Policies in Enterprises: Executive summary. Kent, UK: Centre for Strategy and Evaluation Service.

Evans, Rupert M. 1999. "Increasing minority representation in health care management." *Health Forum Journal* 42 (6).

Federal Glass Ceiling Commission. 1995. Good for Business: Making Full Use of the Nation's Human Capital. Washington, DC: U.S. Department of Labor.

Florida, Richard. 2014. The Rise of the Creative Class—Revisited: Revised and Expanded. New York: Basic Books.

GAO (U.S. Government Accountability Office). 2017. Diversity in the Technology Sector: Federal Agencies Could Impove Oversight of Equal Employment Opportunity Requirements. Available at: https://www.gao.gov/assets/690/688460.pdf. Accessed October 2018.

Guillermina, Jasso, Mark R. Rosenzweig, and James P. Smith. 2000. The Changing Skill of New Immigrants to the United States: Recent Trends and Their Determinants Issues in the Economics of Immigration. Chicago, IL: University of Chicago Press.

Hanson, Gordon H. and Matthew J. Slaughter. 2016. High-Skilled Immigration and the Rise of STEM Occupations in U.S. Employment. Cambridge, MA: National Bureau of Economic Research.

Hatton, Timothy J. and Jeffrey G. Williamson. 2005. "What Fundamentals Drive World Migration?" In George Borjas, Jeff Crisp (eds). 2005. Poverty, International Migration and Asylum. 1st ed, Studies in Development Economics and Policy. London, UK: Palgrave Macmillan UK.

Hatton, Timothy J. and Jeffrey G. Williamson. 2009. Vanishing Third World Immigrants? Cambridge, MA: National Bureau of Economic Research.

Heckler, Margaret. 1985. Report of the Secretary's Task Force on Black and minority health. United States Department of Health and Human Services. Available at: https://minorityhealth.hhs.gov/assets/pdf/checked/1/ANDERSON.pdf. Accessed October 2018.

Holland, Ariel and Latha Palaniappan. 2012. "Problems with the collection and interpretation of Asian-American health data: omission, aggregation, and extrapolation." *Annals of Epidemiology* 22 (6):397-405. doi: 10.1016/j.annepidem.2012.04.001.

Horn, Laura J. and C. Dennis Carroll. 1996. Nontraditional Undergraduates: Trends in Enrollment from 1986 to 1992 and Persistence and Attainment among 1989-90 Beginning Postsecondary Students. Postsecondary Education Descriptive Analysis Reports. Statistical Analysis Report: ERIC.

Huang, Gary, Nebiyu Taddese, and Elizabeth Walter. 2000. "Entry and persistence of women and minorities in college science and engineering education." *Education Statistics Quarterly* 2 (3):59-60.

Hunt, Jennifer. 2011. "Which immigrants are most innovative and entrepreneurial? Distinctions by entry visa." *Journal of Labor Economics* 29 (3):417-457. doi: 10.1086/659409.

Hunt, Vivian, Sara Prince, Sundiatu Dixon-Fyle, and Lareina Yee. 2018. Delivering through diversity. McKinsey & Company. Intel. 2017. Diversity and Inclusion Annual Report: Approaching the First Leg in Intel's Journey. Available at: https://newsroom.intel.com/editorials/2017-diversity-inclusion-annual-report-approaching-first-leg-intels-journey/. Accessed October 2018.

Jaimovich, Nir and Henry E Siu. 2017. "High-Skilled Immigration, STEM Employment, and Non-Routine-Biased Technical Change." In High-Skilled Migration to the United States and Its Economic Consequences. Chicago, IL: University of Chicago Press.

Kim, Mikyong Minsun. 2002. "Historically Black vs. White institutions: Academic development among Black students." *The Review of Higher Education* 25 (4):385-407.

Kochan, Thomas A. 2002."Addressing the crisis in confidence in corporations: Root causes, victims, and strategies for reform." *The Academy of Management Executive* 16 (3):139-141.

Kuenzi, Jeffrey J. 2008. "Science, technology, engineering, and mathematics (STEM) education: Background, federal policy, and legislative action." Available at: https://digitalcommons.unl. edu. Accessed October 2018.

Langdon, David, Mark Doms, Beethika Khan, David Beede, and George McKittrick. 2011. Economics, and Administration Statistics. STEM: Good Jobs Now and for the Future. Esa Issue Brief #03-11.

LaVeist, Thomas A., Darrell J. Gaskin, and Patrick Richard. 2009. "The economic burden of health inequalities in the United States." Available at: https://www.hhnmag.com/ext/resources/inc-hhn/ pdfs/resources/Burden_Of_Health_FINAL_0.pdf. Accessed October 2018.

Murray, Christopher J. L., Sandeep C. Kulkarni, Catherine Michaud, Niels Tomijima, Maria T. Bulzacchelli, Terrell J. Iandiorio, and Majid Ezzati. 2006. "Eight Americas: investigating mortality disparities across races, counties, and race-counties in the United States." *PLoS Medicine* 3 (9):e260.

NAE and NRC (National Academy of Engineering and National Research Council). 2012. Assuring the US Department of Defense a Strong Science, Technology, Engineering, and Mathematics (STEM) Workforce. Washington, DC: The National Academies Press. https://doi. org/10.17225/13467.

NAS, NAE, and IOM (National Academy of Sciences, National Academy of Engineering, and the Institute of Medicine). 2007. Rising Above the Gathering Storm: Energizing and Employing America for a Brighter Economic Future. Washington, DC: National Academies Press. https:// doi.org/10.18226/11463.

NAS, NAE, and IOM. 2011. Expanding Underrepresented Minority Participation: America's Science and Technology Talent at the Crossroads. Washington DC: National Academies Press https:// doi.org/10.17225/12984.

NASEM (National Academies of Sciences, Engineering, and Medicine). 2017a. Building America's Skilled Technical Workforce. Washington, DC: National Academies Press. https://doi.org 10.17225/23472.

NASEM. 2017b. Undergraduate research experiences for STEM students: Successes, Challenges, and Opportunities. Washington, DC: National Academies Press. https://doi.or 10.17225/24622.

NCES (National Center for Education Statistics). 2002. Nontraditional Undergraduates (NCES 2002–012), Institute of Education Sciences, U.S. Department of Education. Washington, DC. Available at: https://nces.ed.gov/pubs2002/2002012.pdf. Accessed October 2018.

NCES. 2017. The Condition of Education 2017. Institute of Education Sciences, U.S. Department of Education. Washington, DC. Available at: https://nces.ed.gov/pubs2017/2017144.pdf. Accessed October 2018.

NCES. 2018. Digest of Education Statistics 2016 (NCES 2017-094). Institute of Education Sciences, U.S. Department of Education. Washington, DC. Available at: https://nces.ed.gov/ pubs2017/2017094.pdf. Accessed October 2018.

NSF (National Science Foundation). 2017. Committee on Equal Opportunities in Science and Engineering 2015-2016 Biennial Report to Congress Broadening Participation in America's STEM Workforce. https://www.nsf.gov/od/oia/activities/ceose/CEOSE%202015-2016%20 Biennial%20Report%20(Final).pdf

National Summit on Competititveness. 2005. Department of Commerce. Summary. Available at: https://www.aip.org/fyi/2005/national-summit-competitiveness. Accessed October 2018.

NSB (National Science Board). 2018. Science and Engineering Indicators 2018. Alexandria, VA. Available at: https://www.nsf.gov/statistics/2018/nsb20181/. Accessed October 2018.

NSB. 2015. Revisiting the STEM Workforce: A Companion to Science and Engineering Indicators 2014. Alexandria, VA: National Science Board.

PCAST (President's Council of Advisors on Science and Technology). 2012. Report to the President. Engage to Excel: Producing One Million Additional College Graduates with Degrees in Science, Technology, Engineering, and Mathematics. Executive Office of the President. Available at: https://obamawhitehouse.archives.gov/sites/default/files/microsites/ostp/pcast-engage-to-excel-final_2-25-12.pdf. Accessed October 2018.

PCAST. 2014. Report to the President. Information Technology for Targeting Job-Skills Training and Matching Talent to Jobs. Executive Office of the President. Available: https://obamawhitehouse.archives.gov/sites/default/files/microsites/ostp/PCAST/PCAST_worforce_edIT_Oct-2014.pdf. Accessed October 2018.

Page, Scott E. 2008. The Difference: How the Power of Diversity Creates Better Groups, Firms, Schools, and Societies. Princeton, N.J.: Princeton University Press.

Palmer, Robert T., Dina C Maramba, and Marybeth Gasman. 2015. Fostering Success of Ethnic and Racial Minorities in STEM. New York, NY: Routledge

Pew Research Center. 2014. "More Hispanics, Blacks enrolling in college, but lag in bachelor's degrees." Available at: http://www.pewresearch.org/fact-tank/2014/04/24/more-hispanics-blacks-enrolling-in-college-but-lag-in-bachelors-degrees/. Accessed October 2018.

Pew Research Center. 2015. "Modern immigration wave brings 59 million to U.S., driving population growth and change through 2065: Views of immigration's impact on U.S. society mixed." Pew Research Center. Available at: http://www.pewresearch.org/wp-content/uploads/sites/5/2015/09/2015-09-28_modern-immigration-wave_REPORT.pdf. Accessed October 2018.

Pew Research Center. 2016. "The demographic trends shaping American politics in 2016 and beyond." Available at: http://www.pewresearch.org/fact-tank/2016/01/27/the-demographic-trends-shaping-american-politics-in-2016-and-beyond/. Accessed October 2018.

Pew Research Center. 2017. "U.S. students academic achievement still lags peers in many other countries." Fact Tank: Pew Research Center, 2017-2002.

Pew Research Center. 2018. "Women and Men in STEM Often at Odds Over Workplace Equity." Chapter 1: Diversity in the STEM workforce varies widely across jobs. Available at: http://assets.pewresearch.org/wpcontent/uploads/sites/3/2018/01/09142305/PS_2018.01.09_STEM_FINAL.pdf. Accessed September 2018.

Putnam, Robert D. 2007. "E pluribus unum: Diversity and community in the twenty-first century: The 2006 Johan Skytte prize lecture." *Scandanavian Political Studies* 30 (157):149-151.

Ramakrishnan, Karthick and Janelle Wong. 2018. "Ethnicity data is critical to address the diverse needs of Asian Americans and Pacific Islander." AAPI Data. Available at: http://aapidata.com/blog/ethnicity-data-is-critical/. Accessed October 2018.

Rodriguez, Carlos, Rita Kirshstein, Lauren Banks Amos, Wehmah Jones, Lorelle Espinosa, and David Watnick. 2012. "Broadening participation in STEM: A call to action." Unpublished report, NSF Grant No. HRD-1059774. Washington DC: American Institutes for Research.

Rothwell, Jonathan. 2013. "The hidden STEM economy." The Brookings Insitution. Washington, DC. Available at: https://www.brookings.edu/research/the-hidden-stem-economy/. Accessed October 2018.

Springer, Molly, Charlotte E. Davidson, and Stephanie J. Waterman. March 2013. Native American Student Affairs Units. In Heather J. Shotton, Shelly C. Lowe, Stephanie J. Waterman, John Garland. 2013. Beyond the Asterisk: Understanding Native Students in Higher Education. Sterling, VA: Stylus Publishing.

Sullivan, Louis W. 2004. "Missing persons: minorities in the health professions, a report of the Sullivan Commission on Diversity in the Healthcare Workforce." Available at: https://depts.washington.edu/ccph/pdf_files/SullivanReport.pdf. Accessed October 2018.

Taniguchi, Hiromi and Gayle Kaufman. 2005. "Degree completion among nontraditional college students." *Social Science Quarterly* 86 (4):912-927.

Tapia, Richard A. 2007. "True diversity doesn't come from abroad." *The Chronicle of Higher Education* 54 (5):B34.

U.S. Census Bureau. 2017. School Enrollment of the Hispanic Population: Two Decades of Growth. Available at: https://www.census.gov/newsroom/blogs/random-samplings/2017/08/schoolen-rollmentof.html. Accessed October 2018.

U.S. Census Bureau. 2018. Demographic Turning Points for the United States: Population Projections for 2020 to 2060. Washington, DC. Available at: https://www.census.gov/content/dam/Census/library/publications/2018/demo/P25_1144.pdf. Accessed October 2018.

U.S. Department of Commerce. 2017. STEM Jobs: 2017 Update. Washington, DC. Available: http://www.esa.doc.gov/sites/default/files/stem-jobs-2017-update.pdf. Accessed October 2018.

U.S. Department of Education. National Commission on Mathematics Science Teaching for the 21st Century. 2000. Before It's Too Late: A Report to the Nation from the National Commission on Mathematics and Science Teaching for the 21st Century. Washington, DC. Available: https://files.eric.ed.gov/fulltext/ED441705.pdf. Accessed October 2018.

U.S. Department of Health and Human Services. 2007. Gaps and Strategies for Improving AI/AN/NA Data: Final Report. Washington, DC: U.S. Department of Health and Human Services, Office of the Assistant Secretary for Planning and Education.

U.S. Department of Health and Human Services. 2014. National Healthcare Disparities Report 2011. Rockville: Agency for Healthcare Research and Quality. Available: https://www.ahrq.gov/sites/default/files/wysiwyg/research/findings/nhqrdr/nhdr11/nhdr11.pdf. Accessed October 2018.

Valantine, Hannah A. and Francis S. Collins. 2015. "National Institutes of Health addresses the science of diversity." *Proceedings of the National Academy of Sciences of the United States of America* 112 (40):12240-12242.

White House (White House Initiative on Asian Americans and Pacific Islanders). 2016. Best Practices for the Disaggregation of Federal Data on Asian Americans and Pacific Islanders. Washington, DC.

3

MSIs and the Students They Serve

"... the graduates of MSIs will be critical to solving the grand chal-
lenges of work in the age of [technology], they will be critical to the
formation of cognitively diverse teams, and they will be important in
bridging communities of privilege and communities in transition."
    – Earl Lewis, Former President, Andrew W. Mellon Foundation

---

KEY FINDINGS

• MSIs play a critical role in training and educating students of color in STEM disciplines.

• MSIs have diverse student bodies, not only in terms of race and ethnicity, but also in income, enrollment intensity, and academic preparation. As a result, standard institutional accountability metrics that fail to consider the influence of important contextual factors inadequately assess the performance of MSIs and their students. Contextual factors to consider may include students' financial circumstances, life stage, commitments to work and family, academic preparation, enrollment intensity, and the resources available at each institution.

• While the role of four-year institutions has been emphasized in MSI research to date, two-year MSIs are also critical actors in providing access to higher education for students of color, and provide important pathways to STEM-related education, training, and careers.

The nation needs to cultivate a larger and more diverse science, technology, engineering, and mathematics (STEM) workforce. Given the rationale outlined in Chapter 2, it can be argued that Minority Serving Institutions (MSIs) are underutilized resources to help address this urgent national need.

Although many MSIs are long established, their role in the nation's higher education system are often overlooked or misunderstood. This chapter provides a closer look at MSIs, their students, and the complex context in which MSIs operate. The chapter begins with an overview of the seven federally recognized types of MSIs, with emphasis (as noted in Chapter 1) on four: Historically Black Colleges and Universities (HBCUs), Tribal Colleges and Universities (TCUs), Hispanic Serving Institutions (HSIs), and Asian American and Native American Pacific Islander Serving Institutions (AANAPISIs). This is followed by a discussion on what makes MSIs diverse, including the ethnic makeup of their student bodies, faculty, and leadership. The chapter concludes with a discussion of the problematic nature of common accountability metrics to measure the performance of MSIs, and what it means to "serve" minority students. Gaining a stronger understanding of MSIs, their faculty, and students will help decision makers, funders, and other stakeholders of higher education and workforce development make more informed decisions on how best to support these institutions as they prepare their students for the workforce.

WHAT ARE MINORITY SERVING INSTITUTIONS?

For more than 180 years, MSIs have had a presence in the higher education landscape, but this presence has expanded rapidly over the past few decades. These institutions now exist across all regions, in nearly every state and territory, and range in terms of size, student populations, physical space, and geographical location (i.e., rural, urban, and suburban) (Figure 3-1).

Based on analyses by the American Council on Education for this report, there are more than 700 federally designated MSIs that represent approximately 14 percent of all degree-granting, Title IV-eligible institutions of higher education.[1] Taken together, they enroll roughly 5 million students, or nearly 30 percent of all undergraduates in U.S. higher education. These institutions carry a significant postsecondary load for the United States and create educational opportunities that in many cases would not otherwise exist (Espinosa et al. 2017; Kim and Conrad 2006; Núñez 2014).

MSIs are traditionally defined by one of two overarching categories: *historically defined or enrollment-defined institutions* (Tables 3-1 and 3-2). Historically defined MSIs were established with the express purpose of providing access to higher education for a specific minority group (Espinosa et al. 2017; Núñez et

---

[1] IPEDS data, collection year 2015. See Appendix F for a table of MSIs and non-MSIs by sector.

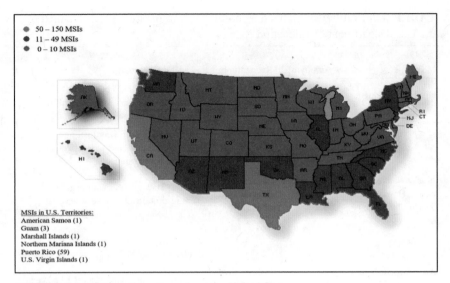

FIGURE 3-1 MSI locations throughout the United States.
NOTE: Image produced in diymaps.net.
SOURCE: Data from the Integrated Postsecondary Education Data System, collection year 2015.

TABLE 3-1 Historically Defined Minority Serving Institutions

MSI Type	Acronym	Federal Recognition	Federal Definition
Historically Black Colleges and Universities	HBCU	Higher Education Act of 1965[a]	Any historically black college or university established prior to 1964, whose principal mission was, and is, the education of Black Americans
Tribal Colleges and Universities	TCU	Tribally Controlled College or University Assistance Act of 1978[b,c]	Institutions chartered by their respective Indian tribes through the sovereign authority of the tribes or by the federal government with the specific purpose to provide higher education opportunities to Native Americans through programs that are locally and culturally based, holistic, and supportive

[a] Higher Education Act of 1965, Pub. L. No. 89-329 (1965).

[b] Tribally Controlled College or University Assistance Act of 1978, Pub. L. No. 95-471 (1978).

[c] TCUs were not established by this legislation, as they are founded by individual Native tribes. Rather, this legislation provides federal support for these institutions.

SOURCE: Adapted from Espinoso et al. (2017).

TABLE 3-2 Enrollment-Defined Minority Serving Institutions, as Defined by the U.S. Department of Education

MSI Type	Acronym	Federal Recognition	Federal Definition
Hispanic-Serving Institutions	HSI	Higher Education Act of 1992[a]	Institutions with 25 percent or more total undergraduate Hispanic full-time-equivalent student enrollment
Alaska Native and Native Hawaiian-Serving Institutions	ANNHI	Higher Education Act of 1998[b]	Alaska Native-Serving Institutions are institutions that have at least 20 percent Alaska Native students. Native Hawaiian-Serving Institutions are institutions that have at least 10 percent Native Hawaiian students Collectively, these institutions are referred to as ANNH institutions
Asian American and Native American Pacific Islander-Serving Institutions	AANAPISI	College Cost Reduction and Access Act of 2007[c,d]	Institutions that have at least 10 percent enrollment of Asian American Pacific Islander students
Predominantly Black Institutions	PBI	Higher Education Opportunity Act of 2008[e]	Institutions that have the following demographics: 1. at least 1,000 undergraduate students 2. at least 50 percent low-income or first-generation-to-college degree-seeking undergraduate enrollment 3. low per-full-time undergraduate expenditure in comparison with other institutions offering similar instruction 4. enroll at least 40 percent African American students[f]
Native American-Serving, Nontribal Institutions	NASNTI	Higher Education Opportunity Act of 2008	Institutions that have at least 10 percent enrollment of Native American students[g]

[a] Higher Education Act of 1992, Pub. L. No. 102-325 (1992).
[b] Higher Education Act of 1998, Pub. L. No. 105-244 (1998).
[c] College Cost Reduction and Access Act of 2007, Pub. L. No. 110-84 (2007).
[d] The AANAPISIs program was expanded under the Higher Education Opportunity Act of 2008.
[e] Higher Education Act of 2008, Pub. L. No. 110-315 (2008).
[f] Note that PBIs are predicated on the institution meeting an enrollment threshold, and HBCUs were established for the primary purpose of educating Black students.
[g] Note that NASNTIs are predicated on the institution meeting an enrollment threshold, and TCUs were established for the purpose of educating Native American students.
SOURCE: Adapted from Espinosa et al. (2017).

al. 2015). They include HBCUs and TCUs. Five other MSI types are federally designated based on student enrollment and institutional expenditure thresholds:

- HSIs,
- Alaska Native-Serving and Native Hawaiian-Serving Institutions (ANNHIs),
- AANAPISIs,
- Predominantly Black Institutions (PBIs), and
- Native American-Serving Nontribal Institutions (NASNTIs).

Two caveats should be highlighted. First, because MSIs enroll substantially diverse communities, they can qualify for more than one category of MSI. For example, based on enrollment numbers, some HBCUs could potentially identify as HSIs (Núñez et al. 2015). Second, there is substantial heterogeneity in institutional characteristics, not only between MSIs but also within each type. (See Box 3-1 for additional discussion.) These caveats should be considered when collecting, analyzing, communicating, and reviewing data on MSIs. In addition, different stakeholders "count" the number of MSIs differently, which has resulted in varied estimates of the total number of MSIs. The U.S. Department of Education's College Scorecard data include institutions as MSIs if they are eligible to

---

BOX 3-1
Diversity within Historically and Enrollment-Defined MSIs

MSIs can broadly be classified as two categories of institutions, historically or enrollment-defined. However, there is substantial institutional diversity within each type of MSI that current legislation and reporting do not address. The heterogeneity in institutional characteristics can be explored from several dimensions, including systemic (e.g., public versus private governance, large versus small enrollments), programmatic (e.g., research- versus teaching-intensive focus, degrees offered), demographic (e.g., the composition of students, faculty, and institutional personnel), resource-related (e.g., institutional capacity), and geographic (e.g., rural versus suburban versus urban settings).

As the nation's population and education system grow more diverse, more enrollment-defined MSIs will emerge, so it is important to have a greater understanding of the institutional diversity among and between MSIs. Such research can lead to more informed decisions on which efforts can best support a particular *type* of MSI and its students. It would also allow for a greater opportunity for MSI leaders, researchers, decision makers, and investors to more appropriately and more equitably compare performance across institutions. (See Chapter 6 for the committee's recommendation to funding agencies to support such efforts.)

SOURCES: Harris (2013), McCormick et al. (2005), Núñez et al. (2016).

apply for federal funding, in a given fiscal year, under Title III and Title V of the Higher Education Act. On the other hand, groups that advocate on behalf of MSIs—particularly MSIs that are enrollment defined—take into account under-graduate enrollment thresholds when identifying MSIs and not federal eligibility under the law. *Note that the data presented in this report come from a variety of sources that may differ in how MSIs are defined or "counted;" each of these sources is identified in the report.*

In pragmatic terms, the term "MSI" has been solidified in the higher educa-tion community through its use by the federal government in its designations and the ability of institutions to receive and/or apply for MSI-specific federal funding. A specified list of allowable activities gears this funding toward institu-tional capacity building, improving student success, and expanding educational opportunities for low-income students (Gasman et al. 2015; Hegji 2017).

A number of historical and contemporary texts go into depth about the beginnings of the various MSI types, including profiles of specific institutions and the overall contributions of MSIs to their students and communities (e.g., Anderson 1988; AIHEC 2012; Núñez et al. 2015; Santiago et al. 2016; Teranishi et al. 2013). What we present here is a *snapshot* view of HBCUs, TCUs, HSIs, and AANAPISIs. Their unique characteristics, and notable or recent activity in STEM, are also discussed. A deeper look at the promising practices to support MSI STEM students on these campuses can be found in Chapter 5.

Historically Defined MSIs

As noted above, HBCUs and TCUs are defined as historical in that they were established with the express purpose of serving specific populations, namely, African Americans and Native Americans, respectively. This historical reference is important given that HBCUs and TCUs came into existence long before they were officially recognized through the Higher Education Act of 1965 and the Tribally Controlled College or University Assistance Act of 1978, respectively (Gasman et al. 2015). These acts set the stage for a new kind of federal support for HBCUs and TCUs. Table 3-1 displays the two historically defined MSI types, their associated acronyms, the pieces of legislation by which each category was established, and their federal definitions.

HBCUs at a Glance

Prior to the Civil War, African Americans were denied access to structured postsecondary education throughout much of the United States. Thus, institutions of higher education with the specific intent to educate students of African descent were established, with Cheyney University of Pennsylvania (1837), Lincoln Uni-versity (1854), and Wilberforce University (1856) representing the nation's first HBCUs (U.S. Department of Education 1991; Thurgood Marshall College Fund

2015). In 1862, the Morrill Act[2] extended higher education opportunities to broad segments of the U.S. population in order to better prepare the nation for a changing economy and society (NRC 1996). This legislation applied to freed citizens only.

After the Civil War, the Freedmen's Bureau[3] and the African Methodist Episcopal Church launched efforts to provide newly freed African Americans with basic needs, including food, medical assistance, and education. These advocates helped establish 70 schools of higher education between 1866 and 1882 (Hawkins 2012). Funding for HBCUs expanded as a result of the Second Morrill Act in 1890,[4] which required segregated public higher education systems to establish land-grant institutions for African American students when such institutions were created for White students only (U.S. Department of Education 1991). Title III of the Higher Education Act of 1965, as amended, defines an HBCU as "any historically black college or university that was established prior to 1964, whose principal mission was, and is, the education of black Americans."[5]

Based on 2016 fall enrollment, 51 public and 51 private two- and four-year HBCUs operate in the United States (National Center for Education Statistics 2018). The majority are in the South; however, HBCUs are also in the Midwest and Mid-Atlantic. They vary in size, curricular focus, traditions, and other characteristics, but they share the mission of preparing and empowering African American students to succeed in higher education. Although HBCUs comprise only 3 percent of all postsecondary institutions, they have shown disproportionate success in graduating African American students, particularly in the STEM fields (Kim and Conrad 2006; UNCF 2017). HBCUs have also long produced a disproportionately large percentage of African American students who go on to earn STEM doctoral degrees (Burrelli and Rapoport 2008; Fiegener and Proudfoot 2013; Sibulkin and Butler 2011; Solórzano and Solórzano 1995).

The success of HBCUs in educating African American students in STEM has been attributed to a number of factors, including the institutions' strong academic and social support networks and culturally responsive teaching approaches. Some observers have argued that one of the most impactful practices of HBCUs is their dedication to maintain an institutional culture of success (e.g., Gasman and Nguyen 2014). (See Chapter 5 for additional strategies used by HBCUs to support student success.) This long-standing commitment to expect, cultivate, and celebrate success has helped HBCUs prepare African American students to reach their full academic potential.[6]

---

[2] The First Morrill Act, 1862, 7 U.S.C. 301 et seq.

[3] Formally known as the Bureau of Refugees, Freedmen and Abandoned Lands, this organization was commissioned by Congress in 1865 (https://www.archives.gov/research/african-americans/freedmens-bureau).

[4] The Second Morrill Act, 1980, 7 U.S.C. 321 et seq.

[5] Higher Education Act of 1965, Pub. L. No. 89-329 (1965).

[6] For additional information on the history of HBCUs and their impact on the success of African Americans in postsecondary education, see Anderson (1988) and UNCF (2017).

HBCUs have a long-standing history and legacy within the higher education landscape, and as a result, social science research on HBCUs is stronger than it is for other MSIs. Nonetheless, many research questions related to HBCUs warrant further exploration, as discussed elsewhere in this report.

TCUs at a Glance

TCUs were established by individual Native American tribes with a core mission to sustain tribal cultures, traditions, and languages, while bringing education, social, and economic opportunities to Native Americans (AIHEC 1999). Following the success of the "self-determination" movement of the 1960s that emphasized self-governance by federally recognized tribes (Cornell and Kalt 2010), Native American leaders restructured tribal higher education to "strengthen reservations and tribal culture without assimilation" (AIHEC 1999). The Navajo Nation created the first tribally controlled college in 1968, now known as Diné College (AIHEC 1999).

TCUs first received federal funding through the Tribally Controlled College or University Assistance Act of 1978. This legislation defines a TCU as "an institution of higher education which is formally controlled, or has been formally sanctioned, or chartered, by the governing body of an Indian tribe or tribes."[7] Today, there are 35 two- and four-year TCUs located primarily in the northern Midwest and Rocky Mountain states.[8] These institutions, most of which are embedded within native, rural communities, serve roughly 30,000 full- and part-time students, including Native American and Alaska Native students, representing more than 250 federally recognized Indian tribes (AIHEC 2018; QEM 2012).

TCUs offer essential sources of educational opportunity for many Native American and Alaska Native students. Culturally relevant support approaches and community engagement are critical components of each TCU's curriculum (AIHEC 1999). At schools with a high population of Native American students, all courses, even those without an explicit cultural focus, are designed from a Native American perspective (AIHEC 1999). As described by Stull et al. (2015), TCUs do not share the same mission as many other higher education institutions, but instead possess a very different history of purpose, investing in efforts to "revitalize Native languages and culture, promote Tribal sovereignty, and further economic growth aligned with Tribal values in the communities they serve" (Stull et al. 2015).

Over the past several decades, STEM-focused programming at TCUs has increased. Grant-funding opportunities and partnerships with federal agencies

---

[7] Tribally Controlled College or University Assistance Act of 1978, Pub. L. No. 95-471 (1978).

[8] The Department of Education collects data on 35 TCUs. Wind River Tribal College (which does not submit data to IPEDS) and Tribal Colleges located in Canada are not included in this tally. Indigenous-focused organizations may provide different total counts of TCUs, which speaks to the complex nature of data collection and reporting for MSIs.

(e.g., the U.S. Department of Agriculture and U.S. Department of Energy) have enabled TCUs to expand their STEM programming; offer new degree options in the fields of information technology, environmental science, and science education; and provide research internship opportunities for their students (Native Science Report 2018; PCAST 2012). (See Chapter 5 for additional strategies used by TCUs to support student success.) Intentional federal legislation and grant programming have served an essential role in stimulating this growth. Notable efforts include the 1996 Executive Order 13021 for Tribal Colleges and Universities,[9] the National Science Foundation's Tribal Colleges and Universities Program, and the 2011 Executive Order 13592[10] for Improving Native American and Alaska Native Educational Opportunities and Strengthening Tribal Colleges and Universities.[11] Although some progress has been made to bolster and sustain STEM success for this traditionally underrepresented population of students, additional investments and resources are needed.

Enrollment-Defined MSIs

In the enrollment-defined or enrollment-driven MSIs, if and when a given institution meets an undergraduate enrollment threshold for a certain population of students, it is designated as the appropriate MSI type. Federal eligibility also requires that these institutions have comparatively low general and educational expenditures, an amount determined annually by the U.S. Department of Education. Other criteria include that they are eligible for Title IV funding[12] and are degree-granting, public or private nonprofit institutions. Established between 1992 and 2008 through various pieces of legislation, there are currently five enrollment-defined MSI types (Table 3-2).

HSIs at a Glance

In 1986, the founding members of the Hispanic Association of Colleges and Universities (HACU) self-defined HSIs as a designated group of colleges and universities with an intentional focus to serve a high population of Hispanic students

---

[9] Executive Order 13021 for TCUs was signed by President William J. Clinton.

[10] Executive Order 13592 for Improving American Indian and Alaska Native Educational Opportunities and Strengthening Tribal Colleges and Universities was signed by President Barack H. Obama.

[11] For additional information on the history of TCUs and their impact on the success of American Indian/Alaska Native students in postsecondary education, see the American Indian Higher Education Consortium (AIHEC 1999) and Guillory and Ward (2008).

[12] Title IV of Higher Education Act of 1965, Pub. L. No. 89-329 (1965); institutions eligible for Title IV funding enter a written agreement with the Secretary of Education allowing participation in Title IV federal financial aid programs, such as grant aid, federal work study, and federal student loans.

(HACU 2012; Valdez 2015).[13] Several years later, the Higher Education Act of 1992 defined HSIs as two- or four-year nonprofit institutions with at least a 25 percent Hispanic undergraduate full-time-equivalent enrollment and a high proportion of students with financial need.[14,15] As shown in Figure 3-2, since then, the number of eligible institutions has grown from 189 in 1994 to 492 in 2016 (HACU 2018). Based on 2016-2017 data, of the 492 HSIs, roughly two-thirds were public and just under one-half were two-year institutions (Excelencia in Education 2018).

HSIs show considerable variability in size and focus, and range from small private institutions to large public research universities. Most HSIs are located in urban metropolitan areas, with a small number in rural areas (Núñez et al. 2016). Some institutions, such as Boricua College in New York, were founded with the mission to serve Hispanic populations; however, the majority have become HSIs because of a fast-growing Hispanic population in and around the local and regional communities that they serve. As a result, the number of HSIs continues to grow as national demographics change, with more HSIs located in regions of the country where Hispanic population growth is concentrated (see Box 3-2). For example, California, Texas, and Puerto Rico are home to greater than 60 percent of all HSIs, and Florida, Illinois, New York, and New Mexico account for roughly an additional 20 percent (Excelencia in Education 2018).

HSIs' contribution to the education of Hispanic students is significant. While HSIs represent 15 percent of all nonprofit colleges and universities, they enroll the majority of Hispanic college students (Excelencia in Education 2018). Some institutions' student bodies are composed of the minimum level of 25 percent Hispanic students, while others, mostly in Texas, California, and Puerto Rico, have student bodies that are 60 to 100 percent Hispanic (HACU 2017). HSIs also show considerable diversity in their non-Hispanic enrollments; ranging from predominantly White to predominantly African American and other underrepresented populations. However, as a whole, HSIs serve larger proportions of African American and Native American students than HBCUs and TCUs, respectively (Núñez et al. 2015).

In recent years, there has been a concerted effort to build the capacity of HSIs to enroll, retain, and graduate more students—especially Hispanic students—in the STEM fields. This initiative includes boosting HSIs' research productivity and contributions to the production of advanced STEM degrees by a growing Hispanic population and student body. In 2017, two pieces of legislation provided guid-

---

[13] Several known HSIs were established with an intentional focus to serve Hispanic students: Boricua College (New York), Colegio Cesar Chavez (Oregon), Eugenio Maria de Hostos Community College (New York), Northern New Mexico College (New Mexico), and National Hispanic University (California, closed in 2015), Puerto Rican institutions, and St. Augustine College (Illinois). See Olivas (1982); Calderón Galdeano et al. (2012); Núñez et al. (2016).

[14] Higher Education Amendments of 1992, 102nd Congress (1991-1992). Became Pub. L. No. 102-325.

[15] This criterion later changed, and the financial status of students is no longer part of the institutional definition.

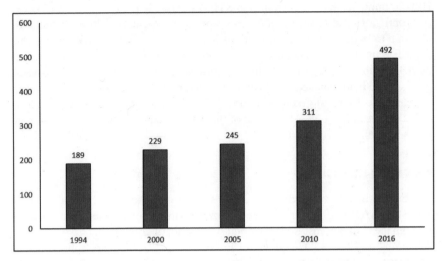

FIGURE 3-2 Number of federally eligible HSIs after the 1992 Reauthorization of the Higher Education Act.
SOURCE: Data adapted from HACU (2018).

BOX 3-2
MSI Growth: The Case of "Emerging HSIs"

As the country's demographics change and grow increasingly diverse, many more MSIs will emerge, making this sector of higher education critical to the nation's educational and workforce goals. Increasing Hispanic settlement in new areas, characterized as the "new Latino diaspora," suggests that more regions will have HSIs soon, as indicated by the growing population of Hispanic college students in states such as Wisconsin, Georgia, Oregon, North Carolina, Nebraska, and Massachusetts.

Using data from 2016 to 2017, Excelencia in Education has identified 333 colleges and universities with between 15 and 24.99 percent Hispanic enrollment that may soon become HSIs, due to their increasing enrollment of Hispanics—calling them "Emerging HSIs." If these 333 Emerging HSIs were to become HSIs tomorrow, that would represent a nearly 68 percent increase in the number of HSIs. Of the institutions that were Emerging HSIs in 1994, the majority had become HSIs by the 2013-2014 academic year. Although HSI status can vary from year to year based on the proportions of Hispanic enrollment, these trends suggest that, once institutions become HSIs, they tend to remain HSIs by maintaining 25 percent undergraduate full-time-equivalent Hispanic enrollment.

SOURCES: Excelencia in Education (2018), Santiago et al. (2015), Wortham et al. (2002), Wortham et al. (2013).

ance to the National Science Foundation (NSF) on how to address the needs of HSIs to improve student outcomes in STEM fields. First, the 2017 Consolidated Appropriations Act (Pub. L. No. 115-31) prompted the establishment of an HSI program to build capacity at institutions that do not typically receive high levels of NSF grant funding. Second, the American Innovation and Competitiveness Act of 2017 (Pub. L. No. 114-329) directed NSF to award competitive, merit-based grants to HSIs to enhance the quality of undergraduate STEM education, and to increase retention and graduation rates for students seeking associate and bachelor's degrees in STEM. At the time of this report, these initiatives were too new to assess their effectiveness.[16]

AANAPISIs at a Glance

Established in the Higher Education Opportunity Act of 2008 (Pub. L. No. 110-315), AANAPISIs were first recognized by the federal government in 2007 through the College Cost Reduction and Access Act of 2007 (Pub. L. No. 110-84). According to the U.S. Department of Education (2017), there are approximately 133 two- and four-year AANAPISIs.[17] Based on 2010 data, they enroll roughly 40 percent of Asian American and Pacific Islander (AAPI) students and award roughly 50 percent of all associate degrees and 25 percent of all bachelor's degrees attained by AAPI college students (CARE 2013; Museus et al. 2018).

To understand the importance of AANAPISIs is to understand their role in educating a fast-growing AAPI population. As a rapidly growing demographic group within the United States, the AAPI population is expected to reach roughly 50 million people by 2060[18] (U.S. Census Bureau 2015). Moreover, between 1979 and 2009, AAPIs experienced a 553 percent increase in two- and four-year college enrollment, a number that is projected to increase by 35 percent, cumulatively, over the next 10 years (Vollman 2017).

Although they have a number of common attributes, AAPI students are a diverse group of individuals. They originate from more than 50 ethnic groups, speak more than 300 languages, and have unique immigration experiences and pathways to and through the U.S. K-12 school system (CARE 2011; U.S. Census Bureau 2017). In addition to ethnic, language, and immigration diversity, the AAPI community is heterogeneous as it pertains to educational attainment, poverty status, generational status, household income, and socioeconomic class (B.M.D. Nguyen et al. 2015; Ramakrishnan and Ahmad 2014).

Although no official grouping of the different ethnicities exists, efforts have been made to group ethnicities based on geographic and cultural boundaries, for example, East Asian (e.g., Chinese, Japanese, Korean, and Taiwanese),

---

[16] For additional background on HSIs and their impact on student success, see Santiago et al. (2016).

[17] Institutions that are eligible for AANAPISI-designated funding.

[18] Calculation from projected Asian and Pacific Islander population; data include Native Hawaiian population. See U.S. Census Bureau (2015, Table 2, p. 9).

Southeast Asian (e.g., Filipino, Cambodian, Vietnamese, and Thai), South Asian (Bangladeshi, Indian, and Pakistani), and Native Hawaiian and Pacific Islander (e.g., Native Hawaiian, Fijian, Guamanian, and Samoan) (B.M.D. Nguyen et al. 2015; Ramakrishnan and Ahmad 2014). Efforts to disaggregate educational data have revealed significant disparities in the educational outcomes and student experiences between these AAPI subgroups (B.M.D. Nguyen et al. 2015; Ramakrishnan and Ahmad 2014). For example, the National Commission on Asian American and Pacific Islander Research in Education determined that when institutional data are disaggregated by AAPI subgroup, clear disparities in degree attainment and rates of student poverty emerge (CARE 2011). In addition, studies have found that student groups from the Pacific Islander and Southeast Asian subgroups, with low numbers, face different challenges of representation and support on campus, as compared to East Asian subgroups with higher representation (B.M.D. Nguyen et al. 2016). Therefore, treating the AAPI community as monolithic creates a mistaken impression that all AAPIs possess the same academic and social needs. This complexity results in further limitations when it comes to understanding AAPI student experiences and academic outcomes at AANAPISIs, and may contribute to a dearth of research on AAPIs as compared to other MSI student groups (Museus and Park 2015).[19] See also Box 2-1 for a discussion on the need to continuously reassess and revise research methods used to examine demographic data.

THE MSI COMMUNITY: A MODEL OF DIVERSITY FOR AMERICAN HIGHER EDUCATION

MSIs offer broad access to higher education for students who might otherwise have limited postsecondary opportunities, including underrepresented racial and ethnic groups, low-income students, first-generation-to-college students, adult learners, and other posttraditional[20] and nontraditional students.[21] As a result, the student bodies at MSIs are the most diverse in the nation, representing what many call "today's student" or the "21st century" student (Lumina Foundation 2015). **MSI learners look very different from those for whom higher education was originally intended. This distinction cannot be overstated when considering the policies and practices—at the federal, state, and institutional levels—needed to support MSIs and MSI students.** In this section, we provide

---

[19] For additional information on AANAPISIs and the students they serve, see Teranishi et al. (2013).

[20] Post-traditional learners are defined as students who are over the age of 25, work full time, are financially independent, or connected with the military. For more information on post-traditional learners, see Soares et al. (2017).

[21] Nontraditional students are generally defined as students with one of the following characteristics: independent, having one or more dependents, being a single caregiver, not having received a standard high school diploma, having delayed enrollment in postsecondary education by a year or more after high school, working full time while enrolled, and/or attending school part time (Brock 2010; Choy 2002; Horn and Carroll 1996; Kim 2002, Taniguchi and Kaufman 2005).

summary profiles of MSI students, including their demographics, financial circumstances, enrollment intensity, and STEM enrollment and degree attainment.

Student, Faculty, and Leadership Diversity at MSIs

Undergraduate Student Body Diversity

MSIs have diverse student bodies, as compared to non-MSIs (Figure 3-3). Across the four MSI types highlighted in Figure 3-3, the racial groups HBCUs and TCUs are associated with serving represented the largest share of all students enrolled at these institutions. On average, students enrolled at public and private two- and four-year HBCUs are overwhelmingly Black or African American, and students at four-year public and two-year public and private TCUs are predominantly Native American or Alaska Native. Likewise, on average, HSIs have a large percentage of Hispanic students within the two- and four-year private and public institutions.

Public and private two- and four-year AANAPISIs have less of a racial/ethnic concentration; however, from a percentage standpoint, AAPI students represent a smaller proportion of America's college student body. For this reason, the AAPI student enrollment threshold for AANAPISI federal designation is much smaller (at 10 percent) than for other MSI types. Still, **across the board, MSIs are the country's most diverse set of institutions in terms of ethnic composition of the undergraduate student body.** This fact is not lost on prospective undergraduate students, and in fact serves as an influential factor in college choice (Box 3-3).

Student Diversity in STEM Disciplines

A review of the U.S. Department of Education's Integrated Postsecondary Education Data System (IPEDS) 2016 fall enrollment data reveals that **a slightly higher percentage of undergraduate students are enrolled in STEM fields at four-year MSIs than at four-year non-MSIs.** The percentage of undergraduates in STEM versus non-STEM is shown in Figure 3-4, broken down by four institutional types: HSIs (43.3 percent STEM enrollment), HBCUs (43.7 percent STEM enrollment), AANAPISIs (48.4 percent STEM enrollment), and non-MSIs (40.0 percent STEM enrollment). Given the dearth of TCU data in IPEDS, the American Indian Higher Education Consortium (AIHEC) provided the committee with supplemental enrollment data from fall 2016, reporting that approximately 13 percent of TCU students are enrolled in STEM programs at four-year TCUs (not pictured).

As shown in Figure 3-5, based on IPEDs 2016 fall enrollment data, African American students represent the vast majority of students enrolled in STEM at four-year HBCUs, at 81 percent. At four-year HSIs, Hispanics represent half

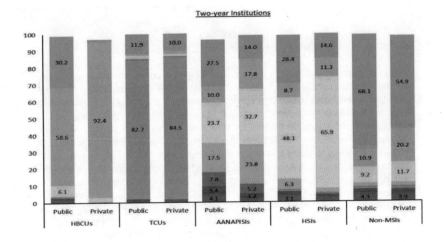

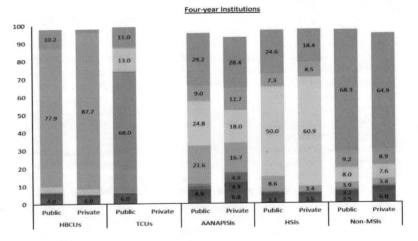

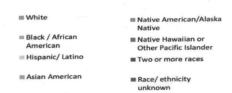

FIGURE 3-3 Percentage distribution of students at MSIs (averages), by race/ethnicity, type and sector, compared to non-MSIs, 2015 data.

NOTE: There are limited data for four-year private TCUs; hence, these data are not included. Percentages below 3 percent were not labeled. See the Annex at the end of the chapter for additional notes.

SOURCE: IPEDS 2015 Fall Enrollment Survey. Analysis by the American Council on Education for this report.

BOX 3-3
Students of Color and College Choice

Understanding the factors that influence college choice may help to inform efforts to support student success. Black et al. (2015) examined the college applications of all Texas public high school graduates in 2008 and 2009. Controlling for individual student academic preparedness and high school characteristics and using advanced statistical techniques, the authors found that African American students in Texas were significantly more likely than White, Asian American, or Hispanic students to apply to a Texas public university. In addition, college application choice for African American, Asian, and Hispanic students was associated with the college's distance from home and, to a much larger extent, the number of same-race students on the college campus. The impact of the racial composition on campus as a determining factor for enrolling in a college or university was most pronounced for low-income African American students, and it was a declining, but still large and significant, factor for African Americans from families with incomes above $40,000 a year.

Similar findings on race and college choice are discussed in a study by Clotfelter and colleagues (2015). Here, the authors examined college attendance within the public University of North Carolina (UNC) system from a cohort of all eighth-grade students in North Carolina's public schools in spring 1999 and spring 2004. The authors found that, controlling for eighth-grade test scores and parental educational attainment, African American students in North Carolina were more likely than Whites with similar backgrounds to enroll in the public UNC system. Furthermore, the authors found that this pattern was largely the result of African American student applications to and enrollments in the five HBCU campuses within the UNC system.

These findings shed light on the importance of a postsecondary institution's demographic profile, mission, and associated potential for a supportive campus climate for some students of color in choosing a college. These factors may be of interest to all institutions of higher education, particularly non-MSIs, that are seeking to increase and/or better support the diversity within their student body.

SOURCES: Black et al. (2015), Clotfelter et al. (2015).

(50.2 percent) of all students enrolled in STEM. Of note, 13.5 percent of STEM students at HSIs are Asian American. At four-year AANAPISIs, Asian American and Pacific Islander students represent 26.5 percent of all students enrolled in STEM; Hispanics are the third largest group (following White students) at 24.3 percent. Across all MSI types, Pacific Islander and Native American/Alaska Native students are the most underrepresented groups in STEM. Not surprisingly, based on AIHEC data provided to the committee, of the 1,263 students enrolled in STEM at four-year TCUs in fall 2016, approximately 93 percent were Native American/Alaska Native (not pictured). In comparison, White students represent the 61.1 percent of students enrolled in STEM at four-year non-MSIs.

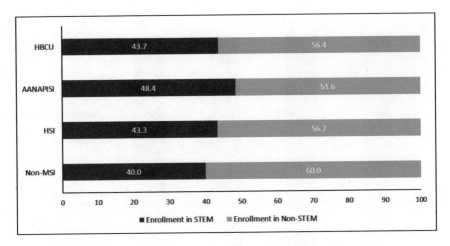

FIGURE 3-4 Percentage of students enrolled in STEM fields versus non-STEM fields at four-year MSIs, compared to four-year non-MSIs, 2016 data.
NOTE: There are limited data for four-year TCUs; hence, these data are not included. See the Annex at the end of this chapter for additional notes. See Appendix F, Table F-2, for data.
SOURCE: IPEDS 2016 Fall Enrollment and Institutional Characteristics data. Analysis by the American Institutes for Research for this report.

Enrollment Intensity and Adult Learners

MSIs reflect another form of diversity in their student bodies: how students pursue college, in terms of enrollment intensity. According to a recent analysis by the American Council on Education (Espinosa et al. 2017), the majority of students at MSIs do not attend college exclusively full time, but rather enroll primarily through mixed enrollment, moving between full-time and part-time status (Table 3-3). Although enrollment data for TCU students were unavailable in this report, data provided by AIHEC demonstrated that a substantial portion of enrolled students attend part time (Table 3-4). Given this pattern of enrollment, it is not surprising that a large number of students who enroll at MSIs, particularly two-year MSIs, are over the age of 25 (see Figure 3-6 for data). These students are often working and are balancing work, school, and family commitments. (See Box 3-4 for a brief discussion on the importance of two-year institutions in higher education.)

The enrollment patterns and proportion of adult learners at MSIs are impor-tant to understand. Institutional policies and practices needed to serve a largely nontraditional student body are very different from those intended to serve stu-dents who enroll right after high school and stay full time through graduation. Serving nontraditional students requires institutions to be more nimble and inno-vative in their educational approach (Arbelo-Marrero and Milacci 2016; Soares et

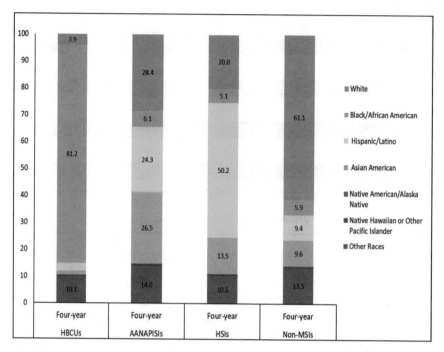

FIGURE 3-5 Percentage distribution of students in STEM at four-year MSIs, by race/ethnicity, type and sector, compared to non-MSIs, 2016 data.
NOTE: Percentages below 3 percent were not labeled. See the Annex at the end of this chapter for additional notes.
SOURCE: IPEDS 2016 Fall Enrollment and Institutional Characteristics data. Analysis by the American Institutes for Research for this report.

al. 2017) and offer more holistic programs and practices, like the ones highlighted in Chapter 5 of this report. It further requires, as discussed in a later section in this chapter, that performance measures take into account the many dimensions of student success for nontraditional and post-traditional learners.

Faculty Diversity

Although not always representative of their student body, full-time faculty members at MSIs are much more diverse than those at non-MSIs (Figure 3-7). HBCUs stand out, in particular, with a faculty body that is overwhelmingly African American. On average, between 41 and 70 percent of faculty at TCUs are Native Americans—figures that vastly exceed proportions of Native faculty at all other institutions. A much higher proportion of Hispanic faculty are employed at two- and four-year HSIs compared to non-MSIs—Hispanic representation is five

TABLE 3-3 Enrollment Intensity Patterns at HBCUs, AANAPISIs, and HSIs

	HBCU			AANAPISI			HSI		
Enrollment Intensity	Public two-year	Public four-year	Private four-year	Public two-year	Public four-year	Private four-year	Public two-year	Public four-year	Private four-year
Percent Enrolled Exclusively Full Time	21	45	56	16	45	71	16	28	49
Percent Enrolled Exclusively Part Time	14	3	1	11	4	3	12	6	6
Percent Enrolled with Mixed Enrollment	65	52	43	73	50	26	72	66	45

TABLE 3-4 Enrollment Intensity Patterns at TCUs

	TCU	
Enrollment Intensity	2-year	4-year
Percentage Enrolled Exclusively Full Time	59.6	67.1
Percentage Enrolled Exclusively Part Time	40.4	32.9

NOTE: Data from 2016 fall enrollment; data include enrollments for Native American/Alaska Native and non-Native students.
SOURCE: Data provided by the American Indian Higher Education Consortium.

times as high at public two-year HSIs and seven times as high at public four-year HSIs, on average.

Turning to faculty diversity in the STEM fields, 2015 data from NSF show varying levels of racial/ethnic diversity at MSIs (Figure 3-8), although their faculty diversity is comparatively notable. Roughly half (48.9 percent) of all STEM faculty at HBCUs were Black/African American, an important statistic given the White majorities at all other MSI and non-MSI types. Asian/Asian Americans represented 22.2 percent of all STEM faculty at AANAPISIs and Hispanics represented 14.4 percent of all STEM faculty at HSIs.

Leadership Diversity

A final point of difference concerns the presence of people of color as senior administrative leaders (i.e., presidents) of colleges and universities (Figure 3-9).

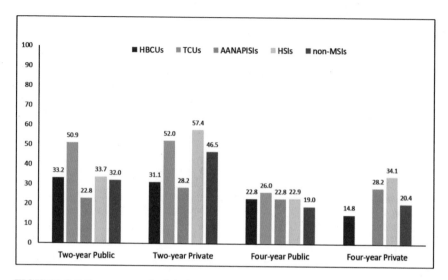

FIGURE 3-6 Percentage of adult learners (aged 25-64) at two- and four-year MSIs, 2015 data.
NOTES: There are limited data for four-year private TCUs; hence, these data are not included.
SOURCE: IPEDS 2015 Fall Enrollment Survey. Analysis by the American Council on Education for this report.

BOX 3-4
The Critical Importance of Two-Year
Institutions and STEM Education

At a time when postsecondary education and training is more important than ever to the American workforce, the nation's two-year institutions provide unparalleled access for those seeking postsecondary education. These institutions are intended to reflect local student demographics and serve the needs of the areas in which they are located. In general, they do not have competitive admissions policies and are open to all students (i.e., open access). Given their educational mission and the students they aim to serve, they are also committed to keeping tuition and fees low. Because of these policies, two-year institutions are a vital resource for communities of color, low-income students, first-generation college students, and adult learners.

The nation's two-year institutions enroll approximately 41 percent of the national college student body and, reflective of the nation's demographics, enroll a large portion of the nation's students of color (based on fall 2016 IPEDs enrollment data). According to the American Association of Community Colleges, the sector enrolls an estimated 43 percent of all African American undergraduates, as well as 52 percent of Hispanic undergraduates, 56 percent of Native American undergraduates, and 40 percent of Asian/Pacific Islander undergraduates, making the

BOX 3-4 Continued

overall student body of two-year institutions the most diverse of any postsecondary sector. Accordingly, many two-year schools are MSIs.

Two-Year Institutions and STEM

Two-year institutions often serve as a starting point, or as a supplement, to traditional four-year baccalaureate degrees, including for students of color. They also play a major role in STEM workforce development and supply a larger portion of STEM workforce training than is generally understood. They offer a wide variety of STEM-focused, vocational-technical programs, some of which are offered as noncredit courses. Many of these programs and courses focus on career development and job training, while others are contract-supported by local businesses who provide students with immediate job placement.

Most of these programs fall into two categories: science and engineering (S&E) and technician. S&E programs (e.g., physical sciences and engineering) aim to prepare students for occupations that often require a bachelor's degree (or greater) for workforce placement. Technician programs (e.g., manufacturing, computer and information science, agriculture, and engineering technology) often prepare students for STEM-related occupations that can be entered with an associate degree or other subbaccalaureate credential, such as short-term certificates.

A Need for Additional Research on Student Success at Two-Year MSIs

Two-year institutions that are MSIs have an important role within American higher education. In 2015, MSIs constituted almost 31 percent of all two-year institutions nationwide; looked at another way, roughly 55 percent of all MSIs are community colleges.[a] Despite this large presence in American higher education, two-year institutions and the students who attend them are vastly understudied in comparison to other higher education institution types. In the MSI literature, in particular, research has been primarily focused on 4-year institutions. Given the rapidly changing demographics of the nation, it is important to have a more complete understanding of student progress at MSIs as a whole.

Additional research on how to increase student success at two-year institutions (e.g., enrollment, persistence, and degree attainment), particularly at MSIs, is an important step toward better understanding which institutional programs, practices, and policies are effectively educating, training, and supporting students of color, and which need to be restructured. Additional research evidence can shed light on the impact that two-year institutions have on the growth and success of the nation's STEM workforce.

---

[a] MSI status is based on federal legislation or the demographics of the enrolled student body. The national total of two-year colleges is 1,269 (1,031 public, 238 private). The national total of MSI 2-year colleges is 391 (320 public, 71 private). The national total of all MSIs is 714.
SOURCE: IPEDS 2015 Fall Enrollment Survey and 2015-2016 College Scorecard data; analysis by the American Council on Education for this report.
SOURCES: AACC (2018), Crisp et al. (2016). Engle and Lynch (2009), Hagedorn and Purnamasari (2012), Ma and Baum (2016), Ma et al. (2017), B.M.D. Nguyen (2015), Nguyen et al. (2015), Mooney and Foley (2011), Starobin et al. (2013), U.S. Department of Education (2015), Van Noy and Zeidenberg (2017).

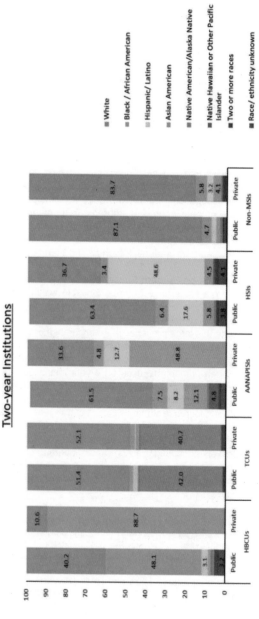

Two-year Institutions

- White
- Black / African American
- Hispanic/ Latino
- Asian American
- Native American/Alaska Native
- Native Hawaiian or Other Pacific Islander
- Two or more races
- Race/ ethnicity unknown

FIGURE 3-7 (Continues)

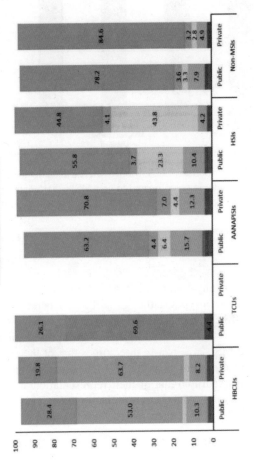

Four-year Institutions

	HBCUs		TCUs		AANAPISIs		HSIs		Non-MSIs	
	Public	Private	Public	Private	Public	Private	Public	Private	Public	Private

HBCUs Public: 28.4, 53.0, 10.3
HBCUs Private: 19.8, 63.7, 8.2
TCUs Public: 26.1, 69.6, 4.4
AANAPISIs Public: 63.2, 4.4, 6.4, 15.7
AANAPISIs Private: 70.8, 7.0, 4.4, 12.3
HSIs Public: 55.8, 3.7, 23.3, 10.4
HSIs Private: 44.8, 4.1, 43.8, 4.2
Non-MSIs Public: 78.2, 3.6, 3.3, 7.9
Non-MSIs Private: 84.6, 3.2, 2.8, 4.9

FIGURE 3-7 Percentage distribution of full-time instructional staff with faculty status at MSIs (averages), by race/ethnicity, type and sector, compared to non-MSIs, 2015 data.

NOTE: There are limited data for four-year private TCUs; hence, these data are not included. Percentages below 3 percent were not labeled. See the Annex at the end of this chapter for additional notes.

SOURCE: IPEDS 2015 Fall Staff Survey. Analysis by the American Council on Education for this report.

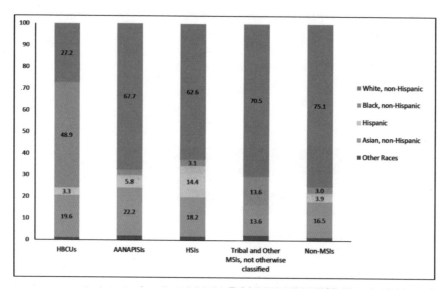

FIGURE 3-8 Percentage distribution of U.S.-trained science and engineering postsecondary faculty at MSIs, by race/ethnicity, compared to non-MSIs, 2015 data.
NOTE: Percentages below 3 percent were not labeled. See the Annex at the end of this chapter for additional notes.
SOURCE: NSF (2015).

Reflecting student and faculty trends, MSI presidents are more diverse when compared to other institution types, although still a low percentage overall. In 2016, 36 percent of MSI presidents were non-White, compared to 17 percent of presidents nationally (Gagliardi et al. 2017). The representation of African American presidents at MSIs was nearly three times that of their representation at non-MSIs (15.2 and 5.6 percent, respectively). The representation of Hispanic presidents at MSIs was quadruple that of their representation at non-MSIs (9.2 and 2.3 percent, respectively). And the representation of Asian American presidents at MSIs was six times that of their representation at non-MSIs (6.2 and 1.0 percent, respectively).

Student Financial Need at MSIs

For all college students, but particularly for many low-income students of color, one of the greatest barriers to obtaining a degree in higher education is the financial cost (Nienhusser and Oshio 2017). Research in fact shows that access to need-based aid is critical to the success of low-income students (Castleman and Long 2016; Perna 2015). This includes access to federal Pell grants, which

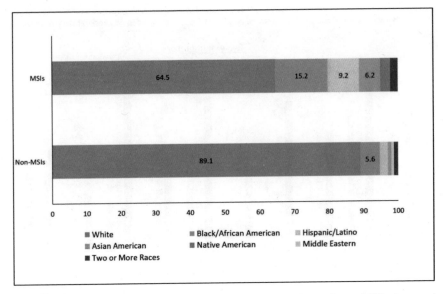

FIGURE 3-9 Percentage distribution of presidents at MSIs and non-MSIs, by race/ethnicity, 2016 data.
NOTE: Percentages below 3 percent were not labeled.
SOURCE: Adapted from Gagliardi et al. (2017).

are awarded to students based on financial need and do not need to be repaid.[22,23] Pell grant awardees are often nontraditional students, including independent students, racial/ethnic minorities, students with family responsibilities, and first-generation-to-college students (U.S. Department of Education 2016).

Indeed, this is precisely the profile of many—and in some cases the majority of—students at MSIs. From a financial need perspective, MSIs are again some of the most diverse institutions in the country. Reflected in Figure 3-10, the majority of students in higher education are awarded some form of financial assistance to subsidize their education costs. However, when comparing the percentage of students awarded Pell grants at MSIs to those at non-MSIs, there are substantial differences, most notably at HBCUs and HSIs. For example, on average, at public four-year HBCUs and HSIs, 65.6 and 50.4 percent of students are Pell grant recipients, respectively, compared to 33.7 percent at public four-year non-MSIs.

---

[22] To review the different options for financial aid from the U.S. Department of Education, see https://www2.ed.gov/fund/landing.jhtml.

[23] For additional information on U.S. Department of Education's federal Pell grants, see https://www2.ed.gov/programs/fpg/index.html.

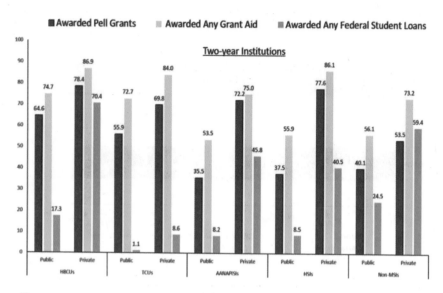

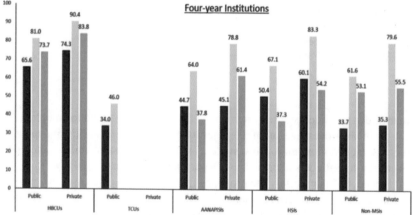

FIGURE 3-10 Percentage of financial aid awarded to undergraduate students at MSIs by type and control, compared with non-MSIs, fiscal year 2015 data.

NOTE: There are limited data for four-year private TCUs; hence, these data are not included. See the Annex at the end of this chapter for additional notes.

SOURCE: IPEDS 2014-2015 Financial Aid Survey. Analysis by the American Council on Education.

Given the low educational and general expenditures, and the overall limited financial resources at MSIs, the sustainability of need-based aid is critical for student success at these institutions. Students are often unable to draw upon family resources to make up the difference when this aid is reduced or withdrawn, and MSIs are generally less equipped to help alleviate students' financial burden of tuition and fees, compared to Predominantly White Institutions. As a result, **federal need-based grants are critical to ensuring access to high-quality higher education, particularly for students of color and even more so for students of color at MSIs.** Any cuts in federal financial aid, such as the Pell grant program, will have significant implications for the educational opportunity and advancement of students of color, including those at MSIs. (See Chapter 6 to review the committee's recommendation to Congress regarding need-based aid.)

CHALLENGES WITH INSTITUTIONAL METRICS

This chapter has described the institutional diversity both within and between MSIs. Yet across the different definitions, federal designations, and funding streams, MSIs share common challenges related to the applicability of traditional performance metrics. Metrics such as retention rate, graduation rate, and postgraduate income are commonly used as across-the-board measures to compare the quality and success of academic institutions. However, as noted, the student bodies at MSIs look very different from those for which higher education was originally intended. As a result, standard metrics of performance are inadequate or do not readily apply.

The U.S. higher education system allows for great diversity in the student pathways taken to obtain a degree or credential, as well as for the life circumstances of students traveling these pathways. **In evaluating the performance of MSIs, particularly MSIs that are less selective or open access, contextual factors must be considered. These factors include students' financial circumstances, life stage, commitments to work and family, and academic preparation.** Many standard accountability metrics fail to take these factors into consideration and are therefore inadequate measures of MSI performance. Such measures also inadequately address the progress of students who attend college part time and students who need to take time away from their studies, common scenarios for low-income students and those balancing work, family, and education (Carnevale et al. 2015; Soares et al. 2017). In many cases, the comparatively limited resources of MSIs mean that they are constrained in how much additional financial support they can offer these students to support retention.

In this respect, graduation rates (measures that look at graduation of full-time students within a certain time period) do not depict the experiences of many students at MSIs—and indeed for students at many other institutions. Comparing terminal graduation rates across institutions as a metric of success puts MSIs at a point of disadvantage and sets up a disparity that labels MSIs as "poorer" quality, or worse, failing in their missions to help students succeed. Many states use per-formance- or outcomes-based funding (POBF) models to allocate funding to the institutions within their states (Jones et al. 2017). When these models rely too heavily on graduation rates and other standardized metrics, they miss many of the other attributes that characterize MSI success (Espinosa et al. 2014; Núñez 2014; Orfield and Hillman 2018; Rodriguez et al. 2012). **When evaluating the success of institutions, including MSIs, it is incumbent on decision makers to understand what the data do and do *not* reveal.**

Research on the effects of state POBF indicates that it has been ineffective at reaching intended goals of raising graduation rates (Dougherty and Reddy 2011). Furthermore, POBF can result in unintended negative consequences, such as diminishing academic standards in order to raise graduation rates, and may penal-ize institutions such as MSIs that provide access to students with fewer resources by reducing institutional resources for those students even further (Dougherty and Reddy 2011; Li 2014). Given that many MSIs have been historically underfunded and enroll relatively large shares of students with lower academic preparation (Flores and Park 2013, 2015; Núñez and Bowers 2011), these schools often need more resources per student to provide sufficient academic and student support, as compared to more selective, Predominantly White Institutions. In light of these findings, researchers have called for institutional metrics to take into account the nation's diverse institutional missions, populations, student needs, and resource constraints, a move that this committee endorses.

As there are multiple steps in the myriad pathways to success, it is important to recognize students' achievements across a diverse set of competencies. As a potential solution to this issue, Li, Gandara, and Assalone (2018) have suggested factoring in other metrics aside from graduation rates, such as student completion of developmental education performance (e.g., supplemental reading and writing courses). Espinosa, Turk, and Taylor (2017) point out that "students enroll in college with a set of unique characteristics, experiences, and backgrounds, as well as changing educational needs and goals" (p. 8), thus urging stakeholders to look at other outcomes, including transfer rates, course completion, and skills enhancement, in addition to graduation rates. They also suggest disaggregating success rates by enrollment intensity, whether full time, part time, or some com-bination, as well as using metrics that expand the time period by which students are tracked, particularly for students who begin at two-year institutions.

Espinosa, Turk, and Taylor (2017) used 2007 cohort data from the National Student Clearinghouse (NSC) to examine MSI student enrollment and outcomes for students who started their postsecondary education at an MSI.[24] Their findings

---

[24] To determine completion rates for two-year institutions, American Council on Education (ACE) used a four-year (or 200 percent of normal time) completion period. For four-year institutions, ACE used a six-year (or 150 percent of normal time) completion period. Throughout their report, ACE notes the substantial difference between the National Student Clearinghouse completion rates for full-time students with the federal graduation rates (Espinosa et al. 2017).

confirm (as discussed above) that the majority of students at MSIs do not attend college exclusively full time, but rather enroll primarily through mixed enrollment, moving between full-time and part-time status. Yet, the federal graduation rate measures students who complete within 150 percent of normal time at their starting institution. Therefore, students who transfer and complete degrees at other institutions are not taken into account in the federal approach to measuring an institution's graduation rate.

The robustness of NSC data allows for tracking students across institutions and enrollment intensities, allowing for a more complete picture of student outcomes. Notably, for each MSI type, the NSC completion rates were substantially higher than the reported federal graduation rates, most notably for full-time students (Tables 3-5 and 3-6).

A 2012 report by the American Institutes for Research examined the role of MSIs in STEM education and recommended specific indicators to measure the success of efforts to broaden the participation of underrepresented groups in

TABLE 3-5 Four-Year Outcomes (200 Percent Normal Time) at Two-Year MSIs: Fall 2007 Cohort

	HBCU	HSI	AANAPISI
NSC Total Completion Rate: Exclusively Full-Time Students	32.1	40.3	42.6
Federal Graduation Rate	13.9	25.5	27.9

NOTE: The federal graduation rate is most comparable to the total completion rate for exclusively full-time students in NSC data.
SOURCE: Espinosa et al. (2017).

TABLE 3-6 Six-Year Outcomes (150 Percent Normal Time) at Four-Year MSIs: Fall 2007 Cohort

	HBCU	HSI	AANAPISI
Private Four-Year			
NSC Total Completion Rate: Exclusively Full-Time Students	66.7	77.9	93.2
Federal Graduation Rate	43.9	49.1	81.0
Public Four-Year			
NSC Total Completion Rate: Exclusively Full-Time Students	61.8	74.1	87.9
Federal Graduation Rate	34.1	42.7	66.2

NOTE: The federal graduation rate is most comparable to the total completion rate for exclusively full-time students in NSC data.
SOURCE: Espinosa et al. (2017).

STEM (AIR 2012). Stakeholders who contributed to the study called for measures that examine STEM degree program quality, establish institutional baselines against which expectations and ultimately outcomes could be derived, and compare like institutions to one another, rather than against institutions who serve a very different student body. Other measures covered in the report include skill development, dispositional and attitude measures, the availability of resources and opportunities, and a given institution's student body diversity (AIR 2012). The Bill & Melinda Gates Foundation, in partnership with the Institute for Higher Education Policy, offers a framework that seeks to address both efficiency and equity in institutional measurement (Engle 2016). The framework offers "a set of metrics that are currently in use by major initiatives to measure institutional performance related to student access, progression, completion, cost, and post-college outcomes. The framework also highlights metrics in use that examine institutional performance in relation to resources (efficiency) and with respect to diverse populations (equity)" (Engle 2016).

In summary, it is important to determine the best possible metrics to most accurately evaluate the success of students at *all* institutions. In an era in which accountability standards and performance-based funding are increasing, it is important not to penalize MSIs by holding them to a standard devoid of their context. The committee is not saying that MSIs should not be held accountable. Quite the contrary. It is because MSIs are serving the underserved in American higher education that they must do it well and do right by the students who walk through their doors.

A new National Academies of Sciences, Engineering, and Medicine report, *Indicators for Monitoring Undergraduate STEM Education* provides a framework and a set of indicators to most effectively determine the status and quality of undergraduate STEM education across multiple years (NASEM 2018). The report describes the limitations of the current national-level indicators system, primarily its ineffectiveness to appropriately track complex student pathways.

Three conclusions from that report are most relevant to the current committee's charge: (1) federal data systems will need additional data on full-time and part-time students' trajectories across, as well as within, institutions; (2) recurring longitudinal surveys of instructors and students are needed; and (3) to monitor progress toward the goal of equity, diversity, and inclusion, national data systems will need to include demographic characteristics beyond gender and race and ethnicity, including at least disability status, first-generation college-going student status, and socioeconomic status. These conclusions bolster this committee's recommendations for a national-level change in metrics to better support MSIs and their students. (See Chapter 6 to review the committee's recommendations to federal and state agencies to improve MSI assessment metrics.)

CONSIDERING WHAT IT MEANS TO
"SERVE" MINORITY STUDENTS

Beyond appropriate accountability metrics lies a final item for consideration, namely, what it means to "serve" the distinct needs of the MSI students discussed throughout this report, as opposed to simply enrolling them. It is clear that serving students means different things to different campuses. Here, too, finding language to define and frame MSIs as a collective group of institutions can be challenging because there is as much diversity across the nation's MSIs as there is across the entire U.S. higher education landscape. The potential range of emphases on missions to serve specific minority populations—for example, between historically designated and enrollment-designated MSIs—illustrates the danger in lumping all MSIs together and points to the need for policy makers, practitioners, and others to consider carefully each MSI within its immediate geographic, social, political, historical, fiscal, and educational context.

The research community has taken note of such differences, with many MSI scholars now engaged in research and dialogue that attempts to further unpack what it truly means to serve students of color. Such research has found that to fully understand how campuses engage in serving minority students, it is often necessary to visit and speak directly with stakeholders. As further discussed in Chapter 5 of this report, observing and engaging with faculty, staff, students, and leaders engaged in STEM disciplines at these institutions reveals organizational behaviors that might otherwise go unrepresented in formally articulated missions or strategic plans.

The implication of being an MSI is that it should serve its target population. In research, policy, and practice, "serving" is often framed as graduating high numbers and shares of that target population, particularly in relation to majority populations at the institution (e.g., García 2017). While graduation and completion rates of minority populations are critical, and should always be considered when understanding an institution's capacity to serve its students, the organizational behaviors that MSIs undertake to promote graduation and completion rates are also important to consider.

Thus, two critical dimensions can constitute an MSI's (or any institution's) approach to serving its students: institutional outcomes and organizational culture (García 2017). Grounded in research on HSIs, the largest, fastest-growing, and most diverse MSI type, García (2017) proposed a typology of HSIs that is useful for understanding variations among other MSIs as well. This typology advances the idea that an HSI that truly serves Hispanic students incorporates an organizational identity that not only promotes Hispanic students' outcomes, but also does so in ways that affirm and support Hispanic students' cultural and familial backgrounds. In contrast, an institution that graduates high shares of its target minority population without having the organizational behaviors that are specifically targeted for that population would not be classified as truly "serving" its students. (See Chapter 5 for a greater discussion on intentionality and strategies to support MSI student success.)

With the expected increases in the number of MSIs, given that Hispanics and Asian Americans are projected to be the fastest-growing ethnic groups in the United States, it is important to consider whether federal funds received by these schools will be used with an intentional purpose to serve and support the students for whom these funds are intended. Going beyond federal definitions of MSIs means taking into account organizational cultures in these institutions as well as their outcomes. Thus, it becomes important to examine and document the everyday and longer-term activities and behaviors that create organizational cultures that can promote minority student success. Given the varied missions of MSIs, the specific dimensions of organizational behavior that "serve" the targeted population of students will vary—and should be celebrated.

CHAPTER ANNEX

Figure 3-3

1. IPEDS data, collection year 2015, were used to create the list of institutions throughout this report for analysis run by the American Council on Education. Data in this report reflect Title IV participating, degree-granting, public and private, nonprofit, two-year and four-year institutions that offered undergraduate degrees. College Scorecard 2015-16 data were used to flag institutions that were eligible to apply for federal MSI funding in that given fiscal year through Title III and Title V of the Higher Education Opportunity Act of 2008. Out of 3,129 total institutions, 714 were eligible for MSI designation. Of these institutions, 76 were eligible for more than one MSI designation.
2. Institutions were classified into a sector based on the institutional category variable and control variable in IPEDS. Within institutional category, all institutions categorized as degree-granting, primarily baccalaureate or above institutions were classified as four-year institutions, and all institutions categorized as degree-granting, not primarily baccalaureate or above and degree-granting, associate's and certificates institutions were classified as two-year institutions. The control variable was used to classify institutions as public or private nonprofit.

Figure 3-4

1. IPEDS data, collection year 2015, were used to create the list of institutions throughout this report for analysis run by the American Council on Education. Data in this report reflect Title IV participating, degree-granting, public and private, nonprofit, two-year and four-year institutions that offered undergraduate degrees. College Scorecard 2015-16 data were used to flag institutions that were eligible to apply for federal MSI funding in that given fiscal year through Title III and Title V of the Higher Education Opportunity Act of 2008. Out of 3,129 total institutions, 714 were eligible for MSI designation. Of these institutions, 76 were eligible for more than one MSI designation.
2. Classification of Instructional Programs (CIP) codes were placed into Science and Engineering categories based on the fields of study classification found in the NSF's "Science and Engineering Degrees: 1966–2012," appendix B, with additions made to cover CIP codes found in the IPEDS completions data that were not included in the NSF taxonomy.

For enrollment, the CIP codes 13.0000, 52.0000, and 22.0101 were classified as "Non-STEM," while the remaining CIP codes were classified as "STEM."

3. For both the completions and enrollment, the racial category "other" is defined as the combination of "nonresident," "race unknown," and "two or more races." Race reporting varies across years in the IPEDS, so information pertaining to Pacific Islanders is not available for all years and would be combined with counts for Asian students.

4. For the enrollment files, we have limited to undergraduate enrollment using the variables LSTUDY and LINE, with criteria that vary by year in accordance with the definition of those variables.

Figure 3-5

1. IPEDS data, collection year 2015, were used to create the list of institutions throughout this report for analysis run by the American Council on Education. Data in this report reflect Title IV participating, degree-granting, public and private, nonprofit, two-year and four-year institutions that offered undergraduate degrees. College Scorecard 2015-16 data were used to flag institutions that were eligible to apply for federal MSI funding in that given fiscal year through Title III and Title V of the Higher Education Opportunity Act of 2008. Out of 3,129 total institutions, 714 were eligible for MSI designation. Of these institutions, 76 were eligible for more than one MSI designation.

2. Classification of CIP codes into Science and Engineering categories was based on the fields of study classification found in the NSF's "Science and Engineering Degrees: 1966–2012," appendix B, with additions made to cover CIP codes found in the IPEDS completions data that were not included in the NSF taxonomy. For enrollment, the CIP codes 13.0000, 52.0000, and 22.0101 were classified as "Non-STEM," while the remaining CIP codes were classified as "STEM."

3. For both the completions and enrollment, the racial category "other" is defined as the combination of "nonresident," "race unknown," and "two or more races." Race reporting varies across years in the IPEDS, so information pertaining to Pacific Islanders is not available for all years, and would be combined with counts for Asian students.

4. For the enrollment files, we have limited to undergraduate enrollment using the variables LSTUDY and LINE, with criteria that vary by year in accordance with the definition of those variables.

Figure 3-7

1. IPEDS data, collection year 2015, were used to create the list of institutions throughout this report for analysis run by the American Council on Education. Data in this report reflect Title IV participating, degree-granting, public and private, nonprofit, two-year and four-year institutions that offered undergraduate degrees. College Scorecard 2015-16 data were used to flag institutions that were eligible to apply for federal MSI funding in that given fiscal year through Title III and Title V of the Higher Education Opportunity Act of 2008. Out of 3,129 total institutions, 714 were eligible for MSI designation. Of these institutions, 76 were eligible for more than one MSI designation.

2. Institutions were classified into a sector based on the institutional category variable and control variable in IPEDS. Within institutional category, all institutions categorized as degree-granting, primarily baccalaureate or above institutions were classified as four-year institutions, and all institutions categorized as degree-granting, not primarily baccalaureate or above and degree-granting, associate's and certificates institutions were classified

as two-year institutions. The control variable was used to classify institutions as public or private nonprofit.

Figure 3-8

1. S&E stands for science and engineering
2. Other race includes non-Hispanics who are Native Americans/Alaska Natives, Native Hawaiians or Other Pacific Islanders, or persons reporting more than one race.
3. Postsecondary institutions are defined as two-year college, community college or technical institute; four-year college or university, other than medical school; medical school (including university-affiliated hospital or medical center); and university-affiliated research institute.
4. Totals for MSIs are not mutually exclusive, as 47 institutions are classified as both AANAPISI and HSI.
5. Faculty is defined as research faculty, teaching faculty, or adjunct faculty working at postsecondary institutions in the United States during the reference period of the first week of February 2015, and reflect part-time and full-time faculty.
6. Some data for TCUs have been suppressed given low sample sizes.

Figure 3-10

1. IPEDS data, collection year 2015, were used to create the list of institutions throughout this report for analysis run by the American Council on Education. Data in this report reflect Title IV participating, degree-granting, public and private, nonprofit, two-year and four-year institutions that offered undergraduate degrees. College Scorecard 2015-16 data were used to flag institutions that were eligible to apply for federal MSI funding in that given fiscal year through Title III and Title V of the Higher Education Opportunity Act of 2008. Out of 3,129 total institutions, 714 were eligible for MSI designation. Of these institutions, 76 were eligible for more than one MSI designation.
2. Institutions were classified into a sector based on the institutional category variable and control variable in IPEDS. Within institutional category, all institutions categorized as degree-granting, primarily baccalaureate or above institutions were classified as four-year institutions, and all institutions categorized as degree-granting, not primarily baccalaureate or above and degree-granting, associate's and certificates institutions were classified as two-year institutions. The control variable was used to classify institutions as public or private nonprofit.

REFERENCES

AACC (American Association of Community Colleges). 2018. Fast Facts 2018. Available at: https://www.aacc.nche.edu/wp-content/uploads/2018/04/2018-Fast-Facts.pdf. Accessed September 2018.

AIHEC (American Indian Higher Education Consortium). 1999. "Tribal colleges: An introduction." Available at: http://www.aihec.org/who-we-serve/docs/TCU_intro.pdf. Accessed October 2018.

AIHEC. 2012. AIHEC AIMS Fact Book 2009-2010: Tribal Colleges and Universities Report. http://www.aihec.org/our-stories/docs/reports/AIHEC_AIMSreport_May2012.pdf. Accessed October 2018.

AIHEC. 2018. "Tribal Colleges and Universities." Available at: http://aihec.org/who-we-serve/index.htm. Accessed October 2018.

AIR (American Institutes for Research). 2012. "Broadening participation in STEM: A call to action." Unpublished report, NSF Grant No. HRD-1059774. Washington, DC.

Anderson, James D. 1988. The education of Blacks in the South, 1860-1935. Chapel Hill, NC: University of North Carolina Press.

Arbelo-Marrero, Floralba and Fred Milacci. 2016. "A phenomenological investigation of the academic persistence of undergraduate Hispanic nontraditional students at Hispanic Serving Institutions." *Journal of Hispanic Higher Education* 15 (1): 22-40.

Black, Sandra E., Kalena E. Cortes, and Jane Arnold Lincove. 2015. "Apply yourself: Racial and ethnic differences in college application." National Bureau of Economic Research. Available at: https://www.nber.org/papers/w21368. Accessed October 2018.

Brock, Thomas. 2010. "Young adults and higher education: Barriers and breakthroughs to success." *The Future of Children* 20 (1):109-132.

Burrelli, Joan and Alan Rapoport. 2008. "Role of HBCUs as Baccalaureate-Origin Institutions of Black S&E Doctorate Recipients. InfoBrief. NSF 08-319." National Science Foundation. https://files.eric.ed.gov/fulltext/ED502482.pdf. Accessed January 2019.

Calderón Galdeano, Emily, Antonio R. Flores, and John Moder. 2012. "The Hispanic association of colleges and universities and Hispanic-serving institutions: Partners in the advancement of Hispanic higher education." *Journal of Latinos and Education* 11 (3):157-162.

CARE (National Commission on Asian American and Pacific Islander Research in Education). 2011. The Relevance of Asian Americans and Pacific Islanders in the College Completion Agenda. Available at: http://www.apiasf.org/CAREreport/2011_CARE_Report.pdf. Accessed October 2018.

CARE. 2013. Partnership for Equity in Education through Research (PEER): Findings from the First Year of Research on AANAPISIs 2013. Available at: http://www.apiasf.org/pdfs/2013_peer_report/APIASF_and_CARE_PEER_Report_June_2013.pdf. Accessed January 2019.

Carnevale, Anthony P., Nicole Smith, Michelle Melton, and Eric Price. 2015. Learning While Earning: The New Normal. Washington, DC: Georgetown University Center on Education and the Workforce.

Castleman, Benjamin L. and Bridget Terry Long. 2016. "Looking beyond enrollment: The causal effect of need-based grants on college access, persistence, and graduation." *Journal of Labor Economics* 34 (4):1023-1073.

Choy, Susan P. 2002. Access & Persistence: Findings from 10 Years of Longitudinal Research on Students. Washington, DC: American Council on Education, Center for Policy Analysis.

Clotfelter, Charles T., Helen F. Ladd, and Jacob L. Vigdor. 2015. Public Universities, Equal Opportunity, and the Legacy of Jim Crow: Evidence from North Carolina. National Bureau of Economic Research. Available at: https://www.nber.org/papers/w21577.pdf. Accessed October 2018.

Cornell, Stephen and Joseph P. Kalt. 2010. American Indian Self Determination: The Political Economy of a Policy That Works. HKS Faculty Research Working Paper Series RWP10-043, John F. Kennedy School of Government, Harvard University. Available at: https://dash.harvard.edu/handle/1/4553307. Accessed October 2018.

Crisp, Gloria, Vincent D. Carales, and Anne-Marie Núñez. 2016. "Where is the research on community college students?" *Community College Journal of Research and Practice* 40 (9):767-778.

Dougherty, Kevin and Vikash Reddy. 2011. The Impacts of State Performance Funding Systems on Higher Education Institutions: Research Literature Review and Policy Recommendations. Columbia University. doi: 10.13140/RG.2.2.22017.25449.

Engle, Jennifer. 2016. Answering the Call: Institutions and States Lead the Way Toward Better Measures of Postsecondary Performance. Bill and Melinda Gates Foundation 22. Available at: https://postsecondary.gatesfoundation.org/wp-content/uploads/2016/02/AnsweringtheCall.pdf. Accessed January 2019.

Engle, Jennifer and Mary Lynch. 2009. Charting a Necessary Path: The Baseline Report of Public Higher Education Systems in the Access to Success Initiative. Education Trust.

Espinosa, Lorelle L., Jennifer R. Crandall, and Malika Tukibayeva. 2014. Rankings, Institutional Behavior, and College and University Choice: Framing the National Dialogue on Obama's Ratings Plan. Washington, DC: American Council on Education.

Espinosa, Lorelle L., Jonathan Turk, and Morgan Taylor. 2017. Pulling Back the Curtain: Enrollment and Outcomes at Minority Serving Institutions. Washington, DC: American Council on Education.

Excelencia in Education. 2018. "Emerging Hispanic-Serving Institutions (HSIs): 2016-2017." Available at: https://www.edexcelencia.org/research/data/emerging-hispanic-serving-institutions-hsis-2016-2017. Accessed October 2018.

Fiegener, Mark K., and Steven L. Proudfoot. 2013. "Baccalaureate origins of U.S.-trained S&E doctorate recipients." InfoBrief, National Center for Science and Engineering Statistics, National Science Foundation.

Flores, Stella M., and Toby J. Park. 2013. "Race, ethnicity, and college success: Examining the continued significance of the minority-serving institution." *Educational Researcher* 42 (3):115-128. doi: 10.3102/0013189x13478978.

Flores, Stella M., and Toby J. Park. 2015. "The effect of enrolling in a minority-serving institution for Black and Hispanic students in Texas." *Research in Higher Education* 56 (3):247-276.

Gagliardi, Jonathan S., Lorelle L. Espinosa, Jonathan M. Turk, and Morgan Taylor. 2017. The American College President Study: 2017: American Council on Education, Center for Policy Research and Strategy; TIAA Institute.

García, Gina A. 2017. "Defined by outcomes or culture? Constructing an organizational identity for Hispanic-serving institutions." *American Educational Research Journal* 54 (1):111S-134S.

Gasman, Marybeth and Thai-Huy Nguyen. 2014. "Historically black colleges and universities (HBCUs): Leading our nation's effort to improve the science, technology, engineering, and mathematics (STEM) pipeline." University of Pennsylvania. Philadelphia, PA.

Gasman, Marybeth, Thai-Huy Nguyen, and Clifton F. Conrad. 2015. "Lives intertwined: A primer on the history and emergence of minority serving institutions." *Journal of Diversity in Higher Education* 8 (2):120-138. doi: 10.1037/a0038386.

Guillory, Justin P. and Kelly Ward. 2008. "Tribal Colleges and Universities: Identity, Invisibility, and Current Issues." In Gasman, Marybeth, Benjamin Baez, and Caroline Sotello Viernes Turner, editors. 2008. Understanding Minority-Serving Institutions. Albany, NY: State University of New York Press.

HACU (Hispanic Association of Colleges and Universities). 2012. 1986-2011: 25 Years of Championing Hispanic Higher Education. A Historical Review and a Glimpse into the Future. Available at: https://www.hacu.net/images/hacu/about/HACU_History_1986-2011F.pdf. Accessed October 2018.

HACU. 2017. HACU List of Hispanic-Serving Institutions (HSIs) 2016-17. Available: https://www.hacu.net/images/hacu/OPAI/2016%20HSI%20list.pdf. Accessed October 2018.

HACU. 2018. 2018 Fact Sheet. Hispanic Higher Education and HSIs. Available: https://www.hacu.net/images/hacu/OPAI/2018_HSI_FactSheet.pdf. Accessed October 2018.

Hagedorn, Linda Serra, and Agustina Veny Purnamasari. 2012. "A realistic look at STEM and the role of community colleges." *Community College Review* 40 (2):145-164.

Harris, Michael. 2013. Understanding institutional diversity in American higher education. John Wiley & Sons.

Hawkins, B. D. 2012. "Echoes of faith: Church roots run deep among HBCUs." Diverse Issues in Higher Education. Available at: https://diverseeducation.com/article/17259/. Accessed October 2018.

Hegji, Alexandra. 2017. Programs for Minority-Serving Institutions Under the Higher Education Act. Congressional Research Service. https://fas.org/sgp/crs/misc/R43237.pdf. Accessed January 2019.

Horn, Laura J. and C. Dennis Carroll. 1996. Nontraditional Undergraduates: Trends in Enrollment from 1986 to 1992 and Persistence and Attainment among 1989-90 Beginning Postsecondary Students. Postsecondary Education Descriptive Analysis Reports. Statistical Analysis Report: ERIC.

Jones, Tiffany, Sosanya Jones, Kayla C. Elliott, LaToya Russell Owens, Amanda E. Assalone, and Denisa Gándara. 2017. Outcomes Based Funding and Race in Higher Education: Can Equity be Bought? New York: Springer.

Kim, Mikyong Minsun. 2002. "Historically Black vs. White institutions: Academic development among Black students." *The Review of Higher Education* 25 (4):385-407.

Kim, Mikyong Minsun and Clifton F. Conrad. 2006. "The impact of historically black colleges and universities on the academic success of African-American students." *Research in Higher Education* 47 (4):399-427. doi: 10.1007/s11162-005-9001-4.

Li, Amy Y. 2014. "Performance funding in the states: An increasingly ubiquitous public policy for higher education." *Higher Education in Review* 11.

Li, Amy Y., Denisa Gándara, Amanda Assalone. 2018. "Equity or disparity: Do performance funding policies disadvantage 2-year minority-serving institutions?" *Community College Review* 46(3), 288–315. https://doi.org/10.1177/0091552118778776

Lumina Foundation. 2015. Who is Today's Student. Available at: https://www.luminafoundation.org/files/resources/todays-student-summary.pdf. Accessed October 2018.

Ma, Jennifer, and Sandy Baum. 2016. Trends in Community Colleges: Enrollment, Prices, Student Debt, and Completion. College Board Research Brief.

Ma, Jennifer, Sandy Baum, Matea Pender, and Meredith Welch. 2017. Trends in College Pricing. New York: The College Board.

McCormick, Alexander C., and Chun-Mei Zhao. 2005. "Rethinking and reframing the carnegie classification." *Change: The Magazine of Higher Learning* 37 (5):51-57. doi: 10.3200/CHNG.37.5.51-57.

Mooney, Geraldine M., and Daniel J. Foley. 2011. "Community colleges: Playing an important role in the education of science, engineering, and health graduates." Available at: http://www.nsf.gov/statistics/infbrief/nsf11317. Accessed October 2018.

Museus, Samuel D., and Julie J. Park. 2015. "The continuing significance of racism in the lives of Asian American college students." *Journal of College Student Development* 56 (6):551-569.

Museus, Samuel D., Raquel Wright-Mair, Jacqueline Mac. 2018. How Asian American and Native American Pacific Islander Serving Institutions (AANAPISIs) Are Creating the Conditions for Students to Thrive. Available at: https://www.indiana.edu/~cece/wordpress/wp-content/uploads/2017/02/Research-Brief-How-AANAPISI-Thrive.pdf. Accessed October 2018.

NASEM (National Academies of Sciences, Engineering, and Medicine) 2018. Indicators for Monitoring Undergraduate STEM Education. Washington, DC: National Academies Press.

Native Science Report. 2018. "Tribal Colleges: An introduction." Available at: http://nativesciencereport.org/introduction/. Accessed October 2018.

National Center for Education Statistics. 2018. "Two and four year Historically Black Colleges and Universities." Available at: https://nces.ed.gov/COLLEGENAVIGATOR/?s=all&ct=1+2&sp=4. Accessed October 2018.

Nguyen, Bach Mai Dolly, Mike Hoa Nguyen, Robert T. Teranishi, and Shirley Hune. 2015. "The hidden academic opportunity gaps among Asian Americans and Pacific Islanders: What disaggregated data reveals in Washington state." Educational Testing Service.

Nguyen, Bach Mai Dolly, Mike Hoa Nguyen, Jason Chan, and Robert T. Teranishi. 2016. "The racialized experiences of Asian American and Pacific Islander Students: An examination of campus racial climate at the University of California, Los Angeles." National Commission on Asian American and Pacific Islander Research in Education. ERIC.

Nguyen, Thai-Huy Peter. 2015. "Exploring Historically Black College and Universities' Ethos of racial uplift: STEM students' challenges and institutions' practices for cultivating learning and persistence in STEM." Available at: http://repository.upenn.edu/edissertations/1105. Accessed October 2018.

Nguyen, Thai-Huy, Valerie Lundy-Wagner, Andres Samayoa, and Marybeth Gasman. 2015. On Their Own Terms: Two-Year Minority Serving Institutions. New York: Center for Analysis of Postsecondary Education and Employment, Columbia University.

Nienhusser, Kenny H., and Toko Oshio. 2017. "High school students' accuracy in estimating the cost of college: A proposed methodological approach and differences among racial/ethnic groups and college financial-related factors." *Research in Higher Education* 58 (7):723-745.

NRC (National Research Council) 1996. Colleges of Agriculture at the Land Grant Universities: Public Service and Public Policy. Washington, DC: National Academy Press. https://doi.org/10.17226/5133.

NSF (National Science Foundation). 2015. National Center for Science and Engineering Statistics, Survey of Doctorate Recipients: 2015. Available at: https://ncsesdata.nsf.gov/doctorate-work/2015/. Accessed October 2018.

Núñez, Anne-Marie. 2014. Counting What Counts for Latinas/os and Hispanic-Serving Institutions: A Federal Ratings System and Postsecondary Access, Affordability, and Success. New York: President's Advisory Commission on Educational Excellence for Hispanics.

Núñez, Anne-Marie and Alex J. Bowers. 2011. "Exploring what leads high school students to enroll in Hispanic-serving institutions: A multilevel analysis." *American Educational Research Journal* 48 (6):1286-1313.

Núñez, Anne-Marie, Sylvia Hurtado, and Emily Calderón Galdeano. 2015. Hispanic-Serving Institutions: Advancing Research and Transformative Practice. New York: Routledge.

Núñez, Anne-Marie, Gloria Crisp, and Diane Elizondo. 2016. "Mapping Hispanic-serving institutions: A typology of institutional diversity." *Journal of Higher Education* 87 (1):55-83. doi: 10.1353/jhe.2016.0001.

Olivas, Michael A. 1982. "Indian, Chicano, and Puerto Rican colleges: Status and issues." *Bilingual Review/La Revista Bilingüe,* 36-58.

Orfield, Gary and Nicholas Hillman 2018. (eds.) Accountability and Opportunity in Higher Education: The Civil Rights Dimension. Cambridge, MA: Harvard Education Press.

PCAST (President's Council of Advisors on Science and Technology). 2012. Report to the President. Engage to Excel: Producing One Million Additional College Graduates with Degrees in Science, Technology, Engineering, and Mathematics. Executive Office of the President. Available at: https://obamawhitehouse.archives.gov/sites/default/files/microsites/ostp/pcast-engage-to-excel-final_2-25-12.pdf. Accessed October 2018.

Perna, Laura W. 2015. "Improving college access and completion for low-income and first-generation students: The role of college access and success programs." Available at: https://repository.upenn.edu/gse_pubs/301. Accessed October 2018.

QEM (Quality Education for Minorities Network). 2012. Promising Practices in STEM Education and Research at Institutions Supported through the National Science Foundation (NSF)'s Tribal Colleges and Universities Program (TCUP).

Ramakrishnan, Karthick and Farah Z. Ahmad. 2014. State of Asian Americans and Pacific Islanders Series: A Multifaceted Portrait of a Growing Population. Washington, DC: Center for American Progress.

Rodriguez, Carlos, Rita Kirshstein, Lauren Banks Amos, Wehmah Jones, Lorelle Espinosa, and David Watnick. 2012. "Broadening participation in STEM: A call to action." Unpublished report, NSF Grant No. HRD-1059774. Washington: American Institutes for Research.

Santiago, Deborah, Morgan Taylor, and Emily Calderón Galdeano. 2016. From Capacity to Success: HSIs, Title V, and Latino Students. Washington, DC: Excelencia in Education. Available at: https://vtechworks.lib.vt.edu/bitstream/handle/10919/83089/FromCapacitytoSuccessLatinoStudents.pdf?sequence=1. Accessed October 2018.

Santiago, Deborah A., Emily Calderón Galdeano, and Morgan Taylor. 2015. "The condition of Latinos in education: 2015 factbook." Excelencia in Education. Available at: https://www.edexcelencia. org/research/publications/condition-latinos-education-2015-factbook. Accessed October 2018.

Sibulkin, Amy E., and J.S. Butler. 2011. "Diverse colleges of origin of African American doctoral recipients, 2001–2005: historically black colleges and universities and beyond." *Research in Higher Education* 52 (8):830-852.

Soares, Louis, Jonathan S. Gagliardi, and Christopher J. Nellum. 2017. "The post-traditional learners manifesto revisited." American Council on Education. Available at: https://www.acenet. edu/news-room/Documents/The-Post-Traditional-Learners-Manifesto-Revisited.pdf. Accessed October 2018.

Solórzano, Daniel G. and Ronald W. Solórzano. 1995. "The Chicano educational experience: A framework for effective schools in Chicano communities." *Educational Policy* 9 (3):293-314.

Starobin, Soko S., Tom Schenk Jr., Frankie Santos Laanan, David G. Rethwisch, and Darin Moeller. 2013. "Going and passing through community colleges: Examining the effectiveness of project lead the way in STEM pathways." *Community College Journal of Research and Practice* 37 (3):226-236.

Stull, Ginger, Demetrios Spyridakis, Marybeth Gasman, Andres Samayoa, and Yvette Booker. 2015. "Redefining success: How tribal colleges and universities build nations, strengthen sovereignty, and persevere through challenges." Center for Minority Serving Institutions.

Taniguchi, Hiromi and Gayle Kaufman. 2005. "Degree completion among nontraditional college students." *Social Science Quarterly* 86 (4):912-927.

Teranishi, Robert T., Dina C. Maramba, and Minh Hoa Ta. 2013. "Asian-American and Native American Pacific Islander Serving Institutions (AANAPISIS)." Fostering success of ethnic and racial minorities in STEM: The role of minority serving institutions. p.168. New York: Rutledge.

Thurgood Marshall College Fund. 2015. "Brief history of HBCUs." Available at: https://tmcf.org/ about-us/our-schools/brief-history-of-hbcus. Accessed October 2018.

UNCF (United Negro College Fund). 2017. HBCUs Make America Strong: The Positive Economic Impact of Historically Black Colleges and Universities. Available at: http:// images.uncf.org/production/HBCU_Consumer_Brochure_FINAL_APPROVED.pdf?_ ga=2.139166256.2045359234.1540825231-851689931.1537544139. Accessed October 2018.

U.S. Census Bureau. 2015. Projections of the Size and Composition of the U.S. Population: 2014 to 2060. Population Estimates and Projections. Current Population Reports. P25-1143. Washington, DC: U.S. Census Bureau. Available at: https://www.census.gov/content/dam/Census/ library/publications/2015/demo/p25-1143.pdf. Accessed October 2018.

U.S. Census Bureau. 2017. American Community Survey and Puerto Rico Community Survey; Code List. Available at: https://www2.census.gov/programssurveys/acs/tech_docs/code_lists/2017_ ACS_Code_Lists.pdf. Accessed September 2018.

U.S. Department of Education. 1991. "Historically Black colleges and universities and higher education desegregation." Office for Civil Rights. Available at: https://www2.ed.gov/about/offices/ list/ocr/docs/hq9511.html. Accessed October 2018.

U.S. Department of Education. 2015. College Scorecard 2015. Available at: https://collegescorecard. ed.gov/. Accessed October 2018.

U.S. Department of Education. 2016. Trends in Pell Grant Receipt and the Characteristics of Pell Grant Recipients: Selected Years, 1999-2000 to 2011-2012. https://nces.ed.gov/pubs2015/2015601. pdf. Accessed January 2019.

U.S. Department of Education. 2017. Asian American and Native American Pacific Islander-Serving Institutions Program. Available at: https://www2.ed.gov/programs/aanapi/index.html. Accessed October 2018.

Valdez, Patrick L. 2015. An overview of Hispanic-Serving Institutions' legislation: Legislation policy formation between 1979 and 1992. In Mendez, J.P., Bonner II, F.A., Méndez-Negrete, J., & Palmer, R.T. (Eds.). Hispanic Serving Institutions in American higher education: Their origin, and present and future Challenges (5-29). Sterling, VA: Stylus. Available at: https://stylus-pub.presswarehouse.com/browse/book/9781620361443/Hispanic-Serving%20Institutions%20 in%20American%20Higher%20Education. Accessed January 2019.

Van Noy, Michelle, and Matthew Zeidenberg. 2017. "Community college pathways to the STEM workforce: What are they, who follows them, and how?" *New Directions for Community Colleges* 178:9-21.

Vollman, Alexandra. 2017. "Asian American students find academic, cultural support at UIC." Available at: http://diversity.uic.edu/news-stories/asian-american-students-find-academic-cultural-support-at-uic/. Accessed October 2018.

Wortham, Stanton, Emerson Fisher, Enrique G. Murillo, and Edmund T. Hamann. 2002. Education in the New Latino Diaspora: Policy and the Politics of Identity. Vol. 2. Westport, CT: Greenwood Publishing Group.

Wortham, Stanton, Katherine Clonan-Roy, Holly Link, and Carlos Martínez. 2013. "Scattered challenges, singular solutions: The new Latino diaspora." *Phi Delta Kappan* 94 (6):14-19.

4

MSI Investment and
Returns on Investment

*"STEM education is a common good. If we don't make the investment
we all suffer. If we don't take advantage of the emerging majority of the
country—[the nation] is going to be in bad shape."*
     – Dr. John Moder, Senior Vice President/Chief Operating Officer,
     Hispanic Association of Colleges and Universities

*"We need the federal government to model the behavior of funding MSIs
so that the industry sector will follow."*
     – Carrie Billy, President and CEO,
     American Indian Higher Education Consortium

KEY FINDINGS

- Despite having fewer financial resources than non-MSIs, MSIs have
  proven successful in providing multifaceted returns on investment,
  which include improving the upward social mobility of their students; expanding the talent pool for the STEM workforce; and supporting the prosperity of local, regional, and national economies.

- Given MSIs' historical inequities in funding and the projections for
  their continued growth, expanded financial investments in MSIs are

---

critical for cultivating the continued success of these institutions and their students, particularly in STEM disciplines. To support greater investment in MSIs, current funding methods need to be reexamined and new, innovative models explored.

- To more effectively measure MSIs' returns on investment, new efforts to increase the clarity, transparency, and accountability of investments are needed.

- There is a critical need for additional evidence-based research on MSIs' returns on investment, including their impact on student education and faculty development, and their role in contributing to local and regional communities and addressing national workforce needs.

The Minority Serving Institutions (MSIs) described throughout this report have committed leaders, dedicated faculty, enthusiastic students, and proud alumni. But like all successful institutions of higher education, the more than 700 MSIs nationwide cannot operate on these strengths alone. Capital resources are critical to establish, support, and scale up the most effective programs and practices to promote the education, sociocultural development, and workforce training of MSI students. (See Chapter 5 for illustrative examples of the most effective programs and practices to promote MSI student success.) Throughout this chapter, we often refer to these resources as "investments" for a reason—adequately supporting MSIs is an investment, from which benefits accrue to the nation.

As described in Chapter 3, MSIs serve a large proportion of nontraditional and low-income students, many of whom self-finance their education and attend school part time while also working and supporting families. Given the profile of their student bodies, many MSIs are constrained by fewer sources of revenue (e.g., tuition and fees, private investments, and endowments) and rely on public funding more than non-MSIs (Nellum and Valle 2015; Nelson and Frye 2016). As part of the committee's charge to review the challenges and obstacles facing MSIs as they execute their missions to prepare students for success, we explored the impact and outcomes of public investments that seek to support MSIs and student success.

This chapter provides an overview of public investments in MSIs, presents a side-by-side comparison of the multiple sources of revenue for MSIs versus non-MSIs, and describes select examples of returns on investment for MSI students, MSI communities, and the science, technology, engineering, and mathematics (STEM) workforce. The chapter concludes with a discussion on the need for new and expanded efforts to invest in MSIs to promote national progress in developing a larger and more diverse STEM-capable workforce.

FEDERAL AND STATE INVESTMENT

Based on 2013 data, federal investment in higher education totaled $75.6 billion, or approximately 2 percent of the federal budget (Pew Charitable Trusts 2015).[1] States collectively provided $72.7 billion, and localities provided $9.2 billion to higher education in 2013, primarily to support institutional operating expenses (Pew Charitable Trusts 2015). In the late 1980s, states provided the greatest amount of funding for postsecondary institutions but have steadily reduced this amount over time, especially during the recession that began in 2008 (Baum 2017; Pew Charitable Trusts 2015). This disinvestment has had serious implications for all institutions of higher education, including MSIs.

Beyond other forms of funding provided to the whole of higher education, MSIs receive targeted federal support by way of direct legislative appropriations. Federal funding to Historically Black Colleges and Universities (HBCUs) and Tribal Colleges and Universities (TCUs) is channeled through formula-based funding from the U.S. Department of Education under Title III of the Higher Education Act (HEA).[2,3] Under formula-based funding, any institution that meets the federal definition of HBCU or TCU may receive a grant rather than go through a competitive process (Hegji 2017). Other institutions, including enrollment-defined MSIs, are eligible for application-based, competitive grant programs from the U.S. Department of Education, many of which are authorized under the amended HEA of 1965.[4] Federal agencies with STEM activities provide additional, targeted funding to MSIs, with an emphasis on institutional capacity building.

U.S. Department of Education

Approximately one-half of the U.S. Department of Education's budget is allotted for investments in higher education (Pew Charitable Trusts 2015). A major source of Department of Education funding for MSIs comes through capacity-building grants under Title III and Title V of the HEA. In 2016, MSI programs

---

[1] Portion of the total federal budget of $3.5 trillion. Calculation is from across all agencies and for all types of institutions, including institutional grants and contracts but excluding student loan programs.

[2] Unlike the enrollment-based MSIs in Title III, HBCUs are not required to meet the low educational and general expenditures nor the specified threshold of needy students to be eligible to receive funding. For additional information, see http://congressionalresearch.com/RL31647/document.php ?study=Title+III+and+Title+V+of+the+Higher+Education+Act+Background+and+Reauthorization +Issues. Accessed October 2018.

[3] Predominantly Black Institutions (PBIs) are unique in that federal funding under Title III, Part A is formula-based funding, similar to that of TCUs and HBCUs. PBIs are also eligible for competitive grant funding under Title III, Part F.

[4] Higher Education Act of 1965, Pub. L. No. 89-329 (1965). As of the drafting of this report, Congress was considering the Promoting Real Opportunity, Success and Prosperity through Education Reform (PROSPER) Act. If passed as submitted, this bill would substantially modify the Higher Education Act and negatively impact funding designated for MSIs.

were appropriated approximately $817 million to help fund more than 900 grants to institutions (Hegji 2017). The grants seek to improve and strengthen institutions' academic quality and provide expanded educational opportunities for low-income students through a specified list of allowable activities that include faculty development, facility construction, and academic programs. As summarized by Espinosa, Turk, and Taylor (2017), funding streams are intended as follows:

- *Title III, Part A—Strengthening Institutions Program.* Helps eligible institutions to expand their capacity to serve low-income students by "providing funds to improve and strengthen the academic quality, institutional management, and fiscal stability of eligible institutions." MSIs that receive funding through Title III, Part A include all MSI types except HBCUs and Hispanic-Serving Institutions (HSIs).[5]
- *Title III, Part B—Strengthening Historically Black Colleges and Universities Program.* Focuses on HBCUs and "provides financial assistance to Historically Black Colleges and Universities to establish or strengthen their physical plants, financial management, academic resources, and endowment-building capacity."[6]
- *Title III, Part F—Hispanic-Serving Institutions – Science, Technology, Engineering, or Mathematics and Articulation Programs.* Aims to increase the number of Hispanic and low-income graduates in STEM fields and to build the quality and quantity of model transfer and articulation agreement programs between two-year HSIs and four-year institutions in STEM fields.[7]
- *Title V, Part A—Developing Hispanic-Serving Institutions Program.* Provides funding to HSIs "to expand educational opportunities for, and improve the attainment of, Hispanic students. These grants also enable HSIs to expand and enhance their academic offerings, program quality, and institutional stability."[8]

To receive Title III or V funding, in addition to meeting predetermined enrollment thresholds (and for Predominantly Black Institutions, size and income thresholds), institutions also must have low educational and general expenditures; that is, in order to receive support, they must demonstrate that they have fewer

---

[5] For more information, see U.S. Department of Education, https://www2.ed.gov/programs/iduestitle3a/legislation.html, accessed October 2018, and Cornell Law School, 20 U.S. Code § 1058: https://www.law.cornell.edu/uscode/text/20/1058#b_1, accessed October 2018.

[6] For more information, see U.S. Department of Education, https://www2.ed.gov/programs/iduestitle3b/legislation.html, accessed October 2018.

[7] For more information, see U.S. Department of Education, https://www2.ed.gov/programs/hsistem/legislation.html, accessed October 2018.

[8] For more information, see U.S. Department of Education, https://www2.ed.gov/programs/idueshsi/legislation.html, accessed October 2018.

resources with which to serve their students.[9] The definition of "low expenditures" is set by the U.S Department of Education annually and is not made publicly available from year to year, although some waivers to these thresholds are accepted,[10] which may impact long-term budgetary projections. In addition, regardless of need, institutions cannot apply for funding under more than one MSI type, even if they qualify as such. For example, if an institution meets the criteria for both an HSI and an HBCU (as does St. Phillips College in San Antonio, Texas), or both an HSI and an Asian American and Native American Pacific Islander Serving Institution (AANAPISI) (as do several institutions in California), it must choose one or the other when applying for federal funding.

While these federal grant programs (with the exception of Title III, Part F) are not specific to STEM, the Title III and V grant programs can be, and are, utilized by MSIs to strengthen their STEM infrastructure and provide specialized programming for STEM students that facilitate retention and graduation in these disciplines. In 2018, the federal omnibus spending bill provided increased support for these programs.[11] The U.S. Department of Education's fiscal year (FY) 2018 budget appropriated $681 million for Title III programs, including those listed above, and $227 million for aid for Hispanic-Serving Institutions.[12] Both programs received a 14 percent increase in discretionary funding, and resulted in an estimated $82 million of new funds for FY 2018. At the time of this report, however, the 2019 White House Administration's budget request proposed a 25 percent *decrease* in aid for Title III programs and a 56 percent *decrease* in Aid for Hispanic-Serving Institutions, compared to 2018 appropriations.[13]

STEM-Focused Investments by Other Federal Agencies

Other federal agencies have established funding streams that specifically support STEM programming and capacity at institutions of higher education, including but not limited to MSIs. The top six sources are the Department of Health and Human Services (DHHS; including the National Institutes of Health), which provides the largest amount, followed by the National Science Foundation, Department of Defense (DoD), Department of Agriculture, Department of Energy, and the National Aeronautics and Space Administration. The total amount awarded across these agencies (including much smaller amounts in about a dozen

---

[9] For more information, see Cornell Law School, reprinted 20 U.S. Code § 1068, https://www.law.cornell.edu/uscode/text/20/1058#b_1, accessed October 2018.

[10] For more information, see Cornell Law School, reprinted 20 U.S. Code § 1068a, https://www.law.cornell.edu/uscode/text/20/1068a#b, accessed October 2018.

[11] The Consolidated Appropriations Act, 2018 (Pub. L. No. 115-141) was enacted by the 115th United States Congress and signed into law by President Donald Trump on March 23, 2018.

[12] U.S. Department of Education, https://www2.ed.gov/about/overview/budget/budget18/18action.pdf.

[13] U.S. Department of Education, https://www2.ed.gov/about/overview/budget/budget19/19action.pdf.

others) for science and engineering activities, including research, education, and infrastructure support, in 2015 was $30.5 billion. Of this total, HBCUs, HSIs, and TCUs (AANAPISIs and other MSI types were not separated out) received $783 million. More than one-half that amount ($539 million) went to only 20 out of the more than 700 MSIs (NSF 2017a). The funding principally supports research and development (R&D), but some programs support fellowships, facilities, and other activities.[14] Box 4-1 provides a few of many examples. Although greater investment is needed, understanding which of these publicly funded programs most effectively serves the national goal of preparing young Americans, including young people of color, to pursue and acquire high-quality STEM degrees, also remains a compelling need.

OVERVIEW OF INVESTMENTS BY MSI TYPE

Another prism through which to look at investment support is by type of MSI. This lens illustrates how decreased or inconsistent public funding can hamper institutions, and how *actual funding* allocations often do not align with the amounts that Congress has authorized.

HBCUs

As is the case for other MSIs, the stability of HBCUs depends on allocations of public investments (Gasman 2010). Although HBCUs are funded through a variety of revenue sources, federal, state, and local allocations provide most of their funding. As shown in Figure 4-1, public four-year HBCUs rely more heavily on federal, state, and local appropriations, grants, and contracts as a source of total revenue than do public four-year non-HBCUs (54 versus 38 percent, respectively). Private four-year HBCUs rely more on net tuition revenue as a source of total revenue than do private four-year non-HBCUs (45 percent versus 37 percent, respectively). Private gifts, grants, and contracts represent a lower proportion of total revenue at HBCUs than at non-HBCUs.

Although federal funding to HBCUs has increased over the past decade, it is not sufficient to meet institutional need (Gasman 2010). Looking across federal agencies during fiscal year 2013 (Table 4-1), HBCUs receive 3 percent or less of each agency's total investment in institutions of higher education, except in the Department of Agriculture. Two important points can be garnered from this table. First, these funds ($172 million), although seemingly substantial, are shared across roughly 100 different HBCUs and are unevenly distributed to only a small subset (Gasman 2010). This suggests that recent allotments of federal investments are not sufficient to meet the needs of the majority of HBCUs. Second, Table 4-1

---

[14] See Chapter 5's section on Public-Private Partnerships for additional discussion on MSI-focused STEM investments.

BOX 4-1
Examples of Federal Programs That Support STEM at MSIs

Department of Health and Human Services, National Institutes of Health
- Minority Access to Research Careers (https://www.nigms.nih.gov/Training/MARC/Pages/USTARAwards.aspx)
- Research Infrastructure in Minority Institutions
- (https://grants.nih.gov/grants/guide/rfa-files/RFA-MD-04-004.html)
- Minority Biomedical Research Support Program (https://www.benefits.gov/benefits/benefit-details/696)

National Science Foundation
- Centers of Research Excellence in Science and Technology (https://www.nsf.gov/funding/pgm_summ.jsp?pims_id=6668)
- HBCU Research Infrastructure for Science and Engineering (https://www.nsf.gov/funding/pgm_summ.jsp?pims_id=6668)
- Partnerships for Research and Education in Materials (https://www.nsf.gov/funding/pgm_summ.jsp?pims_id=5439)
- Hispanic Serving Institutions Program (https://www.nsf.gov/funding/pgm_summ.jsp?pims_id=505512)

Department of Defense
- Research and Education Program for Historically Black Colleges and Universities/Minority Serving Institutions (https://www.arl.army.mil/www/pages/8/FY2018_DoD_HBCUMI_FOA_Research_Education_May252017-FINAL(v2).pdf)
- Historically Black Colleges and Universities/Minority Institutions Science Program (https://basicresearch.defense.gov/hbcu_mi/)
- Minority Serving Institutions, STEM Research & Development Consortium (www.msrdconsortium.org)

U.S. Department of Agriculture
- 1890 Institution Teaching, Research and Extension Capacity Building Grants Program (https://nifa.usda.gov/funding-opportunity/1890-institution-teaching-research-and-extension-capacity-building-grants-cbg)
- Food and Agricultural Science Enhancement Grant (https://nifa.usda.gov/afri-fase-epscor-program)

Department of Energy
- HCBU/MEI Faculty Summer Research Program (https://www.orau.org/ornl/faculty/hbcu-mei-summer-program.htm)

National Aeronautics and Space Administration
- Minority University Research and Education Project (https://www.nasa.gov/offices/education/programs/national/murep/home/index.html)

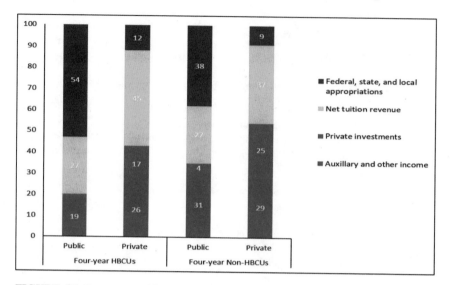

FIGURE 4-1 Percentage of investments by source, public and private (nonprofit) four-year HBCUs and non-HBCUs.
NOTE: Private gifts, grants, and contracts include investment income such as interest on endowments. Percentages were rounded to the nearest whole number (based on source data).
SOURCE: Williams and Davis (2018). ©2018 American Council on Education. Adapted and reprinted with permission.

TABLE 4-1 Federal Investments in Institutions of Higher Education (IHE) and the Percentage of IHE funds Awarded to HBCUs, by Federal Agency, 2013

Federal Agency	IHE	HBCU	Percent HBCU Share
TOTAL Investment	$172,369,578,639	$4,758,941,493	2.8
Department of Education	$139,649,172,390	$4,225,388,454	3.0
Department of Health and Human Services	$17,163,165,640	$156,400,000	0.9
Department of Agriculture	$1,213,525,235	$145,508,729	12.0
National Science Foundation	$5,116,335,618	$92,128,863	1.8
Department of Defense	$3,619,871,702	$25,681,122	0.7
National Aeronautics and Space Administration	$889,110,653	$23,379,116	2.6
Department of Energy	$1,241,285,216	$19,478,488	1.6

NOTE: Table is incomplete. The top six agencies, in terms of IHE investments, are included. Additional agencies provided smaller investments to reach the total investment in the first row.
SOURCE: Adapted from U.S. Department of Education (2015, page 5).

demonstrates that the Department of Health and Human Services (DHHS) and the Department of Defense (DoD) contribute a markedly lower investment in HBCUs compared to other institutions of higher education. These findings shed light on opportunities for HBCUs to explore new, underutilized revenue streams, and for DHHS and DoD to consider new partnership opportunities with HBCUs. Of note, at the time of this report, the White House submitted an overall budget request of $686 billion for DoD ($108 billion more than its authorized budget in FY 2013).[15] This substantial increase in funding suggests HBCUs, particularly the most resource challenged, may find additional investment opportunities in DoD R&D grants and contracts. (See also Chapter 5's discussion on partnerships with government agencies and the committee's recommendations to Congress on expanding federal investments in MSIs.)

In addition to federal funding disparities, the United States has a long history of inequities in *state-level* support for HBCUs (Gasman 2007). Minor (2008) used North Carolina as a recent case in point: in 2007 the University of North Carolina at Chapel Hill and North Carolina State University (both Predominantly White Institutions, PWIs) received approximately $15,700 in state funding per-student, as compared to the approximately $7,800 per student state investment in North Carolina A&T and Fayetteville State University (both HBCUs). The author urged state higher education leaders to be more cognizant of irregular state funding patterns and their potential to worsen inequities in public education.

In addition to fighting for equitable state support, HBCUs are challenged with ensuring that their unique institutional programming and/or educational ventures are not being duplicated at nearby Predominantly White Institutions (Pluviose 2006). Issues with program duplication are said to create unnecessary competition between state institutions and threaten the visibility and potential profitability of HBCUs (Palmer and Griffin 2009; Pluviose 2006). At least one such state case has advanced to the federal court system (Box 4-2).

TCUs

TCUs rely on federal funding as their main source of revenue to a greater extent than other types of MSIs, with greater than 70 percent of revenues coming from federal appropriations (Figure 4-2; see also Nelson and Frye, 2016). Because of the relationship between Native American tribes and the federal government, states are not required to provide funding to TCUs, and many do not. The Tribally Controlled College or University Assistance Act of 1978 (TCCUAA) contains several titles that provide funding to TCUs, although different TCUs have different authorizations and, thus, different types of federal funding (Nelson

---

[15] For more information on the proposed budget for the Department of Defense, see https://dod.defense.gov/News/SpecialReports/Budget2019.aspx, accessed October 2018.

BOX 4-2
Reducing Duplication, Increasing Competitiveness

Leaders of public MSIs that make up the Coalition for Equity and Excellence in Maryland Higher Education have argued not only that there are inequities in state funding, but also that public HBCUs are at a disadvantage when their schools' more innovative courses and curriculum are duplicated at institutions with stronger infrastructures and financial standing. The Coalition contends the duplication of the HBCUs' programs at nearby non-MSI colleges and universities creates an additional barrier for the success and prosperity of HBCUs.

In 2013, a U.S. judge in *Maryland Higher Education v. Maryland Higher Education Commission* ruled that the unnecessary duplication of programs within Maryland's higher education system has shown effects of segregation that the state could not justify. After a failed mediation between the opposing parties, in November 2017, the presiding judge determined that neither proposed remedial plan from the opposing parties would be an effective remedy, and instead proposed a new plan that would support the development of new and unique high-demand programs at HBCUs. When only MSIs are designated for such programs, there is an opportunity for these institutions to develop excellence in areas that enhance their reputation and better position them to attract additional research and education grants and contracts.

The judge's plan indicated that the programs are to be funded by the state rather than the HBCUs, and in addition that institutions are to be awarded appropriate funding for marketing, student recruitment, financial aid, and other incentives over the next 10 years. The judge ordered the appointment of a "special master" to help develop and monitor the implementation of the remedial plan. In 2018, the governor's office responded to the ruling with a proposed financial settlement, although it did not respond to the programmatic issues raised, according to the coalition. The suit remained unresolved as of this writing after more than 5 years. The committee did not learn of any additional federal lawsuits about the potential negative impacts of duplication of MSI programs at Predominantly White Institutions.

SOURCES: Lawyers' Committee on for Civil Rights Under Law (2018), Seltzer (2017).

and Frye 2016).[16] The Bureau of Indian Affairs, within the U.S. Department of the Interior, manages and distributes these funding streams (AIHEC 1999).

TCU federal funding, although tightly regulated, is not without its challenges. Research has suggested that TCU funds are not being appropriated to full TCCUAA-authorization levels (Figure 4-3; see also Nelson and Frye (2016) for additional discussion). Additionally, the mathematical formula used to determine federal funding only allocates funds for Native students (Nelson and Frye 2016).

---

[16] For the language of the Act, see 25 U.S.C. Ch. 20: Tribally Controlled Colleges and Universities Assistance, http://uscode.house.gov/view.xhtml?path=/prelim@title25/chapter20&edition=prelim, accessed October 2018.

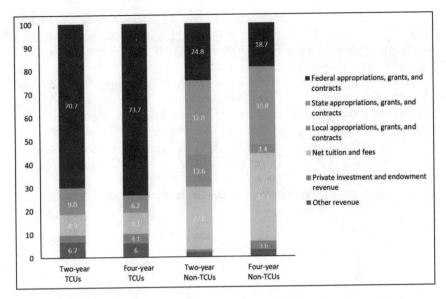

FIGURE 4-2 Percentage of investments by source at TCUs and public non-TCUs.
NOTE: Percentages below 3 percent were not labeled.
SOURCE: Adapted from Nelson and Frye (2016).

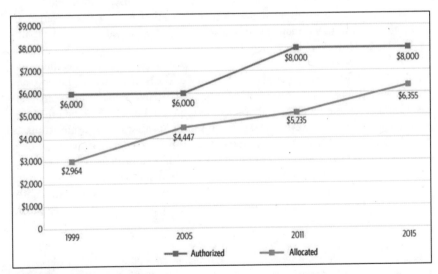

FIGURE 4-3 Federal appropriations per Native student at TCUs, authorized versus allocated.
SOURCE: Adapted from Nelson and Frye (2016); data from Integrated Postsecondary Education Data System.

This is an important concern because, on average, 16 percent of the student population at TCUs is non-Native (Nelson and Frye 2016). This lack of coverage for non-Native students puts additional pressure on TCUs' budgets to fill the revenue gap and support the full student body.

Like most public higher education institutions, TCUs historically have not and currently do not derive a substantial amount of their revenue from private gifts or endowments. Furthermore, as with other MSIs, TCUs are constrained in their ability to raise tuition because of the specific profile of their student population. The majority of students served by TCUs face significant economic barriers such as extremely high rates of poverty and unemployment. More than 75 percent of students attending TCUs are Pell grant recipients, and few participate in the federal student loan programs (AIHEC 2012). (See Chapter 3 for additional discussion on TCU students.)

HSIs

Similar to HBCUs, HSIs are funded through a variety of revenue sources, mostly from federal, state, and local allocations (Figure 4-4). At two-year HSIs, greater than 70 percent of the total external support comes from federal, state, and local sources compared to about 57 percent at non-HSIs. Looking at 4-year institutions, the difference is smaller—46.7 percent for HSIs compared to 42.0 percent for non-HSIs. These data indicate that changes in public budgets would greatly affect HSIs' capacity to prosper, especially for two-year institutions.

With the reauthorization of the Higher Education Act's Title V, Part A in 1998, the federal government increased its commitment to support student success at HSIs. However, since then, the demographics of the United States have changed, and correspondingly, so have the demographics of higher education (Hale 2004; Pew Research Center 2014; U.S. Census Bureau 2017). Not only has there been a dramatic increase in the number of Hispanic students enrolled at all institutions of higher education, but also the total number of HSIs and emerging HSIs have increased as well.[17] **The growth in the number of Hispanic students and the number of HSIs now challenge the ability of federal appropriations, established 20 years ago, to remain aligned with a rapidly growing need.** As potential evidence of this impact, Figure 4-5 demonstrates that per-student state and local investments in two- and four-year HSIs have dropped significantly since 2008. **In light of this evidence, there is an urgent need to reexamine**

---

[17] In 2000, there were 229 federally eligible HSIs, and by 2016 there were 492 (Excelencia in Education 2018; HACU 2018). Using data from 2016 to 2017, Excelencia in Education has identified 333 colleges and universities with between 15 and 24.99 percent Hispanic enrollment that may soon become HSIs, due to their increasing enrollments of Hispanics—calling them "Emerging HSIs" (Santiago and Andrade 2010).

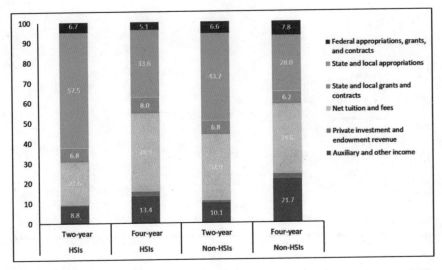

FIGURE 4-4 Percentage of investments by source at public two- and four-year HSIs and non-HSIs.
NOTE: Percentages below 3 percent were not labeled.
SOURCE: Adapted from Nellum and Valle (2015).

and readjust current funding methods to better support these institutions and their students.

AANAPISIs

AANAPISIs are a relatively recent, but growing sector within the MSI landscape. There are approximately 133 two- and four-year institutions that, based on enrollment and income, are eligible to receive AANAPISI-designated funding (Museus et al. 2018); however, in FY 2016, only 25 AANAPISIs received funding through the U.S. Department of Education, for a total of about $8,044,000 (U.S. Department of Education 2018). Many more could be eligible for Title III funding but are not taking the steps to access it, in particular two-year institutions (CARE 2013). In addition, similar to HSIs, a large number of AANAPISIs are two-year institutions and are ineligible for many of the federal R&D programs that serve four-year research institutions. Overall, AANAPISIs rely more on state and local appropriations and less on federal funding than non-AANAPISIs (48.9 percent) (Figure 4-6).

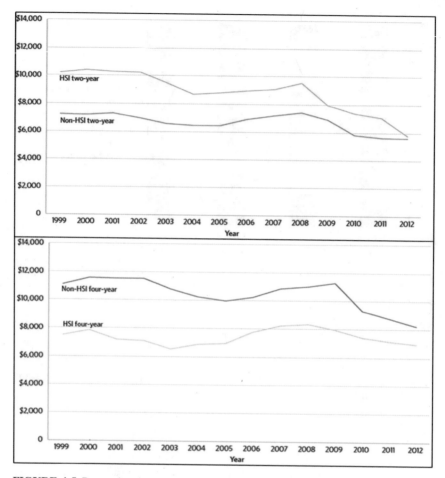

FIGURE 4-5 Per-student investments in public two- and four-year HSIs and non-HSIs, 1999-2012.
SOURCE: Adapted from Nellum and Valle (2015); data from National Forum on Higher Education for the Public Good analysis of Delta Cost Project Database, 1999-2012.

SUMMING IT UP: WHY PUBLIC
INVESTMENTS IN MSIS MATTER

As described in the sections above, MSIs are supported by multiple sources of revenue, including federal, state, and local appropriations; tuition and fees; and, to a lesser extent, endowments and private investments. Given their complex needs, these institutions face substantial resource challenges. Here we highlight two aspects of these challenges: (1) the disparities in how much is invested in MSIs versus non-MSIs, and, as a result, how much MSIs can invest back into

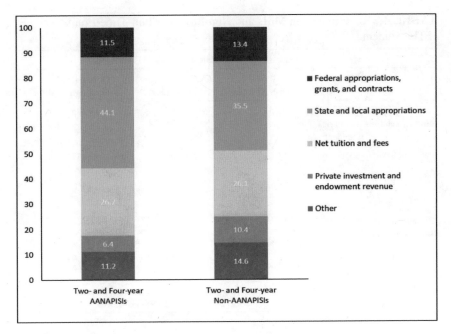

FIGURE 4-6 Percentage of investments by source, AANAPISI and non-AANAPISI public institutions, 2011.
NOTE: See the Annex at the end of this chapter for notes.
SOURCE: Adapted from CARE (2013). National Center for Education Statistics (NCES) and Integrated Postsecondary Education Data System (IPEDS) data.

their institutions versus non-MSIs, and (2) the disparities in endowment assets between MSIs and non-MSIs.

Comparison of Revenue Sources and Allocations for Two- and Four-Year MSIs and Non-MSIs

Four-year MSIs receive less revenue per full-time-equivalent (FTE) student than do four-year non-MSIs; moreover, two-year institutions, both MSIs and non-MSIs, receive far less revenue per FTE student than do four-year institutions (Table 4-2). And expectedly, MSIs in general *spend* less per FTE student than non-MSIs, whether for instruction, academic and social supports, or other aspects that contribute to student success (Table 4-3). The notable disparities in total revenue show that MSIs are working with fewer resources than are non-MSIs, despite enrolling a high percentage of nontraditional and low-income students. Moreover, MSIs have fewer options to raise tuition and fees to offset expenses.

This context challenges MSIs to provide sufficient resources to ensure that they are equipped to meet the standards and expectations for high-quality edu-

TABLE 4-2 Investments in MSIs and Non-MSIs per Full-Time-Equivalent (FTE) Student

	FOUR-YEAR INSTITUTIONS		
	Non-MSI (means)	MSI (means)	Difference in Funding for MSIs
Total revenue (including tuition, excluding auxiliaries and other) per FTE student[a]	$29,833	$16,648	−$13,185
State and local appropriations per FTE student	$4,989	$5,446	+$457
State and local grants and contracts	$1,896	$1,107	−$789
Federal appropriations, grants, and contracts per FTE student (net Pell)[b]	$4,971	$2,249	−$2,722
Private gifts and investment return	$6,586	$863	−$5,723

	TWO-YEAR INSTITUTIONS		
	Non-MSI (means)	MSI (means)	Difference in Funding for MSIs
Total revenue (including tuition, excluding auxiliaries and other) per FTE student[a]	$10,341	$10,192	−$149
State and local appropriations per FTE student	$5,077	$6,142	+$1,065
State and local grants and contracts	$747	$732	negligible
Federal appropriations, grants, and contracts per FTE student (net Pell)[b]	$802	$899	negligible
Private gifts and investment return	$154	$171	negligible

NOTE: See the Annex at the end of this chapter for notes.
SOURCE: Adapted from Cunningham et al. (2014).

TABLE 4-3 MSI and Non-MSI Spending per Full-Time-Equivalent (FTE) Student

	FOUR-YEAR INSTITUTIONS		
	Non-MSI (means)	MSI (means)	Difference in MSI Spending
Total educational and general expenditures[a] per FTE student	$28,806	$16,743	−$12,063
Student services, academic support, and institutional support per FTE student	$8,399	$5,750	−$2,649
Research and public service per FTE student	$6,202	$1,638	−$4,564
Operations and maintenance per FTE student	$2,024	$1,482	−$542
Scholarships and fellowships per FTE student	$959	$1,599	+$640

	TWO-YEAR INSTITUTIONS		
	Non-MSI (means)	MSI (means)	Difference in MSI Spending
Total educational and general expenditures[a] per FTE student	$10,667	$10,592	negligible
Student services, academic support, and institutional support per FTE student	$3,528	$3,629	+$101
Research and public service per FTE student	$210	$153	negligible
Operations and maintenance per FTE student	$960	$963	negligible
Scholarships and fellowships per FTE student	$1,323	$1,696	negligible

NOTE: See the Annex at the end of this chapter for notes.
SOURCE: Adapted from Cunningham et al. (2014).

cation (particularly STEM education), sociocultural development, and relevant research and training experiences for the students. Research has further shown that institutional expenditures have an impact on graduation rates. For example, Webber and Ehrenberg (2010) developed a model to examine the overall effect of four categories of institutional expenditures (instructional, academic support, student service, and research) on graduation rates at HBCUs. The researchers found that higher spending, especially related to instruction and student services, positively influences student outcomes related to persistence and graduation and that institutions with lower numbers of Pell recipients (i.e., wealthier institutions) spend more per student FTE in these categories.

Comparison of Endowment Assets
between Four-Year MSIs and Non-MSIs

In addition to federal and state resources, many institutions maintain endowment funds, defined by the American Council on Education (ACE 2014) as an "aggregation of assets invested by a college or university to support its educational mission in perpetuity." Endowments can provide institutional stability; serve as a source for student financial aid; leverage other sources of revenue; encourage innovation, flexibility, and risk taking; and allow for a longer-term time horizon for improvements to be realized. Much media attention has been given to Ivy League and other institutions with very large endowments, often with the assumption that all institutions of higher education have this resource. However, this is not the case for most public and even many private institutions.

In examining median and mean endowment assets per FTE[18] for four-year MSIs, the data show that MSIs have far lower endowments than non-MSIs.[19] For example, as shown in Table 4-4, the median endowments per FTE in 2015 for four-year public AANAPISIs and especially HBCUs and HSIs were markedly low, as compared to the median endowment per FTE for public four-year non-MSIs. The mean values further unmask the funding extremes between non-MSIs and MSIs. The mean endowment per FTE for public four-year non-MSIs is $16,709, more than twice the mean values per FTE at HBCUs, AANAPISIs, and HSIs. Even the highest endowed MSI would be viewed as poorly endowed when compared to a non-MSI.

Very few funding mechanisms exist to facilitate the creation or enhancement of endowment funds. The HEA presents a few funding opportunities that can be

---

[18] Calculation using IPEDS FY 2015 Finance survey; Examining median endowments per FTE show 50th percentile of endowments for each MSI type. In other words, it shows the median value of endowments for each institutional category, with half of institutions above that value and the other half below that value. Analysis by the American Council on Education.

[19] Only select four-year MSIs are presented due to missing data and low sample sizes for other MSI categories. Non-MSI includes all institutions that were not designated as one of the seven MSI types in the College Scorecard for 2015-2016. College Scorecard was used to determine all institutions that were eligible to apply for federal MSI funding under Titles III and V.

TABLE 4-4 Endowment Assets per Full-Time-Equivalent (FTE) Enrollment by MSI Type (Four-Year Institutions)

	Non-MSI		HBCU		AANAPISI		HSI	
	Public	Private	Public	Private	Public	Private	Public	Private
Endowment Assets per FTE (Mean)	$16,709	$79,934	$5,584	$25,855	$7,715	$24,884	$7,505	$11,691
Endowment Assets per FTE (Median)	$6,707	$22,338	$3,744	$16,389	$5,636	$16,079	$3,844	$6,218
N	416	954	39	38	36	18	68	68

NOTE: See the Annex at the end of this chapter for notes.
SOURCE: IPEDS FY 2015 Finance Survey; Analysis by the American Council on Education for this report.

used to establish or increase institutional endowments. For example, the HEA's Title III-C authorizes the Endowment Challenge Grant program. While not targeted specifically to MSIs, the funds are to be made available to most institutions of higher education with a high concentration of minority students.[20]

In principle, this grant program sounds like an ideal mechanism by which MSIs could realize long-term financial health. However, it has not been funded since fiscal year 1995 and there do not appear to be plans for its reestablishment. Furthermore, if the Endowment Challenge Grant program were active, it would require institutions, even the most financially challenged institutions, to provide nonfederal matching funds equal to the amount of the federal funds provided.[21]

HEA has a few other MSI-focused Title III and V program grants. While these programs can be used to establish or enhance an institution's endowment fund, an institution may not use more than 20 percent of grant monies to do so. In addition, if an institution utilizes the program funds for endowment development, it must provide matching funds from nonfederal sources in an amount equal to or greater than the federal funds provided. The ability of MSIs (and indeed other institutions) to take advantage of such opportunities is limited and, in some cases, impossible, given other pressing, short-term financial priorities. (See Chapter 6 for the committee's recommendation to Congress to support endowment-building programs.)

Public Investments Matter

Given MSIs' historical inequities in funding and the clear projections for continued growth of this sector, there exists a critical need for the nation to reexamine current funding methods and explore new, innovative models of support.

As discussed in Chapters 2 and 3, as the nation's demographic profile evolves, it is in the national interest to proportionally expand investments to the institutions where the majority of the diverse future workforce is being educated and trained—chiefly MSIs. **As the number of MSIs continues to grow, public and private resources and attention must keep pace.** (See Chapter 6 for the committee's recommendation to funding agencies to reconsider current funding methods and to develop new and innovative funding models to better address the needs of MSIs and their students.)

RETURN ON INVESTMENT

A key concern for the committee was the extent to which it is possible to measure MSIs' returns on investment (ROIs) for funders, students, local and regional communities, and the STEM workforce, and, where possible, make ROI comparisons with non-MSIs. Given the overall dearth of research on other

---

[20] For more information on the Endowment Challenge Grants, see Hegji (2017).

[21] For more information on the Endowment Challenge Grants, see Hegji (2017).

aspects of MSIs, the committee was not surprised to find a deficit of economic research (e.g., cost-benefit analyses) on MSIs and their ROIs.

In traditional financial terms, ROI measures the gain or loss generated on an investment relative to the money invested.[22] In recent years, attempts to employ ROI measurements have been made when analyzing the overall benefits of higher education to individuals and to society (Carnevale et al. 2015). Certain efforts focus on ROI by institution, others by major; not surprisingly, different methods of calculations result in different results.[23] Additional studies have presented alternate measures of ROI, including noneconomic ROI for the student such as development of quality mentorships, improved self-esteem, leadership, community engagement, life satisfaction, and intellectual growth (Gallup-Perdue University 2015; Gasman et al. 2017; Nettles 2017; Pew Research Center 2011).

Clearly, measuring ROI when the "product" is a student, the institution itself, the surrounding community, or the nation is a complex endeavor. Certainly, students and families must consider costs and returns when deciding on postsecondary options—to say nothing of the choices for state and federal governments when weighing investments in colleges and universities versus, for example, investments in roads, K-12 education, and health care. But we would argue, and the research highlighted below supports the assertion, that **a range of ROI indicators need to be taken into account when looking at institutions of higher education in general, and MSIs in particular, and that additional research is needed to measure and better understand the economic and social ROIs in higher education.**

The committee examined the research on ROI in terms of the pathways toward education and work in STEM fields, upward mobility and earnings potential, and local and regional impact. It should again be noted that the dearth of overall research for all MSI types has necessitated a less-than-comprehensive look at this topic, despite the high level of interest in higher education ROI by a multitude of stakeholders (Gasman 2017).

Educating the Future Workforce

Given the need to widen pathways of access and opportunity to STEM and STEM-related careers, measuring the extent to which MSIs contribute to the number (and diversity) of STEM graduates prepared to enter the workforce represents one way to examine ROI. Many policy makers and other observers view

---

[22] Return on Investment. BusinessDictionary.com WebFinance, Inc., http://www.businessdictionary.com/definition/return-on-investment-ROI.html, accessed October 2018.

[23] See, for example, Payscale 2018: College ROI Report, https://www.payscale.com/college-roi, and "10 College Majors with Best Starting Salaries," September 25, 2017, *U.S. News and World Report*, https://www.usnews.com/education/best-colleges/slideshows/10-college-majors-with-the-highest-starting-salaries, accessed February 2018.

the federal graduation rate (as derived from the U.S. Department of Education's
IPEDS) as an ROI in terms of student outcomes, with the implication that the
higher the graduation rate of an institution, the better its ROI. However, if graduation rates are indeed to be considered a component of ROI, then it is important to
more accurately reflect degree and credential completions among MSI students.
As noted in Chapter 3, standard institutional metrics such as the federal graduation rate are not sufficiently defined and structured to consider the influence of
important contextual factors (such as students' financial circumstances, life stage,
commitments to work and family, and academic preparation) and inadequately
assess the success of MSIs and their students.

In an effort to look beyond the federal graduation rate, Espinosa, Turk, and
Taylor (2017) examined MSI credential completion via another national data
source: the National Student Clearinghouse (NSC). The NSC data offer a more
complete picture of student enrollment and degree completion at MSIs than
seen in IPEDS, in large part given its ability to track student enrollment patterns
and movement beyond students' starting institution, and over a longer period of
time.[24] As discussed in Chapter 3 (where the NSC analysis is presented), many
MSI students attend college through mixed enrollment, meaning they move between part-time and full-time status. In addition, today's MSI students are mobile
and often attend more than one college; this is especially true for students seeking
a bachelor's degree who start at a community college.

The flexibility to attend part-time and over an extended period is one of
the value-added experiences that many MSIs provide to students. That is, they
are able to offer postsecondary education to those who, for various economic
and family circumstances, cannot attend college as continuous, full-time students—including those who are returning to higher education many years after
high school graduation. In short, MSIs face the challenge of addressing students'
complex sociocultural needs while still meeting the nation's increased demand to
educate a diverse citizenry, including those who will enter the STEM workforce
as teachers, engineers, researchers, and in other capacities.

In addition to providing flexible completion pathways, MSIs are producing
a substantial number of STEM-capable professionals, in part because of the educational, cultural, and environmental support factors described throughout this
report. For example, taken together, HBCUs, HSIs, and AANAPISIs produced
one-fifth of all STEM bachelor's degrees in 2016. Moreover, their individual contributions to STEM degree completions (measured as a proportion of all completions) are on par with non-MSIs, and in the case of HBCUs and AANAPISIs,
exceed non-MSIs in STEM degree production. See Figure 4-7.

---

[24] National Center for Education Statistics and Institute of Education Sciences (U.S.). 2016. Digest
of education statistics. Washington, DC: U.S. Department of Education. Table 326.10. Graduation
rate from first institution attended for first-time, full-time bachelor's degree-seeking students at 4-year
postsecondary institutions, by race/ethnicity, time to completion, sex, control of institution, and
acceptance rate: Selected cohort entry years, 1996 through 2009. Available at: https://nces.ed.gov/
programs/digest/d16/tables/dt16_326.10.asp, accessed October 2018.

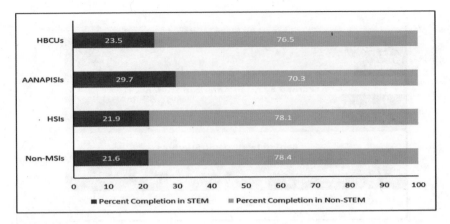

FIGURE 4-7 Total completions in STEM versus non-STEM fields, at MSIs compared to non-MSIs, 2016 data.
NOTE: There are limited IPEDS data for TCUs; hence, these data are not included. See the Annex at the end of this chapter for additional notes. See Appendix F, Table F-3 for the raw data used in calculations.
SOURCE: IPEDS 2016 Completions and Institutional Characteristics data. Analysis by the American Institutes for Research for this report.

When looking at individual racial and ethnic groups (see Figure 4-8), IPEDS 2016 completion data show that HBCUs awarded 15.6 percent of all STEM bachelor's degrees earned by Black students, AANAPISIs awarded 18.8 percent of all STEM bachelor's degrees earned by Asian American students, and HSIs awarded 40.5 percent of all STEM bachelor's degrees earned by Hispanic students. Indeed, many MSIs are listed within the "top 20" rankings of institutions that graduate students of color in STEM disciplines.[25]

Based on 2011-2014 data, 10 HSIs and 10 HBCUs are among the top 20 institutions that award science and engineering degrees to Latinos and African Americans, respectively, and 18 AANAPISIs are among the top 20 institutions that award these degrees to Asian Americans (NSF 2017b).[26] North Carolina A&T State University (a public HBCU) is the top source of African American graduates with engineering bachelor's and master's degrees in the country (Sharpe 2018), and Howard University, Xavier University of Louisiana, and Spelman College (private HBCUs) are the nation's leading suppliers of African American students to U.S. medical schools (AAMC 2018a). The University of Puerto Rico Rio Piedras Campus, Florida International University, University of Puerto Rico Mayaguez Campus, and University of Texas Rio Grande Val-

---

[25] See https://www.nsf.gov/statistics/2017/nsf17310/static/data/tab5-12.pdf, accessed October 2018.
[26] From the same dataset, 14 AANAPISIs were among the top 20 institutions that award science and engineering degrees to Pacific Islanders.

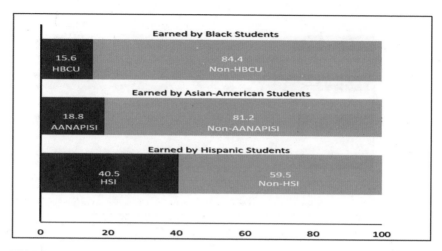

FIGURE 4-8 Percentage total of STEM bachelor's degrees earned by Black students at HBCUs compared to non-HBCUs, Asian American students at AANAPISIs compared to non-AANAPISIs, and Hispanic students at HSIs compared to non-HSIs, 2016 data.
NOTE: There are limited IPEDS data for TCUs; hence, these data are not included. See the Annex at the end of this chapter for additional notes. See Appendix F, Table F-4 for the raw data used in calculations.
SOURCE: IPEDS 2016 Completions and Institutional Characteristics data. Analysis by the American Institutes for Research for the current report.

ley (all HSIs) are among the top suppliers of Hispanic medical students to U.S. medical schools (AAMC 2018b). In short, **the data suggest that MSIs contribute significantly to the STEM talent pool, and that with greater resources, support, and attention, it could be argued that the success of MSIs and their students would only increase.**

There is sufficient evidence to suggest that MSIs are a valued resource for producing the next generation of students of color who are prepared to enroll in STEM graduate education. Because few MSIs are research-intensive, doctoral degree-granting institutions, it is not surprising that in total, MSIs award far fewer STEM doctorates than do non-MSIs. However, a significant number of the Hispanic and African American students who go on to STEM doctoral studies begin their postsecondary education at HSIs and HBCUs, according to 2011-2014 data compiled by the National Science Foundation (NSF 2017c).

For example, between 2011 and 2014, Howard University (a private HBCU) was the nation's second leading producer of African American doctorate holders in science and engineering, and with 175 degrees awarded, was more than twice the University of Michigan-Ann Arbor (a PWI), which produced 82 African American doctorates. Clark-Atlanta University and Jackson State University (both public HBCUs) ranked 14th and 18th among the 20 leading producers of doctorates for African Americans in this same period. In terms of HSIs, Pontifical Catholic University in Puerto Rico ranked third in awarding doctorates to Hispanics in science and engineering, with the University of Puerto Rico, University of Texas-El Paso, Florida International University, and University of California-Irvine also within the top 20 in this same time period (NSF 2017c).

Other research shows that between 2008 and 2012, of the top 50 baccalaureate-origin institutions that produce Hispanic STEM doctorate recipients, nearly one-third (16) were HSIs.[27] Similarly, among the top 40 baccalaureate-origin institutions that produce Hispanic doctorate recipients in engineering, nine were HSIs.[27] Eight of the top 10 baccalaureate-origin institutions that produce African American science and engineering doctoral recipients are HBCUs (Richards and Awokoya 2012), and HBCUs, throughout history, have been a significant source of African American students who go on to earn STEM doctoral degrees (Burrelli and Rapoport 2008; Sibulkin and Butler 2011; Solórzano 1995). This is a particularly salient finding, given that there are far greater numbers of undergraduate students of color enrolled at non-MSIs (see Appendix F, Figure F-1).

These examples support the rationale that MSIs are a significant national resource for producing talent to fulfill the needs of the nation's current and future STEM workforce. Moreover, many are in a position to produce more graduates at all levels.

Income Mobility and Earnings Potential

Most students expect that their college degrees will result in earnings higher than those they would make if they did not earn a degree. While the research confirms this value proposition, especially for STEM graduates (Carnevale et al. 2015), a growing body of literature shows that students who matriculated at MSIs do as well as or better than those who attended non-MSIs when it comes to individual income mobility (Chetty et al. 2017).

Newly available data from the Equality of Opportunity Project—a joint research endeavor of researchers at Stanford, Brown, and Harvard Universities[28]—shed important light on the value of MSIs (and indeed all of higher education) in terms of their role in income mobility for low-income Americans. The researchers define mobility, calculated via a "mobility rate," as a product of a given institution's *access* for low-income students, or "the fraction of its students who come from families in the bottom quintile," and an institution's *success rate*, or "the fraction of students in the bottom income quintile who reach the top quintile" (emphasis in original, Chetty et al. 2017, p. 23).

---

[27] For more detailed information, see HSI STEM Degree Production. (n.d.) Hispanic Association of Colleges & Universities, https://www.hacu.net/hacu/HSIs_and_STEM.asp, accessed February 2018.

[28] See www.equality-of-opportunity.org, accessed October 2018.

Espinosa, Kelchen, and Taylor (2018) examined the mobility rate of HBCUs, HSIs, AANAPISIs, and PBIs[29,30] compared to non-MSIs using Equality of Opportunity Project data. The findings show that across MSI types by higher education sector (i.e., two- and four-year institutions), MSIs do as well as or better than non-MSIs in moving students from the lowest income quintile to the highest income quintile by age 30. The authors found this mobility also holds true when taking into account students who start in the bottom *two* income quintiles and move to the fourth or fifth income quintiles as adults. As these findings suggest, MSIs contribute to the upward income mobility of the students they enroll, reinforcing the ROI proposition of MSIs within their communities and for the nation.

As shown in Table 4-5, MSIs have similar or higher mobility rates than those of non-MSIs. For example, the mobility rate of all four-year MSI types is nearly double (and in some cases triple) that of non-MSIs. In particular, HSIs' mobility rate is 4.3 percent, meaning they move three times as many students from the lowest income quintile to the highest quintile than non-MSIs at 1.5 percent. When looking at the *extended* mobility rate,[31] which takes into account students who start in the bottom two income quintiles and end up in the top two income quintiles as adults, MSIs continue to have higher mobility rates than those of non-MSIs. As with four-year MSIs, two-year MSIs also have higher mobility and extended mobility rates than those of non-MSIs. As such, it is important to note that MSIs contribute to the upward income mobility of their students while operating with fewer financial resources than non-MSIs.

Federal MSI designation and grant funding require enrollment-based MSIs to have low educational and general expenditures (as noted above and in Chapter 3). To examine differences among four-year enrollment-based MSIs[32] and non-MSIs with low resources, the mobility study includes a restricted sample of four-year institutions with expenditures per FTE of $25,000 or less. As shown in Table 4-5,

---

[29] This study analyzes data from the Equality of Opportunity Project to focus on a cohort of students who were born between 1983 and 1985, and who began college in approximately the 2002–2003 academic year. The authors used IPEDS 2002–2003 institutional characteristics data to identify HBCUs and fall enrollment data to identify institutions as HSIs, AANAPISIs, and PBIs if they met the respective student enrollment thresholds in that academic year.

[30] The mobility rate is calculated as the product of admitting a student whose parents are from the bottom 20 percent of the income distribution (bottom income quintile) for all college students' parents *and* having the student earn in the top 20 percent (top income quintile) for all students who entered college that same year. If a college admitted 20 percent of its students from the bottom 20 percent of the income distribution, and 20 percent of those students went on to earn in the top income quintile (top 20 percent), the college mobility rate would be 4 percent (20 percent multiplied by 20 percent equals 4 percent).

[31] An extended mobility rate is the product of the percentage of students who come from families in the bottom 40 percent (two bottom income quintiles) and end up in the top 40 percent (top two income quintiles) as adults.

[32] As previously mentioned, HBCUs are among MSIs that were recognized with the mission to serve a specific demographic group, namely, African American students. Therefore, HBCUs are not required by the federal government to have low educational and general expenditures for federal designation or participation in federal grant programs. As a result, HBCUs were not included in the analysis of this restricted sample.

TABLE 4-5 Student Mobility Rates, by MSI Type and Sector

	Non-MSI	HSI	AANAPISI	PBI	HBCU
Four-Year Institutions					
Mobility Rate	1.5	4.3	3.3	3.5	2.8
Extended Mobility Rate	9.4	20.8	12.1	20.8	19.3
N	948	47	112	11	69
Four-Year Institutions with Low Expenditures ($25,000 per Full-Time Equivalent (enrollment) Student or Less)					
Mobility Rate	1.5	4.4	4.1	3.5	NA[a]
Extended Mobility Rate	9.9	21.5	16.4	20.8	NA[a]
N	714	39	44	11	NA[a]
Two-Year Institutions					
Mobility Rate	1.5	3.2	2.4	1.8	2
Extended Mobility Rate	10.9	17.2	13.4	13.2	13.3
N	604	53	44	40	6

NOTE: See the Annex at the end of this chapter for notes.
SOURCE: Adapted from Espinosa et al. (2018).

even among the lowest-resourced institutions, MSIs still have higher mobility rates than those of non-MSIs.

Analyses by other researchers look at economic mobility and success of MSI students, although not all findings show a clear or always positive picture of mobility by MSI graduates. For example, a comparison of a cohort of students in Texas shows no difference in mobility, as defined above, 10 years out, between Hispanic graduates from comparable HSIs and non-HSIs (Park et al. 2018).[33] In this case, however, it is the *lack* of differential outcomes that the authors deemed noteworthy: "This finding is important, as HSIs are often criticized for having lower graduation rates and, by extension, lower returns on investment for those attending these institutions..." (Park et al. 2018, p. 47). According to research by Chetty et al. (2017), of the top 10 colleges and universities most successful at promoting upward intergenerational mobility, half are HSIs: California State University—Los Angeles (first), University of Texas, Pan American (fifth), Glendale Community College (seventh), South Texas College (eighth), and the University of Texas, El Paso (tenth). The schools that succeed in intergenerational mobility graduate a larger share of students in science and engineering majors,

---

[33] This study analyzed data from restricted-use administrative records from the Texas Education Agency, the Texas Higher Education Coordinating Board, and the Texas Workforce Commission. Source: University of Texas Rio Grande Valley. History of The University of Texas Rio Grande Valley, http://www.utrgv.edu/en-us/about-utrgv/history/index.htm, accessed July 2018.

not surprising given the salary premium placed on STEM jobs in today's work-force (Chetty et al. 2017).

In addition, research on African American graduates of HBCUs versus comparable non-HBCUs shows occupational status and earnings differences, concluding that labor market outcomes are greater for African American gradu-ates from HBCUs (Price et al. 2011; Strayhorn 2015). The economic success of HBCU graduates was also reviewed in a 2017 United Negro College Fund (UNCF) report that analyzed the economic impact of these institutions. Using 2014 data, the researchers determined that the 50,000-plus HBCU graduates will have an estimated $130 billion in total lifetime earnings—56 percent more than they would earn without a college credential (UNCF 2017).[34,35] In sum, **in-creased investments to help bolster the success of MSIs holds great promise for advancing the income mobility of millions of citizens of color.**

The Local and Regional Impact of MSIs

Many MSIs have as a stated or implicit part of their mission to strengthen the local and regional communities in which they are located. From a historical perspective, as described in Chapter 3, HBCUs, TCUs, and some HSIs were established with the express purpose of educating students who had little or no access to mainstream higher education. The goal was to provide postsecondary access to individuals *and* strengthen communities and/or tribal nations through increased educational access and attainment. The 2017 UNCF report discussed above provides an example of how investments in HBCUs and their students generate a "ripple effect" that induces a positive impact on the schools' local and regional communities. Based on 2014 data, HBCUs helped generate more than 134,000 jobs (both on and off campus) for their local and regional economies, and ultimately provided $14.8 billion in total local and regional economic impact.[36] From these findings, the researchers concluded that "HBCUs are economic en-gines in their communities, generating substantial economic returns year after year" (UNCF 2017, p. 4).

When considering local and regional impact, it is important to remember that some MSIs operate within unique contexts, namely TCUs. These institutions ful-fill a dual mission: educating students and addressing Native American tribal pri-orities, such as contributing to not only the economic growth of the reservation, but also community development, and social renewal (Stull et al. 2015). TCUs'

---

[34] The data sources used in this report include the data from the 2013-2014 IPEDS survey, and surveys conducted by the U.S. Bureau of Labor Statistics and The College Board. For more information on the methodology used in this report, see https://secure.uncf.org/page/-/pdfs/HBCU_TechnicalReport_5-17L.pdf?_ga=2.243899520.461513395.1539098147-851689931.1537544139, accessed October 2018.

[35] The $130 billion estimate reflects incremental earnings averaged across degree and certificate programs.

[36] This estimate includes direct spending by HBCUs, as well as the indirect effects of that spending.

impacts explicitly include social and economic benefits beyond the benefits to students and faculty, to encompass collective interests of the surrounding community and tribal nations (Cunningham 2000; EMSI 2015). Most TCUs offer academic programming that has a direct connection to local workforce needs.[37] Such efforts increase students' applicable skill sets, boost their earning potential, and provide incentives for graduates to remain in the community (EMSI 2015; Rainie and Stull 2016). TCUs also offer academic courses that teach vocational skills to improve tribal infrastructure, health courses to improve community well-being, and cultural courses to help maintain long-standing tribal traditions (Rainie and Stull 2016). As a result, TCUs are able to provide economic and noneconomic ROI for their students, tribes, and local and national economies (EMSI 2015).

The same conclusions can be drawn when considering the impact of other MSIs on their local and regional communities, especially those located in places with few national industry partners. In these areas, local communities and local industries play an important role in providing career-related experiences to students. Service learning, community engagement projects, and senior-design projects at MSIs involve students in developing solutions to address challenges in the community. One such example is the UTRGV-Texas Manufacturing Assistance Center's Lean Sigma Academy,[38] where students work on projects from local industries and obtain an industry-recognized certification. Additionally, the UTRGV School of Medicine was created in an effort to teach and prepare medical students to provide health care to the Rio Grande Valley.[39]

Other university and local industry collaborations across the nation involve product design, improvement projects, and prototype design for local start-up companies. (See Chapter 5 for additional examples of MSI-industry partnerships.) More research needs to be done to measure the economic impact of these small-scale university-community partnerships. Indeed, additional evidence may incentivize mayors, governors, and other local and state leaders to evaluate the extent to which larger investments in MSIs can yield economic benefits for communities that extend far beyond the benefits to individual students, faculty, and institutions. (See Chapter 6 for the committee's recommendations to funding agencies to support additional research on this issue.)

---

[37] This may result in TCUs with academic curricula that are less STEM focused, depending on the local and regional needs.

[38] For additional information, see https://www.utrgv.edu/tmac/services/more-services/index.htm, accessed October 2018.

[39] UTRGV School of Medicine, see http://www.utrgv.edu/school-of-medicine/our-story/about-us/index.htm, accessed October 2018.

TARGETED INVESTMENTS IN MSIS AND THE POTENTIAL
FOR INCREASED RETURN ON INVESTMENT

Despite receiving a fraction of the appropriated federal and state funding for higher education and experiencing deep cuts in public education spending, MSIs have shown success in providing ROI for students, the STEM workforce, regional and national economies, and the local communities that surround and support these institutions.

As described in Chapters 2 and 3 of this report, the country's demographics will continue to reflect increases among non-Whites, and more MSIs will emerge. To keep pace, changes in current funding policies and methods are needed to ensure that MSIs have sufficient resources to meet high standards and expectations for educational quality (particularly STEM education), sociocultural development, and research and training, to support the future workforce. Greater resources per FTE would mean an increased capacity to support evidence-based programs and practices that promote and sustain the success of STEM students at MSIs, leading in turn to substantial increases in the ROIs discussed above. (Chapter 5 presents strategies that could productively benefit from increases in such intentional and targeted investments to cultivate a diverse, highly skilled, domestic STEM workforce.)

Although the evidence described in the preceding sections supports the argument for increased funding for MSIs and their students, the committee remains acutely aware that to effectively address the funding deficits and disparities at MSIs, a more dynamic evidence-based approach is needed. One challenge for the argument to create new or expand current funding mechanisms is the lack of clear understanding of how appropriated funding is having an intentional, targeted impact on the outcomes of students of color, particularly those in STEM disciplines (Boland 2018). Over the past few decades, billions of federal dollars have been allocated to MSIs to focus on improving STEM degree production; however, few studies can effectively demonstrate which of these funded programs best serve the national goal of increasing the number of students of color with high-quality STEM degrees, or increasing their presence in the STEM workforce.

The absence of rigorous evidence on availability, use, and effectiveness invites questions about the value of current investments. In light of this, **the committee argues that it is in the best national interest not only to establish new and expand current STEM-focused investments for MSIs, but also to increase the intentionality, clarity, transparency, and accountability of these funds.** More evaluation, and more *nuanced* evaluation, is sorely needed. Evaluations that are adequately funded to determine who is investing, where they are investing, and the measurable impact of these investments (e.g., student academic achievement, workforce readiness, local and regional prosperity, and strengthening the STEM workforce) are critical. (See Chapter 6 for the committee's recommendations to stakeholders on how to address this need.)

CHAPTER ANNEX

Figure 4-7

1. IPEDS data, collection year 2015, were used to create the list of institutions throughout this report for analysis run by the American Council on Education. Data in this report reflect Title IV participating, degree-granting, public and private, nonprofit, two-year and four-year institutions that offered undergraduate degrees. College Scorecard 2015-2016 data were used to flag institutions that were eligible to apply for federal MSI funding in that given fiscal year through Title III and Title V of the Higher Education Opportunity Act of 2008. Out of 3,129 total institutions, 714 were eligible for MSI designation. Of these institutions, 76 were eligible for more than one MSI designation.

2. Total completions includes the following credentials: prebaccalaureate certificates, associate degrees, bachelor's degrees, postbaccalaureate certificates, master's degrees, and doctoral degrees.

3. Classification of Instructional Programs (CIP) codes were placed into Science and Engineering categories based on the fields of study classification found in the NSF's "Science and Engineering Degrees: 1966–2012," appendix B, with additions made to cover CIP codes found in the IPEDS completions data that were not included in the NSF taxonomy. For completions, the racial category "other" is defined as the combination of "nonresident," "race unknown," and "two or more races." Race reporting varies across years in the IPEDS, so information pertaining to Pacific Islanders is not available for all years and would be combined with counts for Asian American students.

4. For the completions data, all CIP codes were converted to current CIP codes using available crosswalks, before applying the classifications based on the NSF taxonomy. The following CIP code conversion required for some IPEDS data files prior to 2004 was added to the crosswalk to convert 1990s to 2000s CIP codes: 8.0199, 8.0299, 8.0899, 8.1299 to 52.19. For the completions data, counts were collapsed across majornum 1 and 2. Completion degree type codes changed slightly in 2010 and later versions of the data, so slightly different groupings were used. For completions data prior to 2010: "3"=Associate, "5"=Bachelor, "7"=Master, "9"=Doctor, "10"=Doctor, "1"=Pre-BA Certificate, "2"=Pre-BA Certificate, "4"=Pre-BA Certificate, "6"=Post-BA Certificate, "8"=Post-BA Certificate, and "11"=Post-BA Certificate. For completions data from 2010 and later: "3"=Associate, "5"=Bachelor, "7"=Master, "17"=Doctor, "18"=Doctor, "19"=Doctor, "1"=Pre-BA Certificate, "2"=Pre-BA Certificate, "4"=Pre-BA Certificate, "6"=Post-BA Certificate, and "8"=Post-BA Certificate.

5. For all but a few runs, data were not filtered using the First Look Report criteria. The First Look Report uses provisional IPEDS data and therefore totals may be slightly different from those reported in other federal reports, though these differences will be minor.

Figure 4-8

1. IPEDS data, collection year 2015, were used to create the list of institutions throughout this report for analysis run by the American Council on Education. Data in this report reflect Title IV participating, degree-granting, public and private, nonprofit, two-year and four-year institutions that offered undergraduate degrees. College Scorecard 2015-2016 data were used to flag institutions that were eligible to apply for federal MSI funding in that given fiscal year through Title III and Title V of the Higher Education Opportunity Act of 2008. Out of 3,129 total institutions, 714 were eligible for MSI designation. Of these institutions, 76 were eligible for more than one MSI designation.

2. Total completions includes the following credentials: prebaccalaureate certificates, associate degrees, bachelor's degrees, postbaccalaureate certificates, master's degrees, and doctoral degrees.

3. Classification of CIP codes into Science and Engineering categories was based on the fields of study classification found in the NSF's "Science and Engineering Degrees: 1966–2012," appendix B, with additions made to cover CIP codes found in the IPEDS completions data that were not included in the NSF taxonomy. For completions, the racial category "other" is defined as the combination of "nonresident," "race unknown," and "two or more races." Race reporting varies across years in the IPEDS, so information pertaining to Pacific Islanders is not available for all years and would be combined with counts for Asian American students.

4. For the completions data, all CIP codes were converted to current CIP codes using available crosswalks, before applying the classifications based on the NSF taxonomy. The following CIP code conversion required for some IPEDS data files prior to 2004 was added to the crosswalk to convert 1990s to 2000s CIP codes: 8.0199, 8.0299, 8.0899, 8.1299 to 52.19. For the completions data, counts were collapsed across majornum 1 and 2. Completion degree type codes changed slightly in 2010 and later versions of the data, so slightly different groupings were used. For completions data prior to 2010: "3"=Associate, "5"=Bachelor, "7"=Master, "9"=Doctor, "10"=Doctor, "1"=Pre-BA Certificate, "2"=Pre-BA Certificate, "4"=Pre-BA Certificate, "6"=Post-BA Certificate, "8"=Post-BA Certificate, and "11"=Post-BA Certificate. For completions data from 2010 and later: "3"=Associate, "5"=Bachelor, "7"=Master, "17"=Doctor, "18"=Doctor, "19"=Doctor, "1"=Pre-BA Certificate, "2"=Pre-BA Certificate, "4"=Pre-BA Certificate, "6"=Post-BA Certificate, and "8"=Post-BA Certificate.

5. For all but a few runs, data were not filtered using the First Look Report criteria. The First Look Report uses provisional IPEDS data and therefore totals may be slightly different than those reported in other federal reports, though these differences will be minor.

Table 4-2

[a] Total revenue is defined as net tuition; state and local appropriations; state and local contracts; federal appropriations, grants, and contracts net of Pell grants; private gifts; grants and contracts; and investment return and revenue from affiliated entities. It excludes auxiliaries, hospital, independent operations, and other sources.

[b] The federal funding amounts are net of Pell grants, consistent with Delta Cost Project's definition (Pell grants were excluded if they were reported as federal grants). This category includes revenue received through acts of a federal legislative body, such as direct funds to specific institutions. It also includes revenue from federal governmental agencies for training, research, or public service activities.

Table 4-3

[a] Education and general expenditures include instruction, research, public service, student services, academic support, institutional support, grants, and operations and maintenance. They exclude auxiliaries, hospital, independent operations, and other expenses.

Table 4-4

1. IPEDS data, collection year 2015, were used to create the list of institutions throughout this report for analysis run by the American Council on Education. Data in this report

reflect Title IV participating, degree-granting, public and private, nonprofit, two-year and four-year institutions that offered undergraduate degrees. College Scorecard 2015-2016 data were used to flag institutions that were eligible to apply for federal MSI funding in that given fiscal year through Title III and Title V of the Higher Education Opportunity Act of 2008. Out of 3,129 total institutions, 714 were eligible for MSI designation. Of these institutions, 76 were eligible for more than one MSI designation.

2. Institutions were classified into a sector based on the institutional category variable and control variable in IPEDS. Within institutional category, all institutions categorized as degree-granting, primarily baccalaureate or above institutions were classified as four-year institutions, and all institutions categorized as degree-granting, not primarily baccalaureate or above and degree-granting, associate's and certificates institutions were classified as two-year institutions. The control variable was used to classify institutions as public or private nonprofit.

Table 4-5

1. There is a small amount of missing data for some measures.
2. A few colleges have multiple MSI designations and thus appear in multiple MSI columns.
3. Federal legislation does not require that HBCUs have low educational and general expenditures to receive federal designation and funding as it does for MSIs predicated on enrollment. Therefore, HBCUs were omitted from the analysis of this restricted sample.
4. The mobility rate is calculated as the product of admitting a student whose parents are from the bottom 20 percent of the income distribution (bottom income quintile) for all college students' parents and having the student earn in the top 20 percent (top income quintile) for all students who entered college that same year. An extended mobility rate is the product of the percentage of students who come from families in the bottom 40 percent (two bottom income quintiles) and end up in the top 40 percent (top two income quintiles) as adults.

REFERENCES

AAMC (Association of American Medical Colleges). 2018a. Undergraduate Institutions Supplying Applicants to U.S. Medical Schools by Applicant Race and Ethnicity, 2017-2018, Table A-2.1. Available at: https://www.aamc.org/download/321446/data/factstablea2-1.pdf. Accessed October 2018.

AAMC. 2018b. Undergraduate Institutions Supplying Applicants to U.S. Medical Schools by Applicant Race and Ethnicity, 2017-2018, Table A-2.3. Available at: https://www.aamc.org/download/321450/data/factstablea2-3.pdf. Accessed October 2018.

ACE (American Council on Education). 2014. Understanding College and University Endowments. Brief answers to questions frequently asked by students, faculty, alumni, journalists, public officials, and others interested in the financial circumstances of American colleges and universities. Available at: https://www.acenet.edu/newsroom/Documents/Understanding-Endowments-White-Paper.pdf. Accessed October 2018.

AIHEC (American Indian Higher Education Consortium). 1999. Tribal Colleges an Introduction. Available at: http://www.aihec.org/who-we-serve/docs/TCU_intro.pdf. Accessed October 2018.

AIHEC. 2012. AIHEC AIMS Fact Book 2009-2010: Tribal Colleges and Universities Report. Available at: http://www.aihec.org/our-stories/docs/reports/AIHEC_AIMSreport_May2012.pdf. Accessed October 2018.

Baum, Sandy. 2017. Examining the Federal-State Partnership in Higher Education. Urban Institute, Education Policy Program. Available at: https://www.luminafoundation.org/files/resources/examining-the-federal-state-partnership-in-higher-education.pdf. Accessed October 1, 2018.

Boland, William. 2018. "The higher education act and minority serving institutions: Towards a typology of Title III and V funded programs." *Education Sciences* 8 (1):33.

Burrelli, Joan and Alan Rapoport. 2008. "Role of HBCUs as Baccalaureate-Origin Institutions of Black S&E Doctorate Recipients." InfoBrief. NSF 08-319. National Science Foundation. Available at: https://files.eric.ed.gov/fulltext/ED502482.pdf. Accessed October 2018.

CARE (National Commission on Asian American and Pacific Islander Research in Education). 2013. "Partnership for Equity in Education through Research (PEER): Findings from the First Year of Research on AANAPISIs 2013." Available at: http://www.apiasf.org/pdfs/2013_peer_report/APIASF_and_CARE_PEER_Report_June_2013.pdf. Accessed October 2018.

Carnevale, Anthony P., Ban Cheah, and Andrew R. Hanson. 2015. The Economic Value of College Majors. Washington, DC: Georgetown University Center on Education and the Workforce.

Chetty, Raj, John N. Friedman, Emmanuel Saez, Nicholas Turner, and Danny Yagan. 2017. "Mobility Report Cards: The Role of Colleges in Intergenerational Mobility," Working Papers 2017-059, Human Capital and Economic Opportunity Working Group. Available at: https://ideas.repec.org/p/hka/wpaper/2017-059.html. Accessed October 2018.

Cunningham, Alisa Federico. 2000. Tribal College Contributions to Local Economic Development. Washington DC: American Indian Higher Education Consortium. Available at: http://www.aihec.org/ourstories/docs/reports/TC_contributionsLocalEconDevmt.pdf. Accessed October 2018.

Cunningham, Alisa, Eunkyoung Park, and Jennifer Engle. 2014. Minority-serving institutions: Doing more with less. Washington, DC: Institute for Higher Education Policy. Available at: http://www.ihep.org/sites/default/files/uploads/docs/pubs/msis_doing_more_w-less_final_february_2014-v2.pdf. Accessed October 2018.

EMSI (Economic Modeling Specialists International). 2015. The Economic Value of American Indian and Alaska Native Tribal Colleges & Universities. An Analysis of the Economic Impact and Return on Investment of Education. Available at: http://www.aihec.org/our-stories/docs/reports/EconomicValue-AIAN-TCUs.pdf. Accessed October 2018.

Espinosa, Lorelle L., Jonathan Turk, and Morgan Taylor. 2017. Pulling Back the Curtain: Enrollment and Outcomes at Minority Serving Institutions. Washington, DC: American Council on Education. Available at: https://www.acenet.edu/news-room/Documents/Pulling-Back-the-Curtain-Enrollment-and-Outcomes-at-MSIs.pdf. Accessed October 2018.

Espinosa, Lorelle L., Robert Kelchen, and Morgan Taylor. 2018. Minority Serving Institutions as Engines of Upward Mobility. Available at: https://www.acenet.edu/news-room/Documents/MSIs-as-Engines-of-Upward Mobility.pdf. Accessed October 2018.

Excelencia in Education. 2018. "Emerging Hispanic-Serving Institutions (HSIs): 2016-2017." Available at: https://www.edexcelencia.org/research/data/emerging-hispanic-serving-institutions-hsis-2016-2017. Accessed October 2018.

Gallup-Purdue University. 2015. Great Jobs, Great Lives: The Relationship Between Student Debt, Experiences and Perceptions of College Worth. Gallup-Purdue Index 2015 Report. Available at: https://www.wfyi.org/files/wfyi/files/gpi-report-2015-09-25-2015.pdf. Accessed October 2018.

Gasman, Marybeth. 2010. Comprehensive Funding Approaches for Historically Black Colleges and Universities. University of Pennsylvania Graduate School of Education and North Carolina Central University, Available at: http://repository.upenn.edu/gse_pubs/33. Accessed October 2018.

Gasman, Marybeth. 2017. The Return on Investment for Minority Serving Institutions. Edited by M. Gasman, A. Castro Samoya, and M. Nettles. Policy Information Report and ETS Research Report Series No. RR-17-57. Princeton, NJ: Educational Testing Service.

Gasman, Marybeth, Benjamin Baez, Noah D. Drezner, Katherine V. Sedgwick, Christopher Tudico, and Julie M. Schmid. 2007. "Historically black colleges and universities: Recent trends." *Academe* 93 (1):69-77.

Gasman, Marybeth, Andrés Castro Samayoa, and Michael Nettles. 2017. "Investing in student success: Examining the return on investment for minority-serving institutions." *ETS2 ETS Research Report Series* 2017 (1):1-66.

HACU (Hispanic Association of Colleges and Universities). 2018. "2018 fact sheet. Hispanic higher education and HSIs." Available at: https://www.hacu.net/hacu/HSI_Fact_Sheet.asp. Accessed October 2018.

Hale, Frank W. 2004. What makes racial diversity work in higher education: Academic leaders present successful policies and strategies. Sterling, VA: Stylus Publishing, LLC.

Hegji, Alexandra. 2017. Programs for Minority-Serving Institutions Under the Higher Education Act. Congressional Research Service. Available at: https://fas.org/sgp/crs/misc/R43237.pdf. Accessed October 2018.

Lawyers' Committee on for Civil Rights Under Law. 2018. Available at: https://lawyerscommittee.org/press-release/state-maryland-attempts-remedy-decades-mistreatment-harming-historically-black-institutions/. Accessed October 2018.

Minor, James T. 2008. Contemporary HBCUs: Considering Institutional Capacity and State Priorities: A Research Report. East Lansing, MI: Michigan State University, College of Education, Department of Educational Administration.

Museus, Samuel D., Raquel Wright-Mair, and Jacqueline Mac. 2018. How Asian American and Native American Pacific Islander Serving Institutions (AANAPISIs) Are Creating the Conditions for Students to Thrive. Available at: https://www.indiana.edu/~cece/wordpress/wp-content/uploads/2017/02/Research-Brief-How-AANAPISI-Thrive.pdf. Accessed October 2018.

Nellum, Christopher J., and Katherine Valle. 2015. "Government investment in public Hispanic serving institutions." American Council on Education. Center for Policy Research and Strategy. Available at: https://www.acenet.edu/news-room/Documents/Government-Investment-in-Public-Hispanic-Serving-Institutions.pdf. Accessed October 2018.

Nelson, Christine A., and Joanna R. Frye. 2016. Tribal College and University Funding: Tribal Sovereignty at the Intersection of Federal, State, and Local Funding. Minority Serving Institutions Series. Available at: http://aihec.org/who-we-serve/docs/ACE-CPRS_TCU-Funding.pdf. Accessed October 2018.

NSF (National Science Foundation). 2017a. National Center for Science and Engineering Statistics. Federal Science and Engineering Obligations to Universities and Colleges Declined 2% in FY 2015, Table 4. Available at: https://www.nsf.gov/statistics/2017/nsf17318/nsf17318.pdf. Accessed October 2018.

NSF. 2017b. National Center for Science and Engineering Statistics. Women, Minorities, and Persons with Disabilities in Science and Engineering: 2017. Special Report NSF 17-310. Arlington, VA. Table 5-12. Top 20 Academic Institutions. Available at: https://www.nsf.gov/statistics/2017/nsf17310/static/data/tab5-12.pdf. Accessed October 2018.

NSF. 2017c. National Center for Science and Engineering Statistics. 2017. Women, Minorities, and Persons with Disabilities in Science and Engineering: 2017. Special Report NSF 17-310. Arlington, VA. Table 7-22. Top 20 academic institutions awarding S&E doctoral degrees, by race or ethnicity of U.S. citizen and permanent resident minority recipients: 2011–14. Available at:https://www.nsf.gov/statistics/2017/nsf17310/static/data/tab7-22.pdf. Accessed October 2018.

Palmer, Robert T. and Kimberly A. Griffin. 2009. "Desegregation policy and disparities in faculty salary and workload: Maryland's Historically Black and Predominately White Institutions." *Negro Educational Review* 60.

Park, Toby J., Stella M. Flores, and Christopher J. Ryan. 2018. "Labor market returns for graduates of Hispanic-Serving Institutions." *Research in Higher Education* 59 (1):29-53.

Pew Charitable Trusts. 2015. Federal and State Funding of Higher Education: A Changing Landscape. Washington, DC. Available at: https://www.ewtrusts.org//media/assets/2015/06/federal_state_funding_higher_education_final.pdf. Accessed October 2018.

Pew Research Center. 2011. "Is College Worth It? College Presidents, Public Assess Value, Quality and Mission of Higher Education." Social & Demographic Trends. Available at: http://www.pewresearch.org/wp-content/uploads/sites/3/2011/05/higher-ed-report.pdf. Accessed October 2018.

Pew Research Center. 2014. "More Hispanics, blacks enrolling in college, but lag in bachelor's degrees." Available at http://www.pewresearch.org/fact-tank/2014/04/24/more-hispanics-blacks-enrolling-in-college-but-lag-in-bachelors-degrees/. Accessed October 2018.

Pluviose, David. 2006. "Civil rights panel: Duplication threatens Black colleges." *Diverse Issues in Higher Education* 23 (8):8.

Price, Gregory N., Omari H. Swinton, and Omari H. Swinton. 2011. "The relative returns to graduating from a Historically Black College/University: Propensity score matching estimates from the National Survey of Black Americans." *The Review of Black Political Economy* 38 (2):103-130.

Rainie, Stephanie Carroll, and Ginger C. Stull. 2016. Reframing Return on Investments for Tribal Colleges and Universities: Aligning Analyses with Tribal Priorities and Educational Missions. Philadelphia, PA: Penn Center for Minority Serving Institutions, Graduate School of Education, University of Pennsylvania. Available at: https://cmsi.gse.upenn.edu/sites/default/files/TCU%20paper%20final_0.pdf. Accessed October 2018.

Richards, David A. R., and Janet T. Awokoya. 2012. Understanding HBCU Retention and Completion. Frederick D. Patterson Research Institute, United Negro College Fund. Available: https://files.eric.ed.gov/fulltext/ED562057.pdf. Accessed October 2018.

Santiago, Deborah A., and Sally J. Andrade. 2010. "Emerging Hispanic-Serving Institutions (HSIs): Serving Latino Students." Excelencia in Education (NJ1).

Seltzer, Rick. 2017. "Ending segregation through duplication." Inside Higher Education. Available at: https://www.insidehighered.com/news/2017/11/10/judge-issues-long-awaited-ruling-black-colleges-maryland. Accessed October 2018.

Sharpe, Rhonda Vonshay. 2018. "The top producers of African-American graduates." *Diverse Issues in Higher Education* 35(1):15-19.

Sibulkin, Amy E., and J. S. Butler. 2011. "Diverse colleges of origin of African American doctoral recipients, 2001–2005: historically black colleges and universities and beyond." *Research in Higher Education* 52 (8):830-852.

Solórzano, Daniel G. 1995. "The doctorate production and baccalaureate origins of African Americans in the sciences and engineering." *Journal of Negro Education*. 64(1):15-32.

Strayhorn, Terrell L. 2015. Return on Investment Analysis for Black Graduates for Historically Black Colleges and Universities: Insights from Three Studies. In Return on Investment Convening, edited by Center for Higher Education Enterprise. Available at: https://cmsi.gse.upenn.edu/sites/default/files/HBCU.final%20paper.pdf. Accessed October 2018.

Stull, Ginger, Demetrios Spyridakis, Marybeth Gasman, Andrés Castro Samayoa, and Yvette Booker. 2015. Redefining Success: How Tribal Colleges and Universities Build Nations, Strengthen Sovereignty, and Persevere Through Challenges. Available at https://cmsi.gse.upenn.edu/sites/default/files/MSI_TBLCLLGreport_Final.pdf. Accessed October 2018.

UNCF (United Negro College Fund). 2017. "HBCUs make America strong: The positive economic impact of Historically Black Colleges and Universities." Available at: https://www.uncf.org/hbcu-impact. Accessed October 2018.

U.S. Census Bureau. 2017. "School enrollment of the Hispanic population: Two decades of growth." Available at: https://www.census.gov/newsroom/blogs/random-samplings/2017/08/school_enrollmentof.html. Accessed October 2018.

U.S. Department of Education. 2015. White House Initiative on Historically Black Colleges and Universities, 2013 Annual Report to the President on the Results of the Participation of Historically Black Colleges and Universities in Federal Programs.

U.S. Department of Education. 2018. "Asian American and Native American Pacific Islander-Serving Institutions Program." Funding Status. Available at: https://www2.ed.gov/programs/aanapi/funding.html. Accessed October 2018.

Webber, Douglas A., and Ronald G. Ehrenberg. 2010. "Do expenditures other than instructional expenditures affect graduation and persistence rates in American higher education?" *Economics of Education Review* 29 (6):947-958.

Williams, Krystal L., and BreAnna L. Davis. 2018. Public and Private Investments and Divestments in Historically Black Colleges and Universities. Washington, DC: American Council on Education.

5

Promising Strategies That Contribute to STEM Student Success

"We succeed, if they succeed."
— Administrator at San Diego State University

"The focus must shift from access to success."
— Administrator at Mission College

KEY FINDINGS

- Intentionality is a critical component in the design and implementation of programs, policies, and practices that effectively improve the academic success and career preparation of students of color at MSIs.

- Students of color in STEM fields benefit from strategies that enhance the accountability and success of institutional leadership, offer a culturally supportive campus environment, provide easily accessible academic and student supports, offer sustained mentorship, and create authentic research and other learning experiences that mirror the world of work through partnerships with employers and with other organizations.

- Exposure to undergraduate research experiences remains a predictor of successful outcomes for students of color in STEM, including the pursuit of postgraduate STEM education and careers.

- Mutually beneficial public- and private-sector partnerships can serve as an alternative mechanism for MSIs to secure new educational, research, and workforce training opportunities for faculty and students, increase institutional capacity, and expand their current network.

- Rigorous evaluations of the promising programs and institutional initiatives at MSIs are needed. This quantifiable evidence can be used to inform MSI leaders, policy makers, and public and private funders of the necessary investments to ensure that MSIs keep pace in offering the educational experiences necessary for student success.

The committee's charge included two compelling research questions:

1. *What are examples of model programs on Minority Serving Institution (MSI) campuses that have demonstrated strong evidence of success in producing quality science, technology, engineering, and mathematics (STEM) graduates?*

2. *What are the key components of these programs that promote student success?*

Providing straightforward answers to these questions is challenging. MSIs, like other institutions, implement an eclectic mix of evidence-based and promising (albeit not rigorously evaluated) programs, practices, and strategies. The programs range from large, established, federally funded initiatives to small, newly launched, faculty-piloted efforts. Unfortunately—as is the case with many higher education programs, interventions, and extracurricular support activities—most lack clear, quantifiable evaluations, often the result of limited resources and institutional capacity for assessment, data collection, analysis, and communication. A lack of designated grant funding and the overall challenge to evaluate programs as a collective contribute to the inadequacy of data. (See Chapter 6 for the committee's recommendations to public and private funders to support the evaluation of MSIs and the promising strategies and effective programs they use to support their students.)

The limited evidence base for such interventions and programs complicated the committee's examination to meet its statement of task. Thus, while we identified and drew lessons from programs that had undergone rigorous external evaluation, we also considered those that show promise based on more experiential and/or anecdotal evidence. In addition, many STEM-focused programs reviewed by the committee had objectives and outcomes of student success not always directly tied to the degree production referred to in the first question above, making it difficult to determine common trends or primary principles for effectiveness. For this reason, the committee employed a broader definition of student success (see Box 5-1).

Despite these challenges, the committee carried out a comprehensive search to find effective programs, practices, and strategies. As detailed in this chapter, we were able to reach consensus on a number of key interventions and conditions that we judged beneficial to STEM students of color at MSIs when designed and offered with *intentionality*, that is, tailored to recognize and address student strengths and challenges across academic, social, and financial dimensions.

BOX 5-1
Definition of Student Success in STEM

From our research efforts, the committee identified two commonly used categories of success:

- *Academic success*: Interpreted as consistently high or measurable improvements in individual grades, grade point average, or increases in course pass rates over a specific period of time, and other academically defined demonstrations of success.
- *STEM pathway success*: Demonstrated by marked increases in measures of enrollment, persistence, retention, and completion of degrees and credentials in STEM fields or the pursuit of postbaccalaureate STEM education (e.g., graduate school) or employment in a STEM-related field.

The term *student success* is a complex concept, as individuals take multiple pathways to success. In addition, given the great diversity of students attending MSIs, many of the standard metrics of success are inadequate because they fail to take into consideration important contextual factors that impact MSI students. In light of this, researchers have begun to examine alternate ways to define and contextualize measures of success for postsecondary students overall, and students of color in particular. These include, but are not limited to, social mobility, skill development, dispositional and attitude measures, and advancements in intra- and interpersonal skills (e.g., growth mindset and self-efficacy).

For the purposes of this report, the committee applied a comprehensive definition of the term student success, including the use of the aforementioned categories.

SOURCES: AIR (2012), Carmichael et al. (2016), Carpi et al. (2017), Espinosa et al. (2014), Espinosa et al. (2018), Flores and Park (2013), Gasman and Nguyen (2016), Kim and Conrad (2006), May and Chubin (2003), Merisotis and Kee (2006), NASEM (2017a) Núñez (2014), Rochat (2015).

COMMITTEE RESEARCH PLAN

The committee's search for evidence-based and promising programs included a comprehensive literature review, discussions informed by nine MSI site visits, expert testimony and presentations at two open-session meetings, and committee members' own research expertise and experiences working with and on MSI campuses. This effort is described below and summarized in Box 5-2.

Literature Review

The committee commissioned a literature review by the University of Pennsylvania's Center for Minority Serving Institutions (the Penn Center), summarized here and detailed more fully in Appendix E. A tiered review encompassed three areas of focus: (1) STEM education for students of color across higher education (MSIs and non-MSIs), (2) student success at MSIs (STEM and non-STEM), and (3) student success in STEM at MSIs. Using committee-directed criteria and casting a wide net of search terms, the Penn Center identified and analyzed more than 170 studies for common themes or lessons learned. See Appendix E for additional details.

The focus of the first literature search sought evidence on *what works* pertaining to supporting the success of underrepresented minorities in STEM education, not necessarily at MSIs. This search uncovered 78 publications of various types; reflective of the aforementioned concerns about the available evidence, most relied on self-reported data rather than more rigorous, external evaluations. Other constraints were that some studies, including randomized controlled trials, were not isolated to STEM and/or MSIs. Nonetheless, this initial review pointed to three recurring themes: the *importance of undergraduate research experience*

BOX 5-2
Committee's Research Plan

The committee consulted, reviewed, and deliberated on various sources of evidence. These sources included, but were not limited to,

- Results from a *commissioned literature search*, conducted by the study's consultants at the University of Pennsylvania's Center for Minority Serving Institutions,
- Findings resulting from committee discussions informed by *nine MSI site visits*,
- Expert testimony and presentations of data and information at *two open-session meetings*, and
- Committee members' own *research expertise and experiences* working with and on MSI campuses.

in STEM education, the *role of peer support groups* to improve student persistence, and *the impact of a flexible curriculum structure* on students' persistence in STEM.

The second literature search focused on evidence for specific MSI practices, policies, and/or programs that support students' success, although not necessarily limited to STEM. Most of this literature was designed to understand MSIs and their contributions to higher education. The majority of the publications employed a case study methodology and were multisite in nature. A small number used propensity score matching, mainly focused on degree attainment. Across the 30 studies identified, a significant number highlighted the benefits to students when MSIs offer *culturally relevant approaches to learning, developmental education when needed*, and an *environment that promotes college completion and success*. Regardless of MSI type and the racial and ethnic makeup of students served, many of the interventions focused on the need to help students embrace their full identities, the power of culturally relevant assignments in retention efforts, the importance of collaboration over competition, and the vital nature of peer support and peer-to-peer mentoring.

The third literature search was the most focused: STEM education for students of color at MSIs. Again, although the aim was to include quasi-experimental design and experimental design studies, most of the studies conducted were case studies. The emergent themes included the importance of *sustained and personalized faculty and peer mentoring*, the opportunity to *engage in research*, the *value of early recruitment* (precollege) and the importance of summer bridge programs, the opportunity to engage in *STEM-related extracurricular and community activities, an emphasis on sequenced and comprehensive courses*, and the need for *counseling and other supports to help students make successful transitions* to graduate school and the STEM workforce.

Site Visits

Subgroups of the committee conducted site visits to MSIs across the nation. While it would have been valuable to visit more schools, time and financial resources required tough decisions on which institutions to visit. The nine MSIs visited were selected from a list of nominated institutions culled from discussions with key stakeholders in the study.[1] It was important to visit public and private, large and small, as well as two- and four-year institutions. Four MSI types (Historically Black Colleges and Universities (HBCUs), Hispanic Serving Institutions (HSIs), Tribal Colleges and Universities, and Asian American and Native American Pacific Islander Serving Institutions were represented in this effort. Commit-

---

[1] Nominations were accepted from MSI advocacy and association groups, including the United Negro College Fund, Hispanic Association of Colleges and Universities, American Indian Higher Education Consortium, Asian & Pacific Islander American Scholarship Fund, and University of Pennsylvania's Center for Minority Serving Institutions.

tee members held private, group interviews with administrators, faculty, alumni, students, and community stakeholders at Dillard University (Louisiana), Mission College (California), Morgan State University (Maryland), North Carolina A&T State University (North Carolina), Salish Kootenai College (Montana), San Diego State University (California), University of Texas Rio Grande Valley (Texas), West Los Angeles College (California), and Xavier University (Louisiana). Using a structured set of questions, the conversations varied by campus, but each provided valuable insights to the study's charge. See Appendix C for additional details on the committee's site visits.

Common themes that surfaced during conversations with faculty and administrators on these nine campuses included a *passion for the mission* of providing a high-quality education for their students and preparing them for a successful future, and a *continual search for innovative ways* to do so; a *commitment to creating an expectation of success* while also fostering a *supportive and caring community*; and the need to weigh ambitious aims against *limited resources*. Many MSI faculty and staff find themselves stretched thin, balancing research and teaching loads with other responsibilities that they recognize as vital, such as outreach, resource development, mentoring, and other responsibilities.

Presentations and Committee Discussions

Complementing the literature review and site visits, the committee hosted two public meetings to gather insight from educators, researchers, advocates, policy makers, public and private funders, and other relevant stakeholders of higher education. Invited panelists representing MSIs University of Alaska Anchorage and South Texas College[2] provided important testimony and data to the committee. (See Appendix B for meeting agendas.) In sum, the speakers presented *a holistic view of the academic, social, and financial concerns of students*; the need for *evaluations, including better data,* to point to what is working; and the *struggle to fund opportunities* that could benefit students and institutions.

The committee members deliberated on findings from the literature reviews, site visits, and presentations alongside their own experiences as faculty, administrators, partners, researchers, and/or alumni of MSIs. These rich and diverse sources notwithstanding, we acknowledge the limitations of the research evidence on current strategies to promote STEM student success, especially at MSIs.

Some resources provided stronger, more empirically based evidence than others. In the vast majority of the research (including peer-reviewed research), data-driven findings specific to outcomes in STEM at MSIs were not available. The reasons behind this paucity are not limited to the topic at hand. As noted in another recent National Academies study focused on STEM in higher education

---

[2] The University of Alaska Anchorage is a public, four-year Alaska Native-Serving and Hawaiian-Serving Institution. Texas South College is a public, two-year Hispanic-Serving Institution.

(NASEM 2018), the reasons include the challenges in determining appropriate measures of impact (particularly among MSIs—see Chapter 3) and in isolating the effects of a particular intervention that is undertaken alongside others, and the higher costs and ethical concerns associated with research designs to isolate those effects, especially in light of MSIs' student needs and limited resources. Another challenge is the difficulty of gathering data on longitudinal effects as students leave an institution (whether to transfer to a four-year school, go on to further graduate study, or enter the workforce). And last but definitely not least, the costs of undertaking evaluative research, especially when not included in a grant or other funding source, are difficult for an MSI to incur when so many other, immediate financial needs compete for scarce resources. (See Chapter 6 for the committee's recommendations for additional evidence-based research related to MSIs.)

INTENTIONALITY

Many of the programmatic and institutional efforts identified by the committee, such as mentorship or peer tutoring, are not new or unique to MSIs. However, what is novel about the committee's task is the opportunity to examine these efforts through the lens of their potential impact on the nation's future STEM workforce, in an MSI context. **A common theme that emerged from the committee's investigations and subsequent deliberations on these efforts is what the committee has described as** *intentionality.*

Intentionality, as defined by the committee, is a calculated and coordinated method of engagement used by institutions, agencies, organizations, and the private sector to effectively meet the needs of a designated population, in this case within a given higher education institution. Intentionality drives the creation of programs, practices, and policies that are tailored to recognize and address student differences across multiple dimensions: academic, financial, social, and with cultural mindfulness. Intentionality takes into account such student needs, as well as student strengths and attributes; in other words, students are not viewed as problems to fix but talent to cultivate.

As described in Chapters 3 and 4, many students enrolling at MSIs are nontraditional students,[3] have families with few discretionary financial assets, have had limited opportunities to access robust academic offerings and support systems, or come from high schools with low levels of college and career guidance and counseling services (Conrad and Gasman 2015). As a result, many of these students enter postsecondary education with the need for support services

---

[3] Nontraditional students are generally defined as students with one of the following characteristics: independent, having one or more dependents, being a single caregiver, not having received a standard high school diploma, having delayed enrollment in postsecondary education by a year or more after high school, working full time while enrolled, and/or attending school part time (Brock 2010; Choy 2002; Horn and Carroll 1996; Kim 2002, Taniguchi and Kaufman 2005).

that go beyond access to quality classroom instruction. MSIs that design their programs and services with an intentional focus on addressing the holistic needs of their students see greater student success in terms of academic outcomes and workforce readiness (Museus et al. 2011; Palmer et al. 2015).

From its analysis of the evidence base, the committee concluded that programs demonstrating the most promise in enhancing the success of students of color, particularly those in STEM fields, are intentional. They assess the social, cultural, and academic needs of the student population they serve; articulate clear objectives for their programs; implement evidence-based strategies to achieve program goals (e.g., leadership buy-in and support, designated staffing, maintenance of appropriate facilities, secured funding, and/or established partnerships); attempt to assess program outcomes through data collection, performance monitoring, and the use of data to inform future program development; and cultivate opportunities for program sustainability and growth (e.g., incorporation into institutional strategic plans and/or budgets, alumni and community outreach, and policy work and advocacy).

Some MSIs have articulated goals of intentionality through their mission and vision statements and charters. Arizona State University (ASU), for example, adopted a charter in 2014 that embodies this idea: "ASU is a comprehensive public research university, measured not by whom it excludes, but by whom it includes and how they succeed; advancing research and discovery of public value; and assuming fundamental responsibility for the economic, social, cultural and overall health of the communities it serves."[4] ASU is an enrollment-defined Hispanic Serving Institution; thus, demographics and not historical precedent determine its designation as an MSI. The charter reflects an intentional embrace of how it sees its role in relation to its students and the community.

Achieving intentionality is a challenge. In fact, after a comprehensive review of the literature, the committee determined that many minority- and STEM-focused programs fail to achieve all aspects of intentionality and, as a result, are unable to *effectively or efficiently* move the needle to increase the success of students of color in STEM. Combined with the current funding challenges for MSIs (see Chapter 4 for a detailed discussion), we consider it especially vital that MSIs—and other stakeholders in the MSI education system, including employers, federal and state governments, and private foundations—invest their resources in classroom, laboratory, student support services, and strategies that embody intentionality.

To further explore how intentionality manifests itself to support students of color at MSIs, the committee identified seven core strategies, described below with illustrative examples. We also highlight six programs in this chapter that employ one or more of these strategies: (1) Achieving the Dream, a national non-profit that aims for whole-system transformation at two-year institutions; (2) the

---

[4] See https://president.asu.edu/about/asucharter.

Alaska Native Science and Engineering Program, a University of Alaska program with a focus on a middle school through graduate STEM education for Alaska Natives; (3) A Student-Centered ENtrepreneurship Development (ASCEND) program, a program to encourage student entrepreneurship in biomedical sciences at Morgan State University; (4) the Building Infrastructure Leading to Diversity (BUILD) Initiative, funded by the National Institutes of Health to support biomedical research capacity (including ASCEND); (5) Louis Stokes Alliances for Minority Participation (LSAMP) Program, a long-standing National Science Foundation (NSF) initiative to build the STEM pipeline; and (6) Math Engineering Science Achievement (MESA), another longstanding program with a goal of successfully transitioning STEM students from community colleges to four-year institutions. (See Appendix D for links to additional program details on the illustrative examples and the six highlighted programs.)

The diversity of these initiatives, in terms of structure, scale, goals, and funding, show many possibilities, but no one-size-fits-all formula exists to foster success.

STRATEGIES TO PROMOTE STUDENT SUCCESS

Drawing on the concept of intentionality, and review of the research and other inputs, the committee identified seven core strategies or interventions that appear the most promising for cultivating and supporting the success of MSI students in STEM fields, with an emphasis on undergraduate students:

- Dynamic, multilevel, mission-driven leadership;
- Institutional responsiveness to student needs;
- Campus climates that support a sense of belonging for students;
- Student-centered academic and social supports;
- Effective mentorship and sponsorship;
- Undergraduate research experiences; and
- Mutually beneficial public- and private-sector partnerships.

Many of these strategies are not novel to the MSI community; however, with a focus on intentionality, each of these practices can be replicated (or, as appropriate, adapted) and brought to scale at MSIs to bolster the success of students of color and enrich the campus community at large. Furthermore, they are interrelated: mission-driven leadership will help foster a positive campus climate, strong partnerships can provide research experience and mentorships, and the like.

These seven strategies are described in the remainder of this chapter, with illustrative examples. (Appendix D compiles these examples, with website links for further information.) They are offered as illustrations for MSIs and their stakeholders (i.e., federal and state governments, business and industry, foundations, and others) to adopt or adapt to support MSI students, particularly those in STEM, in their sphere of influence. MSIs have also been innovative in experimenting with new programs to prepare their students for success in the future. Although not always based on hard evidence, these programs reflect the desire to experiment and think outside the box (Conrad and Gasman 2015). **Given the diversity and rapid growth of the MSI sector, established MSIs may find new promising ideas here that support their efforts to recruit and retain students, while newly emerging MSIs can become aware of the most effective strategies to support the success of their rapidly changing student demographics.**

Many of the examples highlighted below are national or regional programs implemented at multiple institutions. The committee thus offers an additional caveat, recognizing that the impact of a particular program may rise or fall at a specific institution depending on institutional buy-in, infrastructure and capacity, available funding, competing ventures, and other contextual considerations. In addition, many (but not all) of the programs discussed below lack formal evaluations and impact assessments, or are largely based on anecdotal evidence. As such, the committee refers to these multisite and single-site programs as *promising* programs to support MSI students. In the future, assessment and evaluation data can be used to modify the programs and their institutional support structures to enable them to thrive, extend their reach to additional students, and be replicated or adapted elsewhere.

Dynamic, Multilevel, Mission-Driven Leadership

"[To achieve student success], faculty need to understand the continuum of progress, invest in the success of their students, and understand the current student."
                                        –Administrator at Morgan State University

"[This school] has enjoyed consistent leadership from the top."
                     –Faculty Member at North Carolina A&T State University

Strong leadership at MSIs is critical for student success. Together, the president, governing boards, and senior administrators are the key drivers for determining the progress of the institution. They have the responsibility to establish and promote the institution's culture of success, organize institutional priorities, serve as prominent figures in their local and regional communities, and determine the most effective policies and practices to support the educational and sociocultural success of enrolled students (Palmer et al. 2018). MSI leadership—its challenges, successes, and recommended best practices—is not a highly researched or reviewed topic in the higher education literature. Although recent progress has been made (e.g., Palmer et al. 2018), many of the committee's conclusions regarding MSI leadership come from MSI site visit communications and personal expertise.

In their research, the committee learned that leadership at MSIs needs to be proactive and creative (Whittaker and Montgomery 2012). At site-visits it was stressed that leadership needs to be faithful to the vision of the institution as one that serves one or more specific populations of underrepresented students; committed to academic and social supports that reflect intentionality; and steadfast in a desire to develop and maintain a culture of transparent communication, trust, and accountability. Furthermore, given the need for alignment of strategic priorities and governance practices with operational management, a shared commitment between the head of the institution (i.e., president or chancellor) and its board of trustees is of paramount importance (Commodore et al. 2018; Hodge-Clark 2017). MSI leadership needs to be committed to promote and preserve the institution's mission and its unique culture and climate (Toldson 2013). Such leadership may need to be creative and flexible when encountering environmental and fiscal barriers and pursue "outside-the-box" opportunities to support student success.

Strong leadership at MSIs and non-MSIs requires many of the same qualities, yet anecdotal evidence suggests that there is a notable difference in the *level* and *nature* of leadership that is needed at MSIs. As discussed in Chapter 4, there are substantial differences between the resources available for MSIs as compared to non-MSIs. Given the paucity of resources and challenges in building institutional capacity, when leading in these environments it is critical to be both strategic and operational in focus (Schexnider 2013). MSI administrators "wear multiple hats" while seeking out new ways to advance the institution's mission. As observed at several site-visit locations, leadership duties and responsibilities are often widely distributed, akin to principles of a "shared leadership" (Kezar and Holcombe 2016). MSI STEM faculty and staff are often tasked with or take it upon themselves to create, manage, and advocate for important institutional initiatives, in addition to their teaching loads, research, and administrative demands. To support their needs, MSI faculty and administrators stressed the importance of transparent communication across committees and other formal and informal channels, and the involvement of senior leadership.

An institutionalized culture of "we are all in this together" was the common thread observed among leadership at MSIs. Establishing a supportive institutional environment for the faculty and engaging them as highly invested stakeholders, as well as implementing programmatic efforts to break down institutional silos and establish collaborative leadership, shows evidence of success for institution-wide transformations (Blake 2018; Godreau et al. 2015; Wilson-Kennedy et al. 2018). As an example, to support the development and launch of a comprehensive plan to transform and advance STEM research and education on its campus, North Carolina A&T State University's faculty and administrators utilized a *collaborative leadership approach*—a strategic method that breaks down institutional silos and fosters connectivity across multiple levels and disciplines to establish widespread change (Kezar and Holcombe 2016).

Some institutions seeking to instill change take a "top-down" approach, starting at the governance level and permeating all levels of leadership, from the head of the institution to other senior executive level management. Alternatively, others follow a "bottom-up" approach, initiated at the faculty level with the aim of gaining the support of senior leadership. Both approaches were viewed as effective when leadership was not siloed, but distributed in the end, necessitating effective and transparent communications channels and a culture of respect for differing roles and responsibilities. Xavier University of Louisiana provides an illustrative example of the use of these approaches. Many of the people interviewed during the committee's site visit credited the vision of the institution's president and the efforts of the director of the PreMed Office, both recently retired, in laying the foundation of a campus culture that combines high expectations and personal relationships. Given that Xavier University is among the top schools in the country in the number of African American graduates who go on to U.S. medical schools, with an acceptance rate well above the national average, its leadership, appears to have played a critical role in cultivating the educational success of Xavier students.

Thinking long term, to continue to support the complex needs of MSIs, it is important for MSIs to be mindful of new and creative ways to prepare the next generation of MSI leaders, to support widespread professional development for institutions' faculty and staff, and to be strategically engaged in succession planning (Hodge-Clark 2017; Pickens 2010). As an example, the leadership of the University of Alaska-Anchorage's Alaska Native Science and Engineering Program (ANSEP), described in Box 5-3, developed a program to support the advancement of faculty to cultivate new leaders in STEM fields and provide examples of success to which students can aspire. Recognizing a need for Alaska Native faculty development and growth, Herb Schroeder, ANSEP founder and vice provost, established a "Grow Your Own Ph.D." component of the program, providing opportunities to send faculty to out-of-state institutions to earn doctoral degrees. As discussed in the committee's public meeting, he then negotiated an agreement with the University of Alaska's administration to ensure acceptance of these faculty members into tenure-track positions within the College of Engineering upon their return.

As another example, the San Diego State University's (SDSU's) Building on Inclusive Excellence Hiring Program allocates five tenure-track positions to qualified candidates who meet criteria aligned with SDSU's commitment to diversity. Thus, the leadership acknowledges the contributions of faculty members who engage with students (through service, teaching, mentoring, research, etc.) and who demonstrate expertise in cross-cultural communication and collaboration.

The committee's recommendations for how MSI leaders and their stakeholders can cultivate a pipeline of forward-looking, mission-driven MSI leaders, MSIs, and their stakeholders are presented in Chapter 6.

BOX 5-3
The Alaska Native Science and Engineering Program[a]

The Alaska Native Science and Engineering Program (ANSEP) is a longitudinal education model that supports students underrepresented in the Alaska STEM workforce, particularly Alaska Natives and nonurban students. ANSEP was established in 1995 at the University of Alaska-Anchorage with a single student, and has since grown to support more than 2,000 students.

The program starts in the sixth grade and continues through high school and beyond, leading to undergraduate and graduate degree programs in STEM. A middle school academy and a STEM career explorations program serve middle schoolers, followed by an acceleration academy for high school students, a summer bridge program for incoming freshman, a University Success program, and a graduate success program. By design, each of these components helps to address the cultural and academic needs of the student population.

The Urban Institute, a nonprofit research organization, has conducted several evaluations of the ANSEP program to evaluate the students' progress and the program's overall success. In 2013 and 2014, using data collected from interviews, surveys, and student records, an evaluation determined that ANSEP has produced a multilevel impact on the Alaskan K-12 system, University of Alaska, and the local and regional STEM workforce. Notable outcomes of success related to enrollment, retention, and graduation include the findings that 98.7 percent of Summer Bridge participants were admitted to degree programs at the University of Alaska, with 76.7 percent admitted into B.S. degree programs in STEM majors.[b]

A 2015 evaluation found that 66.4 percent of all University Success participants completed[c] (34.7 percent) or were enrolled (31.7 percent) in STEM B.S. degree programs; among those who graduated, 92 percent received B.S. degrees in STEM. There are also notable outcomes of success related to employment: Within 1 year of graduation, 84 percent of University Success participants reported being employed, with the vast majority employed in STEM or STEM-related occupations (88 percent). Another 10 percent of students reported enrollment in graduate school. In addition, 44 percent of matched survey respondents[d] reported a median salary of $40,000 to $59,000 (not constant dollars) during their first year of employment after school, with another 44 percent reporting salaries greater than $60,000. In comparison, according to the evaluation, the mean income of American Indian/Alaska Native and Native Hawaiian/Pacific Islander college graduates 1 year after graduation across all STEM fields was around $43,000. In sum, ANSEP has shown positive outcomes on STEM degree completion and postgraduate earnings once graduates are in the STEM workforce.

---

[a] See http://www.ansep.net/.
[b] Among those individuals whose entry-level information was available to researchers.
[c] Using data from students who receive a B.S. or B.A. degree at least 8 years after first enrollment.
[d] Based on alumni survey responses matched to university records data.

Institutional Responsiveness to Student Needs

"Students have a dogged perseverance. They will face a lot of challenges."
–Administrator at Salish Kootenai College

"We are meeting students where they are."
–Administrator at West Los Angeles College

The core, and indeed intentional, mission for many MSIs is to help their students successfully address potential academic, financial, and social challenges, and empower them to succeed (Gasman and Conrad 2013). Enhanced responsiveness to student needs can be facilitated by building institutional capacity and supporting a culture of inquiry that is focused on data collection and evaluation (Chaplot et al. 2013; Museus and Jayakumar 2011). Achieving the Dream, highlighted in Box 5-4, is an example of an initiative that uses data to improve student support programs and services across institutions.

As discussed in Chapter 3, MSIs educate a largely nontraditional student body. Not surprisingly, managing basic needs, such as transportation, health care, food, and housing, poses an additional challenge for many MSI students. In fact, many students who drop out of school do so largely because of social and financial challenges, as opposed to academic ones (Cahalan and Perna 2015).

Many schools, including MSIs, have instituted technology-based, Early Alert systems. The systems track student attendance, academic performance, and behaviors, so schools can use these data to help students before they fail or drop out. Critical to their effectiveness, according to one study (Hanover Research 2014), is how an institution uses the information as part of a larger strategy to support students once they have been "flagged." At Salish Kootenai College, the committee learned that the Early Alert system is located within a broader Department of Student Success to serve as the link between student services and college faculty.

Other notable examples of support uncovered during the committee's site visits include the following:

- Alternative staff work schedules to assist students who need flexible access to certain supports (for example, counseling offices open beyond the typical Monday-to-Friday, 9-to-5 schedule);
- Increased course offerings to support students who need to repeat a class, but do not want to lose a year of academic time waiting for the opportunity to reenroll;
- Open educational resources to provide free online teaching, learning, and resource materials for educators and students;
- Access to technology and STEM Centers that provide students with online course materials, software, computers, and printers;

BOX 5-4
Achieving the Dream[a]

Achieving the Dream (ATD) is a national nonprofit organization begun by the Lumina Foundation and seven partner organizations in 2004. Currently, the ATD network consists of 220 two-year institutions (both MSI and non-MSI) in 40 states. ATD institutions embark on whole-college transformation to support a student-centered culture that promotes student success. The program strives to use evidence-based practices to improve teaching and learning, engagement and communication, strategy and planning, policies and practices, leadership and vision, data and technology, and equity. As examples of its approach, ATD advocates a Holistic Student Supports Approach, rather than offering disparate services. Its Institutional Capacity Assessment Tool helps institutions evaluate how they are functioning across these dimensions and then use data derived from the tool, as well as other data collected by the institution, to improve decision making.

A 2016 review of the program, supported by the Strada Education Network, used Gallup-USA Funds associate degree data to compare outcomes of associate degree holders from 15 ATD colleges with associate degree-holders from non-ATD schools on measures of employment rates, job satisfaction, quality of life, and collegiate experiences. The study found ATD alumni more likely to feel engaged at work (42 percent for ATD graduates versus 33 percent for non-ATD graduates) and more likely be thriving in purpose and financial well-being than students who did not graduate from ATD schools. Overall, nearly 3 in 10 ATD graduates (29 percent), compared with fewer than 1 in 5 associate degree holders nationally (17 percent), are considered emotionally attached to their institution. Nearly one-third of ATD graduates (31 percent)—significantly higher than associate degree holders nationally (22 percent)—strongly agree that their institution prepared them well for life outside of college. In addition, within ATD institutions, the perceptions of African American and Hispanic graduates were similar to those of White and nondisaggregated Asian graduates in terms of feeling prepared for life outside school. These findings suggest that ATD supports the success of underrepresented community college students.

SOURCE: Gallup Inc. 2018
[a] See http://www.achievingthedream.org/.

- Transportation and housing assistance to alleviate costs for students enrolled at campuses located in remote geographic regions or in regions where the cost of living is high;
- Capped tuition and fees to lessen the financial burden on students; and
- Health care services and food pantries to help ensure that basic needs are being met.

Institutional support may also include online and/or distance learning, evening, weekend, and/or hybrid courses (i.e., combination of in-person and virtual instruction), coupled with tailored tutoring sessions and co-instruction (Crockett 2014; Drew et al. 2015; Drew et al. 2016; Mosina 2014; QEM 2012). For example, NetLAB technology at West LA College allows students to remotely access course materials when it is most convenient for their schedules. In addition, noncredit instruction at West LA is offered free to students to facilitate the transition into credit programs, career and technical education, or employment without incurring tuition costs for courses that carry no credits. As another example, cloud-based learning management systems like Schoology, used at Salish Kootenai College among other institutions, connect faculty, students, and administrators and allow for the creation and management of shared content and resources.

Some MSIs, particularly those with large shares of students whose first or primary language is not English, have implemented programs (in STEM and non-STEM) to harness the linguistic resources that students bring to the classroom. An example of leveraging students' linguistic assets is the Visionlearning Project, a system of free open educational STEM learning modules and other resources available in English and Spanish (Carpi and Mikhailova 2003).

At the University of Texas Rio Grande Valley (UTRGV), the B3 (bilingual, bicultural, and biliterate) Institute is committed to enhancing coursework by delivering it bilingually or in Spanish, and by integrating community-engaged teaching, research, and service. A bilingual program that originated at the former University of Texas Pan American (now part of UTRGV) offered an advanced composition course that engaged migrant students and their families in telling oral histories of their communities (Alvarez and Martínez 2014). Indeed, opportunities to do hands-on, culturally relevant research enhances the student experience (Thao et al. 2016). These programs help students strengthen their writing and oral communication skills, and increase the sense of connectivity to the university community (Alvarez and Martínez 2014; García and Okhidoi 2015).

While most of these programs and interventions are not specific to STEM majors, nor should they be, they offer the types of institutional support that STEM students need in order to thrive in their courses and laboratories.

Campus Climates That Support a Sense of Belonging for Students

"Diversity is our strength."
　　　　　　　　　　　　　　　　　　　–Administrator at Mission College

"They [the students] really are our own."
　　　　　　　　　　　　　　　　　　　–Board Member of Salish Kootenai College

"We need to educate each other—one person, one student at a time."
　　　　　　　　　　　　　　　　　　　–Faculty Member at Mission College

An inviting and nurturing campus climate that supports a fundamental sense of community and culture, together with an institution that enables students to find and learn from each other, that provides holistic support, and that builds students' confidence, is key to fostering student success at MSIs (Brown 2011; Locks et al. 2008; Perna et al. 2009; Tachine et al. 2017; Whittaker and Montgomery 2012).

In aligning campus climate goals with leadership and institutional responsiveness strategies, faculty and staff at MSIs aim to cultivate climates that are supportive and inclusive. In fact, many highly academically qualified minority students who could attend more selective institutions report that they attend MSIs for this very reason (e.g., Santiago 2007). The emphasis on historical and cultural heritage is a motivation to attend HBCUs for many African American students, many of whom report they were encouraged by family members or teachers who themselves attended HBCUs, given their supportive environments (Freeman 2005; McDonough et al. 1997).

Several studies have found that MSIs cultivate a sense of family for their students (Conrad and Gasman 2015; Nguyen 2015). This sense goes beyond providing comfort and familiarity. It has been shown to facilitate interactions with faculty, grow students' academic self-confidence and sense of belonging (Allen et al. 2007; Cuellar 2014; Chun et al. 2016; Williams Pichon 2016), and, in turn, lead to positive learning outcomes (Slovacek et al. 2012).

Some institutions place a strong emphasis on creating safe spaces, supporting students' identities, and recognizing the desire of MSI students to engage with their communities. Many MSIs demonstrate considerable innovation through student-centered coursework that encourages talent development for students from diverse backgrounds. Often, this coursework weaves in culturally relevant approaches to leverage the cultural, community, linguistic, and related strengths that students bring with them to the classroom (Cole et al. 2011; Conrad and Gasman 2015; García et al. 2017; Hurtado et al. 2015). For example, faculty at HSIs have been shown more likely than those at non-HSIs to engage their students through strategies like collaborative learning and reflective journaling, each of which has been shown to increase success for students of color (Felder and Brent 2016; García and Okhidoi 2015; Hurtado et al. 2015).

At Salish Kootenai College, leadership and faculty provide students with a culturally congruent education by weaving the livelihood and vitality of the Native American community into the curriculum. At the University of Texas Rio Grande Valley, community-engaged research projects and programs, such as the NSF-funded Stimulating Hispanic Participation in the Geosciences program, have an embedded service learning component that allows for students and student organizations to give back to the community, in addition to training and workforce development goals.

Another crucial aspect of establishing and maintaining a supportive climate is building an equity-oriented culture that promotes equitable educational engagement, participation, and success (Dowd and Bensimon 2015; Museus and

Jayakumar 2011; Rubel 2017). Laying the foundation for a culture of equity and promoting communication among students, faculty, staff, administration, and board members is a current challenge faced by many emerging MSIs. The success of these initiatives is highly dependent on institutional commitment, political will, and visible leadership support for policies and practices aimed at closing gaps.

Mission College, for example, is creating an equity framework that guides its work in developing a collaborative infrastructure that aims to engage and drive the entire campus community toward an optimally inclusive and equitable environment. Mission also invites students to participate in the PUENTE Community College Program (active at roughly 70 community colleges across California) and its academic support, counseling, and mentoring services that seek to increase the number economically disadvantaged students who earn degrees from four-year institutions.

Project LEARN (Leading & Energizing African American Students to Research and Knowledge) at West Los Angeles College was established in 2011 to improve the educational outcomes of African American males. Today, Project LEARN is a community of faculty mentors, student mentors, and support staff who are committed to the academic success of all students. The program provides students with academic counseling and advising, mentoring, tutoring, and workshops and seminars focused on personal and professional skills development.[5] Addressing the transition to college by nontraditional students is the Troops to Engineers (T2E) program at San Diego State University; T2E is designed to ensure a successful transition of military men and women—many of whom come from communities of color—to college and, ultimately, to future STEM careers. SDSU's College of Engineering offers specialized services to veteran and active duty students including internships, counseling and academic support, and consideration of academic credit for military training.

Several schools have instituted STEM learning communities. Not exclusive to MSIs (or to STEM), learning communities (LCs) are "organized academic communities focused on a theme relevant to students. Students who participate in an LC are often housed together, take academic classes together, and are provided with educational and cultural programs to enhance the academic curriculum and social integration" (Carrino and Gerace 2016, p. 3). Research has shown that LCs can facilitate the academic success and persistence of their members (see, for example, Carrino and Gerace 2016). During the site visit at North Carolina A&T University, the committee learned about the STEM Theme House, a living learning community, supported through the North Carolina Louis Stokes Alliance for Minority Participation (LSAMP) (described in more detail in Box 5-5). Students must submit a personal state-

---

[5] In addition to Project LEARN, West Los Angeles College offers several other cohort programs to support student progress. See http://www.wlac.edu/Academic/Cohort-Programs.aspx, accessed October 2018.

ment to be considered; academic, personal, and professional development activities are designed to build their sense of community.

Entities such as the California Community Colleges' Success Network and the National Institute for Transformation and Equity (NITE) are resources that MSIs use to create communities of practice and build more inclusive college campuses.[6] For example, NITE uses tools, such as the Culturally Engaging Campus Environments survey, to gain a comprehensive understanding of how to best foster campus environments that value diversity, equity, and inclusion.[7]

Student-Centered Academic and Social Support

"It is worth it to be the absolute best that we can be for our students."
–Faculty Member at the University of Texas Rio Grande Valley

Deficiencies in academic preparation are a well-studied barrier to the success of students of color in STEM. As reported in the 2015 National Assessment of Education Progress study, African American, Hispanic, and American Indian/ Alaska Native 12th-grade students consistently score lower than their White counterparts on mathematics and science assessments[8] (Nation's Report Card 2018a,b). Similar patterns are observed when examining the results of the 2014 Technology and Engineering Literacy assessment (Nation's Report Card 2018c). Given the outcomes of these assessments and longevity of the pattern of results, some researchers suggest that the national K-12 education system does not appropriately prepare underrepresented students for continued education in the STEM fields as compared to their White counterparts (Gainen 1995; May and Chubin 2003; Meling et al. 2012). A number of factors have been implicated in contributing to this gap in performance, such as segregated schooling, resource disparities, poor funding, and unavailability of qualified teachers (May and Chubin 2003; Orfield et al. 2017; Ushomirsky and Williams 2015). While a comprehensive look at these issues is beyond the scope of the current study, the committee found that strong academic transition and support programs at MSIs are essential to the future success of their students in STEM.

Holistic approaches at MSIs that integrate academic *and* social support can be especially effective at fostering environments that promote persistence and STEM degree attainment among students of color. Successful strategies at MSIs include providing comprehensive developmental education opportunities (e.g., bridge programs and supplemental instruction), employing culturally relevant

---

[6] See http://3csn.org/ and https://www.indiana.edu/~cece/wordpress/ for more details, accessed October 2018.

[7] See https://www.indiana.edu/~cece/wordpress/cece-model/, accessed October 2018.

[8] In comparison to 2013 12th-grade math scores, there were no significant changes in the percentages of students at or above Proficient for any reported ethnic group. In comparison to 2009, there were no significant changes in the average 12th-grade science scores for any reported ethnic group.

BOX 5-5
The Louis Stokes Alliances for Minority
Participation (LSAMP) Program[a]

LSAMP was established in 1991 by the National Science Foundation. LSAMP was initially created to answer a charge from Congress to "undertake or support a comprehensive science and engineering education program to increase the participation of minorities in science and engineering."[b] Its primary objective is to increase the quality and quantity of students of color who earn bachelor's degrees in STEM fields and who pursue STEM-related graduate studies in order to increase the number of underrepresented minorities in the STEM workforce. LSAMP has funded access to summer bridge programs, undergraduate research, opportunities to attend and present at scientific conferences, tutoring and peer study groups, and scientific internships (Merriweather et al. 2017).

A quantitative assessment of LSAMP outcomes data was conducted by The Urban Institute and published in 2006 (Clewell 2005). It determined that the average overall undergraduate performance of LSAMP awardees, as measured by GPA, was significantly greater than their counterparts (i.e., a national comparative sample of non-LSAMP underrepresented minorities, and White and nondisaggregated Asian students). The data also revealed LSAMP participants were more likely to take STEM coursework following their undergraduate education and more likely to enroll in graduate programs or pursue advanced degrees in STEM than their counterparts.

A 2012 review of the University of Texas System LSAMP Program demonstrated success in bolstering the quantity and quality of students who obtained degrees in STEM-fields from 1992 to 2012. Data from the program's fourth phase

---

pedagogies, and designing course sequences that smooth transitions through introductory math, science, and other gateway courses (Conrad and Gasman 2015; Gasman and Conrad 2013; Parker 2012). Institution-supported bridge programs are among the most long-standing and highly effective efforts to support college readiness among students of color. So too, supplemental instruction can help students master course content, especially in introductory STEM classes that assume a certain level of secondary background and/or move through concepts quickly. Faculty, peer, and near-peer mentoring are often embedded or designed to occur alongside such supports (mentorship and sponsorship are considered as a separate, although interrelated strategy below). Coordination across various efforts or departments and sustained institutional commitment strengthen these supportive environments (Chun et al. 2016; Hrabowski III and Maton 2009; Maton et al. 2012; Maton et al. 2016; NAS, NAE, and IOM 2011).

Successful approaches at MSIs that provide academic support emphasize the following:

(2007 to 2012) showed all 242 students enrolled in the program graduated with a B.S. STEM degree; about one-third (70 students) went on to an M.S./Ph.D. program, of whom 53 had received an advanced degree as of 2018 (personal communication with administrators at University of Texas Rio Grande Valley).[c]

In addition to its impact on its students, LSAMP has had a positive impact on participating institutions. Data compiled by The Urban Institute suggest that participation enabled institutions to expand their capabilities to develop and support undergraduate STEM talent. Participation also produced a change in institutional culture (i.e., the intentionality element). For example, faculty reported greater cultural competency and awareness, which motivated them to reflect more on the teaching strategies they use to reach their students. LSAMP also helped create "a community feel" on campus, providing an opportunity for students to take part in a social network of tutors, peers, and role models. Finally, LSAMP institutions reported enhanced student support systems and the creation of learning centers; restructured STEM curriculum; strengthened faculty research proposals; and increased partnerships, relationship building, and collaboration with other institutions.

---

[a] See https://www.nsf.gov/funding/pgm_summ.jsp?pims_id=13646.

[b] It is important to note that these data reflect success within The University of Texas System LSAMP, an alliance of both two- and four-year MSIs and non-MSIs. However, based on 2016 enrollment data, two-thirds of the enrolled undergraduates in The University of Texas System are minorities (UTSystem.edu/Fast Facts).

[c] In comparison to 2013 12th-grade math scores, there were no significant changes in the percentages of students at or above Proficient for any reported ethnic group. In comparison to 2009, there were no significant changes in the average 12th-grade science scores for any reported ethnic group.

- Positive reframing of the academic and cultural assets of students, rather than a deficit orientation that far too often dominates perceptions of students of color by faculty, staff, and others;
- Gathering data about what students need to learn to advance in their education and develop their skills, which can require faculty to adjust their pedagogies;
- Connecting students with peer mentors to foster collaboration rather than competition; and
- Linking traditional academic affairs functions (such as instruction) to traditional student affairs functions (such as advising) to construct a more holistic approach to guiding students along their postsecondary trajectories (e.g., Conrad and Gasman 2015).

Bridge Programs

Numerous types of bridge programs exist to provide academic support to students who require guidance and enhanced preparation for college-level coursework. Some are designed to enhance recruitment, engagement, and retention of high school students with weak or underdeveloped secondary school educations, while others support community college students who are transitioning to a four-year college. Bridge programs at MSIs are often constructed as intensive precollege summer or first-semester experiences to prepare students for the academic and social differences between high school and college. They typically have two components: (1) skills development, including preparation for college math, science, engineering, or technology courses, and (2) environmental transitioning, including initiatives that support the development of "soft skills" such as time management and intra- and interpersonal communication (Slade et al. 2015). These programs may also help to expose students to current and future STEM career opportunities (Merisotis and Kee 2006). In general, bridge programs have been associated with increased likelihood of academic success for students of color (Ghee et al. 2016; Harrington et al. 2016; Murphy et al. 2010; Strayhorn 2011; Tsui 2007).

The committee encountered many bridge program models on the nine site visits. The Center for Academic Success and Achievement Academy Summer Bridge Program at Morgan State University, for example, is designed to ease the transition from high school to college for students whose academic profile and performance suggest the need for early intervention to bolster their potential for success in college. Another program at Morgan State University, the Pre-Freshman Accelerated Curriculum in Engineering (PACE) Program, is a 5-week comprehensive and intensive summer program. PACE students complete fundamental coursework in physics, chemistry, mathematics, English, and computer science, which is meant to increase the probability of a successful freshman year. There is also a research rotation component. This program allows students to become acclimated to college life, and engage with professors, peers, and tutors.

San Diego State University's college readiness program, the Freshman Academic Success Track (FAST), is mandatory for all California, first-time freshman with developmental educational needs in English. The program prepares students to excel in their classes at SDSU and is offered during the summer, prior to the start of fall classes. Another transition program is the SDSU Bridges Program, which assists students to make the transition from one of three community colleges to SDSU's 4-year baccalaureate programs. Bridges@SDSU supports students who are underrepresented in the biomedical and behavioral sciences and/or populations disproportionately affected by health disparities. Sponsored through the National Institutes of Health (NIH) Bridges to the Baccalaureate Program, the overarching goal of the program is to enhance the diversity of the biomedical research workforce.

Supplemental Instruction

Data show that attrition rates are highest among students who intend to major in a STEM discipline, particularly in their first two years of study (Carpi et al. 2013; Gainen 1995), and that a wide variety of social, academic, and economic factors contribute to these elevated rates (Carpi et al. 2013; Slade et al. 2015; Tinto 1993). Particularly relevant for students of color is an unfavorable academic institutional experience. Evidence shows that traditional classroom curriculum and standard lecture formats often create a competitive environment and fail to provide opportunities for active participation or collaboration among students, which are important considerations in creating opportunities for academic success by minority students (and indeed all) (Conrad and Gasman 2015; Gainen 1995; Gasman et al. 2017; Seymour and Hewitt 1997; Twigg 2005; Wieman 2017). Indeed, diversification of and improvements to teaching methods can be employed to help retain students of color in STEM fields because "uninspiring introductory courses" are often cited as a factor for those students who switch majors (PCAST 2012).

To support engagement and retention of students of color in STEM, one of the most common and well-researched academic supports is supplemental instruction (SI) (Meling et al. 2012; Meling et al. 2013). SI was first developed in 1973 at the University of Missouri–Kansas City to address attrition issues among minority students (Widmar 1994) but has taken many forms, one of which is referred to as Treisman's model or simply "mathematical workshops" (Fullilove and Treisman 1990). There are many variations on the SI theme; however, they all focus on collaborative learning, group study, and interaction among peers.

Well-constructed, appropriately funded, and mindfully implemented SI and related tutoring initiatives continue to positively influence the success of students of color (Conrad and Gasman 2015; Gasiewski et al. 2012; May and Chubin 2003; Meling et al. 2012). In addition to promoting increased student success (e.g., improved retention and graduation rates) in the STEM fields, these interventions also promote higher confidence levels and critical thinking competence (Barlow and Villarejo 2004; Bowles and Jones 2004; Bowles et al. 2008; Congos 2002; Wilcox and Koehler 1996).

The committee learned of a number of promising SI programs but cannot point to a specific evidence-based model that encompasses STEM supplemental instruction for students of color at MSIs. With this caveat, SDSU has shown success with a supplemental instruction course, in which the sessions integrate course content with basic study skills and are facilitated by former, high-achieving students. Another form of SI encountered by the committee was the Embedded Tutoring Program at Mission College. This program supports a tutor in the classroom who provides more individualized attention and assistance during class activities to help improve students' understanding and engagement. Embedded tutors are, most commonly, students who have successfully completed the course previously. The tutors are also required to complete peer tutor and mentoring training.

Broader programs, such as the California Guided Pathways Project, that focus on institution-wide approaches that emphasize student-centered support systems, are structured to facilitate institutional capacity building through a shared knowledge network. Research has shown that peer-to-peer learning enhances student connection and interest in coursework (Meling et al. 2012; Tagg 2003). Peer-assisted tutoring has further been shown to minimize the stigma that may come with seeking help (Conrad and Gasman 2015; Engle and O'Brien 2007).

The National Center for Academic Transformation has developed a model to provide assistance with entry-level mathematics courses called the Emporium Model. It is in place at North Carolina A&T, among other institutions (including MSIs and non-MSIs, two-year and four-year institutions). It uses commercially available interactive software combined with personalized assistance from an instructor. Students must commit to mandatory class meetings and out-of-class, online homework to participate. An NSF-funded evaluation of the Emporium Model on student attitude, self-efficacy, effort, and performance was launched in 2018.[9]

Importantly, although these types of programs have shown success (Meling et al. 2012; Meling et al. 2013; Toven-Lindsey et al. 2015), the need for funds to sustain and institutionalize them continues to be a serious concern. Also needed are institutionalized efforts to support the professional development of faculty (e.g., updating curriculum, adjusting pedagogies, and employing diversity and mentorship training). South Texas College has recognized this need and has established the Rio Grande Valley (RGV) STEM Faculty Institute. Funded by Educate Texas' Texas Regional STEM Degree Accelerator program, the RGV STEM Faculty Institute provides professional development opportunities for faculty to learn innovative, culturally mindful instructional strategies to better support the success of their students.

Effective Mentorship and Sponsorship

"Being relatable to the students is really important."
                              –Faculty Member at Salish Kootenai College

"We are all helping each other."
                              –Student at West Los Angeles College

"Teamwork makes the dream work!"
                              –Student at Xavier University of Louisiana

---

[9] For more information, see https://nsf.gov/awardsearch/showAward?AWD_ID=1818710&HistoricalAwards=false, accessed September 2018.

"[The professors] believed in me even when I didn't believe in myself and [they will] push you to greatness."
                                        –Student at West Los Angeles College

Mentoring has been described as an experienced person (mentor) guiding a less experienced person (mentee) toward a specific goal (Eby et al. 2007; NASEM 2017b).[10] Mentorship—including sponsorship, peer mentorship, and tiered mentorship—is a common strategy used at MSIs to promote student success in the STEM fields. During its site visits, the committee observed deep investment in infrastructures, both formal and informal, that support effective mentoring of MSI student populations. Moreover, many students and alumni reported that mentoring received from faculty and administrators was integral to their success, in many instances citing them as "sponsors" who not only advised them, but also actively advocated on their behalf in ways that advanced their careers.[11]

Research has in fact shown that mentoring is particularly effective for students of color, citing the power of faculty-student bonds and the opportunities to explore and clarify students' professional goals (Byars-Winston et al. 2015; Crawford et al. 1996). Faculty attitudes toward students can greatly impact student outcomes (Hubbard and Stage 2009), and the *quality* of faculty-student mentorship has great bearing on student achievement (Carlone and Johnson 2007). Findings from research conducted on a large national sample of students indicate that African American undergraduates at HBCUs have more sustained and personal interactions with faculty in developing their interests and skills in science than their counterparts at Predominantly White Institutions (PWIs) (Hurtado et al. 2011; Kim and Sax 2018).

In conjunction with a culture of faculty-student mentorship, faculty diversity can have a significant impact on STEM student success at MSIs (and indeed all institutions). Higher ratios of minority faculty in comprehensive institutions is positively associated with the number of students of color who pursue doctorates in the STEM fields (Hubbard and Stage 2010). Findings from a qualitative study of professors of color in STEM at PWIs reveal that mentorship played a significant role in their pursuit of academic attainment and long-term success in STEM fields, and that these experiences helped to shape the way they mentor contemporary cohorts of students of color in STEM (Griffin et al. 2010). While minority faculty should not take sole responsibility for mentoring students of color, they often serve as "institutional agents" (Stanton-Salazar 1997) or role models for their students, possessing an intrinsic ability to affirm and develop the talents that students of color bring to the STEM classroom (e.g., Museus et al. 2011).

---

[10] Of note, a National Academies of Sciences, Engineering, and Medicine consensus study report on "The Science of Effective Mentoring in Science, Technology, Engineering, Medicine, and Mathematics (STEMM)" is scheduled for release in 2019.

[11] See Hewlett (2013) for a larger discussion on sponsorship.

To increase an institution's capacity for effective mentorship, faculty and staff, particularly majority faculty and staff, could benefit from additional professional development. As an example, Xavier University's Center for the Advancement of Teaching and Faculty Development trains faculty to more effectively mentor and advise undergraduate students, especially those engaged in research. The center hosts faculty workshops to provide background in mentoring philosophy, mentor-mentee communication, goal and expectation setting, stereotype threat/implicit bias, issue identification and resolution, and best practices for good mentoring and advising. In addition, The National Research Mentoring Network (NRMN), a NIH-funded nationwide consortium of biomedical professionals and institutions, is another example of a structured resource with which MSIs can partner to increase their capacity for effective mentorship.[12]

The beneficial impacts of mentoring are often apparent in sustained and personalized faculty and peer mentoring throughout the undergraduate experience (Byars-Winston et al. 2015; Haeger and Fresquez 2016; Hurtado et al. 2017; NAS, NAE, and IOM 2011; Toven et al. 2015). Centers and other spaces where these relationships can be cultivated, such as peer-assisted study sections or specialized (e.g., by field or year in school) peer mentoring programs, are prevalent at MSIs (Conrad and Gasman 2015). This strength of peer mentoring, in particular, is likely due to a culture of students holding other students accountable for engaging in their education, which can be even more powerful than similar messages from faculty or administrators.

For example, Xavier University of Louisiana's Peer Mentoring Program promotes academic success and persistence by pairing incoming freshmen with upperclassmen, and student mentors and mentees with faculty advisors. San Diego State University's Aztec Mentoring Program established a joint partnership between the offices of Career Services and Alumni Engagement, and connects alumni and professional mentors with juniors, seniors, and graduate students. The University of Texas Rio Grande Valley Student Mentoring and Research Training (SMART) program provides graduate students the opportunity to serve as mentors to undergraduate students. During the fall semester, SMART mentors participate in professional development and mentoring workshops, and in the spring, they mentor and provide guidance to a project team composed of at least three undergraduate students. Formative evaluations are conducted throughout the program, and SMART mentors and project teams are required to complete a final poster presentation at an annual symposium. Institutionalized mentorship initiatives such as these show great promise in supporting sustained success for MSI students.

---

[12] See https://nrmnnet.net/about-nrmn-2/ for more details on the NRMN, accessed July 2018.

Undergraduate Research Experiences

"This is about building the scientific infrastructure of America."
–Alumni/Community partner at Dillard University

In the STEM fields, exposure to undergraduate research is one of the best predictors of degree completion and success in postgraduate education and careers. Research mentoring programs in STEM broadly call for the pairing of students on a one-on-one or very small group basis with a faculty member conducting research. This allows students to develop close relationships with faculty and see themselves as budding scientists. More holistic programs also provide students with professional development, academic and career counseling, graduate program application assistance, and other resources, in addition to research mentorship.

Evidence suggests that the two most effective components of undergraduate research experiences are (1) deep immersion into the culture of laboratory research that supports critical-thinking and communication skill enhancement, laboratory technical skill development, co-authoring publication(s), and attending a professional conference, and (2) participation in a sustained, rather than short-term, research experience (Russell et al. 2007; Thiry et al. 2011). Authentic research programs provide students opportunities to engage in research from beginning to end—identifying research problems, designing effective and efficient experiments, giving presentations about their work, co-authoring publications, and contributing findings to the longer-term questions being addressed by the faculty sponsor's research laboratory (NASEM 2015a, 2017b).

Moreover, an engaged research faculty mentor is critical to promoting student success (Aikens et al. 2017; Byars-Winston et al. 2015; Carpi et al. 2013; Carpi et al. 2016; Daniels et al. 2016; Eagan et al. 2013; Maton et al. 2012; NASEM 2015a; Russell et al. 2007; Santiago 2007; Slovacek et al. 2012). Longstanding evidence suggests that undergraduate research, coupled with high-quality faculty engagement or mentoring, leads to the retention of students of color in STEM and promotes changes in self-efficacy and self-actualization that foster postgraduate STEM success (Byars-Winston et al. 2011; Chemers et al. 2011; Espinosa 2011; Hurtado et al. 2009; NASEM 2015a, 2017b; Ward et al. 2014).

The benefits of undergraduate research are clear. Specific examples of student success as a result of participation in undergraduate research include investment of more time and effort into students' studies, increases in persistence and retention rates in STEM, and increases in grade-point averages and graduation rates (Barlow and Villarejo 2004; Espinosa 2011; Gregerman et al. 1998; Jones et al. 2010; Maton et al. 2000). Cognitive gains that contribute to self-efficacy, self-confidence, and intrinsic motivation to learn are further benefits (Carpi et al. 2017; Hunter et al. 2007; Lopatto 2007; Ryder et al. 1999; Seymour et al. 2004). Moreover, students gain valuable insight about the working world of science, including the day-to-day demands on scientists and the process and principles of conducting research (Bauerand Bennett 2003; Crawford et al. 1996; Lopatto 2004; Russell et al. 2007; Seymour et al. 2004).

Other studies show that undergraduate research participants were more likely to pursue graduate education and gain acceptance into graduate school than non-researchers (Alexander et al. 1998; Alexander et al. 2000; Bauer and Bennett 2003; Crawford et al. 1996; Hathaway et al. 2002; Jones et al. 2010; Maton and Hrabowski 2004; Russell et al. 2007; Summers and Hrabowski 2006). A recent study from Carpi et al. (2017) also found a significant increase in postgraduate STEM enrollment specifically as a function of participation in research. These changes were linked to demographics and show the impact of an undergraduate research opportunity. While White and Asian students were more likely to already have postgraduate expectations at the onset of college, Black and Hispanic students were more likely to report changes in expectations toward increasing interest in postgraduate STEM education as a result of research participation.

Of the institutions visited by the committee, few had an infrastructure or formal policies in place to support undergraduate research experiences for students on or off campus. Several faculty members noted that they frequently need to "sponsor" students and turn to their own personal networks to organize and secure students' research experiences. Some better-resourced and more research-focused MSI campuses (e.g., SDSU) *do* have undergraduate research programs in place, either through success at obtaining external funding or by dedicating internal resources to such programs. The Leadership Alliance, a consortium of leading research and teaching institutions that engages nearly 300 undergraduates in research experiences every year, was cited by some as a critical partner in ensuring that students were able to pursue research experiences, albeit on a different campus (Ghee et al. 2016; LaVallie et al. 2013). Partnerships with industry (as discussed later on in this chapter) also provide opportunities for research experiences.

The National Institutes of Health's Building Infrastructure Leading to Diversity (BUILD) Program awards grants to increase biomedical research capacity through undergraduate research training and mentorship at institutions with less than $7.5 million in NIH funding and a student population of at least 25 percent Pell grant recipients (see Box 5-6). The initial phase of the program supported the development of experiments at 10 institutions in collaboration with research-intensive and pipeline institutions across the United States. The ASCEND program at Morgan State University in Baltimore is one of these 10 projects. An acronym for A Student Centered Entrepreneurship Development training model, ASCEND is designed to build a cadre of biomedical researchers who are familiar with the root causes of health disparities and are highly competent to address them see Box 5-7).

BOX 5-6
Building Infrastructure Leading
to Diversity (BUILD) Initiative[a]

The National Institutes of Health's Building Infrastructure Leading to Diversity (BUILD) Program launched in 2014. It and several other initiatives are part of the Diversity Program Consortium, created in part to address studies that showed the role of race and ethnicity in the likelihood of NIH research funding. BUILD awards aim to achieve simultaneous impact at the student, faculty, and institutional levels by investing in approaches to transform undergraduate research training and mentorship. The initial phase supported the development of experiments at 10 institutions that, in turn, collaborate with nearly 100 research-intensive and pipeline institution partners across the United States.[b]

To be eligible for the BUILD program, primary institutions must have less than $7.5 million in total NIH research project grant funding, and a student population of at least 25 percent Pell grant recipients. Two MSIs visited by the committee are among the 10 BUILD awardees. Morgan State's ASCEND model aims to build a cadre of biomedical researchers who are familiar with the root causes of health disparities and are highly competent to address them. At Xavier University, the BUILD-funded Project PATHWAYS has set up four "cores" to strengthen student and faculty research.

A comprehensive evaluation is planned through NIH's Coordination and Evaluation Center. In order to evaluate the overall project, data collected between 2013 and 2019 will be used. A multimethods quasi-experimental longitudinal evaluation will emphasize stakeholder participation and collaboration around major evaluation questions and short- to long-term outcome measures known as "Hallmarks of Success." Data were collected from each BUILD site through national surveys from the Higher Education Research Institute at the University of California, Los Angeles, with annual follow-up surveys, site visits, and other data collection. The approach will compare changes in the Hallmarks within institutions for biomedical students who participated versus those who did not participate in the BUILD program, as well as between institution patterns of biomedical students at the BUILD sites, and matched institutions that were not BUILD grantees.

---

[a] See https://www.nigms.nih.gov/training/dpc/pages/build.aspx.
[b] For a full list of the awardees and their projects, see https://www.nigms.nih.gov/training/dpc/pages/build.aspx. Accessed September 2018.

In addition to BUILD and LSAMP, a number of research programs are available to MSIs.[13] However, they all require that MSIs have a sufficient infrastructure to implement the programs and compete effectively for scarce federal

---

[13] These programs include, but are not limited to: Maximizing Access to Research Careers Program Undergraduate Student Training in Academic Research, Minority Biomedical Research Support Initiative for Maximizing Student Development, Historically Black Colleges and Universities Undergraduate Program, Improving Undergraduate STEM Education: Hispanic-Serving Institutions, and the Research Initiative for Scientific Enhancement.

BOX 5-7
A Student-Centered ENtrepreneurship
Development (ASCEND) Program[a]

The ASCEND program at Morgan State University in Baltimore is working to accomplish what its acronym stands for—A Student-Centered ENtrepreneurship Development training model. It is 1 of 10 projects awarded five-year grants as part of the NIH BUILD Initiative. The committee discussed this on-the-ground example of BUILD during its site visit to Morgan State.

Housed within the university's Division of Research and Economic Development, ASCEND is designed to support students, faculty, and institutional infrastructure. Students have the opportunity to participate in a Summer Research Institute and develop independent research proposals. An annual cohort of 20 ASCEND Scholars conducts research and receives additional mentoring and postgraduate support. A Student Research Center supports students' interest in health research. Faculty, especially junior faculty, gain skills in grant writing and receive support for pilot projects and conference travel, as well as support to design and/or redesign courses and curricula. As for institutional capacity building, ASCEND has provided support for a core laboratory, research equipment, enhanced library resources, and research training space.

Another aspect of the five-year, $23 million, NIH-funded project is to strengthen partnerships with researchers and the research infrastructure at Johns Hopkins University, the University of Maryland, and the NIH Intramural Program; with "pipeline partners," including Baltimore City Public Schools and community colleges; and with community groups to conduct community-based health research.

A comprehensive external evaluation is planned through NIH's Coordination and Evaluation Center. Some preliminary assessments have taken place. Students' self-perception of their research knowledge and skills were tested before and after participation in the Summer Research Institutes and showed substantial perceived increases. In terms of science identity (which encompasses students' goals and confidence related to science), ASCEND Scholars had a higher mean score than the control group. The first cohort of ASCEND scholars finished their program in May 2017, and five of the six students had postgraduate plans. (No data were available for 2018 ASCEND Scholar graduates.)

---

[a] See https://www.morgan.edu/ASCEND.

---

research dollars, a point further addressed in the section on partnerships below. Other federally funded research programs include the Summer Undergraduate Research Fellowships, supported by the National Institute of Standards and Technology, and the U.S. Department of Education's TRIO Programs and the Minority Science and Engineering Improvement Program. Again, MSIs must compete for these funds (against both MSIs and non-MSIs), and those that have the infrastructure necessary to craft competitive proposals and contracts are more likely to win the grants and contracts. Thus, an overriding priority for any MSI that seeks to create federally funded research opportunities for its students is to consider how to build and sustain a campus system that enables it to successfully win research awards.

The Program for Research Initiatives in Science and Math (PRISM) at John Jay College, City University of New York, launched with federal funding in the early 2000s, is an example of what students of color at an MSI can accomplish through an undergraduate research program (Carpi et al. 2017). The concept began in 2001 with three students who received partial credit to conduct sustained, mentored research on campus, and support scientific conference travel; all three went on to successfully earn Ph.D.s, compared with just five John Jay undergraduate students in total over the previous decade. Over time, PRISM has grown to about 25 participants each year and provides stipends, conference support, professional development, and one-on-one mentoring to students. Some 80 students, more than half from underrepresented groups, have now moved on to postbaccalaureate STEM degrees. In one survey, more than two-thirds of students without previous intentions to pursue a postgraduate STEM degree credited their PRISM research experience with this new goal (Carpi et al. 2017). Also of note, PRISM has contributed to an increase in external funding for faculty research and other benefits to the institution (Carpi and Lents 2013; Carpi et al. 2017). Recognizing the impact of the program, the college has dedicated supportive resources and partially institutionalized the effort, including the hiring of a full-time Associate Director and investing in science laboratories.

As research experiences become more common and available, especially at top-tier research institutions, more graduate and professional-degree programs expect that their applicants have such experience, regardless of their undergraduate college. This expectation disadvantages students who attend nonresearch institutions or have limited or no access to research opportunities. These programs are arguably necessary, but many MSIs are insufficiently resourced, in terms of available financial support and laboratory infrastructure, to offer high-quality research experiences to students. This compounds the disadvantages to STEM students of color at MSIs, by excluding them from the research training needed to succeed in graduate school or the workforce. Carpi et al. (2017, p. 190) state, "Thus, while the trend toward undergraduate participation in research may benefit the state of science education nationally, there is an inherent danger of exacerbating current disparities in minority representation if care is not taken to support these experiences at institutions that may not presently be able to afford them." **The committee identified a lack of opportunity for authentic, high-quality undergraduate research at MSIs as a very significant concern—and targeted its recommendations at securing additional resources, including funding, to address this shortcoming.**

Mutually Beneficial Public-Private Partnerships

A public-private partnership typically involves a contractual agreement between a public agency (federal, state, or local) and a private entity (Farquharson et al. 2011). Partnerships, as described here, are further characterized by MSIs partnering with the private sector, with nonprofit organizations, or with other higher education institutions. Some successful partnerships are formal relationships, while others start informally, perhaps by a faculty member with ties to a nearby business or government agency or with alumni who reconnect with their alma mater.

The past few decades have seen the growth of STEM-related partnerships between academia and government agencies at all levels, with for-profit businesses spanning Fortune 500 companies to local businesses and start-ups, and with nonprofits ranging from community organizations to those with a global reach. The most successful partnerships appear to be those that have a clear mission and meaningful roles and responsibilities through which all parties benefit. For MSIs, partnerships can provide alternative mechanisms for securing education and research funding, increasing capacity, and expanding their network, while broadening STEM educational opportunities for students and faculty and supporting their transition into the STEM workforce (Parthenon-EY Education 2017; Perkmann et al. 2013). Federal and state agencies benefit when a partnership allows them to tap into new research and innovative thinking, achieve greater efficiency completing tasks and requirements, save taxpayer dollars, improve the quality of services and products, train the future workforce, and support the prosperity of the nation. Businesses look to partnerships to enhance specific enterprises (such as using a company's own laboratories and research and development (R&D) centers, or identifying talent for recruitment) and increase intellectual property. Most profit-driven companies base their decision making on financial metrics; thus, to be sustainable for the long term, partnerships must provide benefits beyond engaging in philanthropy or public relations to include short- or long-term returns on investment. Nonprofits, including STEM professional societies, provide networking opportunities that strengthen job prospects for students, who may ultimately contribute to the vitality of the organization as members. For other nonprofit organizations, partnering with MSIs can help achieve goals such as increasing opportunities and access for people from historically underrepresented populations.

The committee faced challenges when identifying an evidence base for successful or promising public and private partnerships and their outcomes. This lack of evidence may be due to the informality of some of these partnerships or a lack of clear outcome assessments and reporting. The examples of partnerships highlighted below demonstrate the promise of mutual benefit. In particular, they highlight the opportunity for MSI students to have access to stronger, more rigorous, and more relevant research experiences, noted in the previous section as an important component for STEM success.

While MSIs can be a prime resource for partnerships, they often lack the capacity to effectively market themselves for highly competitive ventures. Generally speaking, MSIs' Offices of Sponsored Programs, if in place, are limited in terms of staff, knowledge of government acquisition processes, resources for marketing and compliance, and ability to influence faculty to pursue research grants and contracts (Pickens 2010). However, as indicated by the programs highlighted throughout this chapter, there is much to learn from the nimbleness of certain MSIs and their ability to be flexible and responsive to new opportunities.

To explore these new avenues for funding and educational opportunities for STEM students, an institutional culture change needs to occur. Building new infrastructure, prioritizing leadership training and professional development for faculty and staff, and embracing modern ways of thinking all must happen for successful implementation of these partnerships. (The committee's recommendations for new and expanded partnerships with MSIs are presented in Chapter 6.)

Illustrative Examples of Partnership with MSIs

Government Partnerships

The federal government, which funds the preponderance of STEM opportunities for MSIs, uses a wide range of procurement mechanisms (e.g., contracts, grants, cooperative agreements, etc.) to establish partnerships with extramural research entities that align with federal agency priorities. (See Table 5-1 for brief descriptions of available mechanisms for partnerships with government agencies.) Federal agencies that have established relationships with MSIs include (but are not limited to) the Department of Defense (DoD), Department of Energy (DOE), NIH, National Aeronautics and Space Administration (NASA), National Oceanic and Atmospheric Administration (NOAA), NSF, National Institute of Standards and Technology, and the Department of Education.

NASA, for example, utilizes multiple funding mechanisms to establish strategic partnerships with MSIs. NASA's Minority University Research and Education Activity Project (MUREP) awards multiyear grants and cooperative agreements to MSIs to enhance the institutions' research, academic, and technology capabilities, and to provide authentic STEM engagement related to the NASA mission.[14] One such initiative is the MUREP STEM Engagement (MSE) portfolio. The goal of the MSE portfolio is to increase the retention and completion rates of undergraduate degrees awarded in NASA-related STEM disciplines. Through MSE, NASA conducts educator institutes at its 10 centers and offers professional development for MSIs. NASA's most recent MUREP initiative,

---

[14] Education Performance Reports FY 2014, National Aeronautics and Space Administration, https://www.nasa.gov/offices/education/programs/national/murep/about/index.html, accessed July 2018.

TABLE 5-1 Types of Mechanisms Available for Collaborative Research
Partnerships

Type of Agreement	Agreement or Mechanism	Primary Purpose
Research Partnership Agreements	Cooperative Research and Development Agreement (CRADA)	Contract for collaborative research (e.g., production of commercial technologies). Provides opportunities for faculty and students to conduct high-level research in top-tier federal laboratories and participate in contractual science and technology programs
	Nontraditional CRADA	CRADA tailored for specialized purposes (e.g. clinical trial partnerships, materials transfer)
	Cooperative Agreement	Used for collaborative research projects that are exploratory in nature
	Collaborative Research/ Technology Alliance (CRA/CTA)	A special form of cooperative agreement that emphasizes multidisciplinary collaboration and often combines government, industry, and university partners
Resource-Use Agreements	Commercial Test Agreement	Allows partners to test materials, equipment, models, or software using government laboratory equipment
	Test Service Agreement	Allows partners to purchase testing services for materials, equipment, models, or software from government laboratories
	User Facilities Agreement	Enables partners to conduct research experiments on unique government laboratory equipment and facilities.
Personnel Exchange Agreements	Intergovernmental Personnel Act (IPA) Assignments	Used for exchanges of federal laboratory and university personnel
	Joint appointments	Allows university or federal laboratory personnel to be employed at multiple institutions
Educational Agreements	Educational Partnership Agreements	Used to allow government laboratories and universities to work together to develop educational programs that further both partners' missions
	Fellowship, Internship, and Sabbatical Leave Programs	A variety of mechanisms available for students and research professors, including summer internships and fellowships and faculty leave programs

TABLE 5-1 Continued

Type of Agreement	Agreement or Mechanism	Primary Purpose
Other Partnership Agreements	University Affiliated Research Center (UARC)	Long-term partnerships that create a university-led research center to meet the Department of Defense's needs
	Centers of Excellence	An Air Force mechanism that is similar to that of the UARC
	Other Transaction Authority	Provides authorized agencies the flexibility to fund research and development projects without the terms, conditions, and regulations that accompany typical contracts, grants, or cooperative agreements
	Small Business Innovation Research (SBIR)	
	Small Business Technology Transfer (STTR) programs	SBIR and STTR provide federal research and development funding to small business or nonprofit research institutions

SOURCE: Adapted from Gupta et al. 2014.

MUREP for Sustainability and Innovation Collaborative,[15] is a two-year cooperative agreement that offers workshops for teams of MSIs and nonprofit organizations to help establish a sustainable infrastructure and build their capacity to be competitive for federal funds and, in particular, NASA grants and contracts. Another initiative, the MUREP Institutional Research Opportunities (MIRO) program is an agency-wide higher education activity that engages underrepresented populations.[16] MIRO was established to strengthen and develop the research capacity and infrastructure of MSIs in areas of strategic importance and to add value to NASA's mission and national priorities.

Certain federal agencies have the authority to maintain partnership programs for MSIs. For example, NIH's National Institute on Minority Health and Health Disparities fosters collaborations between MSIs and medical- and/or research-based organizations through its Research Centers in Minority Institutions (RCMI) program.[17] NASA, as another example, has an agency-wide goal of 1 percent of all total contract value of prime and subcontracting awards for acquisitions

---

[15] See https://nspires.nasaprs.com/external/viewrepositorydocument/cmdocumentid%3D614506/solicitationId%3D%7B60093581-F392-DAED-9821-67D191A898C4%7D/viewSolicitationDocument%3D1/EONS%202018%20APPENDIX%20H_MUSIC_Ammended%203-13-18.pdf, accessed October 2018.

[16] See https://www.nasa.gov/sites/default/files/atoms/files/2014_miro_508.pdf, accessed October 2018.

[17] See https://www.nimhd.nih.gov/programs/extramural/coe/rcmi.html, accessed October 2018.

to HBCUs/MSIs (approximately $160 million), which represents a significant opportunity for institutions to participate on NASA contracts.[18] Other agencies, such as the General Services Administration and the Department of Commerce's Minority Business Development Agency, have launched efforts to enhance MSI competitiveness for federal research and development awards, and through training and funding opportunities plan to support MSI-public agency partnerships, Mentor Protégé programs, career development, and STEM entrepreneurship.[19] NOAA has established the Educational Partnership Program with Minority-Serving Institutions, a federal STEM education workforce program,[20] and more recently, the U.S. Department of the Army's Edgewood Chemical and Biological Center has launched the MSI STEM Research & Development Consortium (MSRDC)[21] (see Box 5-8 for an additional description of MSRDC). Other areas of opportunity for federal agencies and MSIs to partner are in large-scale, collaborative ventures, such as University Affiliated Research Centers or Federal Funded Research & Development Centers. [22] These centers exist at major institutions of higher education, and the potential for MSIs to lead or serve a greater role in these partnerships could be further explored.

The establishment of these types of federal programs provides important opportunities to address national research priorities *and at the same time promote* success at MSIs (NRC 2014). Overall, however, there are only scattered examples of federal agencies that have made intentional efforts to establish MSIs as leading members of government-funded research partnerships. A large portion of the nation's MSIs do not engage in high levels of research activity, and typically federal investments are geared toward training programs rather than research grants or contracts. This may be due, in part, to the language used in federal Broad Agency Announcements (BAAs). BAAs are competitive solicitations issued by federal agencies to inform industry and academia of available funding opportunities for basic and applied research, and development ideas. BAAs do not include specific incentives, mandates, or effective measurements of MSI participation, and without this language few agencies have championed for the inclusion of the MSI community. Given that sponsoring agencies have points of authority to articulate interest for greater MSI inclusion (particularly during the procurement planning process), herein lies an opportunity to foster MSI participation in federal programs and build research capacity in measurable ways. The use of incentives in evaluation criteria and subcontracting goals, and procurement language that

---

[18] See https://osbp.nasa.gov/hbcu-mi/index.html, accessed October 2018.

[19] See https://www.mbda.gov/page/2018-mbda-broad-agency-announcement and https://osbp. nasa.gov/docs/event-presentations/2018_02/speaker/1345_GSA-and-DON_Networking-Federal-Agencies-panel-TAGGED.pdf, accessed October 2018.

[20] See https://www.noaa.gov/office-education/epp-msi, accessed October 2018.

[21] See https://www.msrdconsortium.org/about/, accessed October 2018.

[22] See https://www.nsf.gov/statistics/ffrdclist/ and http://acqnotes.com/acqnote/industry/urac, accessed October 2018.

BOX 5-8
MSI STEM Research and Development
Consortium (MSRDC)[a]

The MSRDC was established in 2015 by the U.S. Army Research Development Engineering Command's Edgewood Chemical and Biological Center (ECBC) to serve as a consortium of universities to engage in basic, applied, and advanced research and development programs. The MSRDC consists of more than 50 MSIs and a growing number of collaboration partners that represent major research institutions and industry stakeholders. Among the program's objectives are to enhance research and educational capabilities of MSIs, improve research facilities at MSIs, and create a robust pipeline of research and development projects to address the science and technical priorities of the Department of Defense and other federal agencies. The program is entrepreneurial in nature, its projects are pursued and funded on technical merit, and the mechanism for success is continuous marketing effort and good science ideas.

The program provides MSIs access to a 10-year Cooperative Agreement contract with an unfunded ceiling of $86 million, and, based on key performance indicators, the Cooperative Agreement is renewable after seven years. This type of program agreement fulfills four distinct objectives: (1) it increases MSI-agency engagement as lead investigators, (2) it eliminates idle time associated with traditional Broad Agency Announcements processes, (3) it builds MSI's research and development capacity over a longer horizon when science and technology priorities change with agency missions, and (4) it expands agencies' access to a national MSI research and development enterprise. It is the program's hope that participation in MSRDC will grow and support innovation and entrepreneurship efforts, increase the number of graduates from MSIs engaged in prioritized federal research efforts, and magnify the presence of MSIs as a resource for diverse STEM talent.

Agencies that are currently participating in the MSRDC program include Army Materiel Systems Analysis Activity; the Armament Research Development and Engineering Center; the Communications Electronics Research Development and Engineering Center; the Defense Threat Reduction Agency; the Department of Homeland Security; ECBC; and the Office of the Deputy Assistant Secretary of Defense for Nuclear, Chemical, and Biological Defense.

---

[a] See https://www.msrdconsortium.org/about/.

---

emphasizes inclusion, could lead to increased opportunities for MSIs to secure federal grants and contracts, as prime or subrecipients.

In addition to the language in BAAs, over the course of the committee's site visits, a number of other barriers to establishing MSI and federal research partnerships were revealed. First, complex bureaucratic processes and time-intensive tasks place an enormous burden on already resource-challenged MSIs, as compared to PWIs and/or research-intensive institutions that often have dedicated staff or offices to manage these processes. A second barrier is unfamiliarity with

MSI-specific federal research grants, programs, and contracted research opportunities, as described earlier. Moreover, MSIs without proven track records in demonstrating their ability to implement and manage grants or contracts may be at a competitive disadvantage for funding compared with institutions that have established such credentials.

As already noted, this deficit in the ability for many MSIs to successfully compete for and secure large federal grants and contracts results in fewer opportunities for their faculty and students, as compared to PWIs, to participate in state-of-the-art research or secure work experiences in areas of science, engineering, and medicine. This, in turn, affects MSI students' marketability in the 21st-century career marketplace. As such, there are important areas primed for stakeholder investment and support. These include efforts to (1) increase MSI knowledge of and participation in the federal budgeting and planning process and (2) foster relationships between MSI faculty and grants office officials with agency leaders and program officers to help bridge the knowledge gaps pertaining to agencies' research priorities and relevant partnership opportunities. Partnerships between MSIs and academic, research, or industry stakeholders—stakeholders with a larger, more established network within the federal research community—could facilitate MSI success in these areas.[23]

Given the nation's urgent need to expand its domestic STEM-capable workforce and the poised position of MSIs as a national resource for STEM talent (see Chapter 2 for additional discussion), substantial increases in the number and type of *MSI-specific* public-private partnerships could help to bolster domestic achievements in STEM. However, as discussed in Chapter 4, to support the advancement and growth of *MSI*-specific public-private partnerships, it is important to obtain a clear profile on the current federally funded initiatives at MSIs and their return on investment for the institutions, students, and STEM workforce. **Efforts to enhance the clarity, transparency, and accountability for all STEM-focused federal appropriations available to MSIs could inform future partnership initiatives and help to determine which are most needed, underfunded, or unexplored**. (See Chapter 6 for the committee's recommendation to Congress on this issue.)

Business Partnerships

Private-sector partnerships include opportunities for MSI student scholarships, paid workforce experiences, internships, and/or mentorships that focus on

---

[23] As an example of ongoing efforts to address this need, in 2018 the DoD's Defense Threat Reduction Agency, the Army Research Laboratory, the Naval Research Laboratory, and the National Academies of Sciences, Engineering, and Medicine co-hosted two one-day, no-cost workshops for MSIs. The goal of the workshops was to increase MSI knowledge of DoD research priorities and budget processes, foster relations between MSI faculty and program managers, and to spur research engagement.

student and faculty development. These partnerships can also support positive engagement with the MSI leadership, faculty, and students, and as described later, influence the institution's STEM curriculum. These initiatives could have lasting effects, *provided that aggressive and intentional steps are taken by both industry and MSIs to nurture and grow such partnerships* (Burge et al. 2017).

National partnerships. Companies such as Intel, Google, Boeing, Northrup Grumman, Apple, Facebook, Airbnb, Salesforce, Microsoft, and Hewlett Packard have launched STEM initiatives and supplier diversity programs focused on promoting a diverse workforce. Some of these initiatives include partnerships with MSIs, but there is an opportunity to do more. In February 2018, Congresswoman Alma Adams (Democrat, North Carolina) and Congressman Bradley Byrne (Republican, Alabama), co-chairs of the Bipartisan Historically Black Colleges and Universities (HBCU) Caucus, helped to launch a HBCU Partnership Challenge to the private sector. This challenge opens an opportunity for businesses to create, expand, or strengthen partnerships with HBCUs, to provide greater engagement and support for their missions. Based on current reports, industry partners that have accepted this challenge include Amazon, Intel, Regions Bank, Dell, Inc., GM Financial, Nielsen, Pandora, AnitaB.org, and Volvo Group North America.[24] Similar efforts across all MSI types could have a substantial impact on the STEM education and outcomes of success for students.

As an example of industry initiatives, in 2017, Boeing pledged to invest $300 million in employees, infrastructure, and local communities to advance the skillset of current employees and to help develop and diversify the future STEM workforce. As part of this pledge, Boeing plans to invest $6 million in a partnership with Thurgood Marshall College Fund and several HBCUs, as well as an investment of $11 million in a partnership with NSF.[25] In 2013, Google launched a program called Google in Residence (GIR) at Howard University (a HBCU) (Washington et al. 2015). Now at 10 HBCUs, this program was designed to increase the interest and retention of underrepresented students in computer science disciplines, and to reform computer science and coding programs at HBCUs to meet industry needs (Google 2018; Washington et al. 2015). In fall 2018, GIR plans to expand its program to three additional schools, including two HSIs (Google 2018).

The Northrup Grumman Corporation and Northrop Grumman Foundation also channel support to MSIs through a number of different avenues. For ex-

---

[24] Based on the most recent data available, the Bipartisan Historically Black Colleges and Universities (HBCU) Caucus is comprised of 72 bipartisan members of Congress. For more information, see https://adams.house.gov/bipartisan-historically-black-colleges-and-universities-hbcu-caucus, accessed September 2018.

[25] For more information, see https://www.tmcf.org/tmcf-in-the-news/boeing-announces-6-million-investment-in-thurgood-marshall-college-fund/14475 and http://boeing.mediaroom.com/news-releases-statements?item=130293, accessed October 2018.

ample, Northrup Grumman supports the National Society of Black Engineers (NSBE) Integrated Pipeline Program, a program that provides engineering students at Florida A&M, Howard, and North Carolina A&T State (all HBCUs) with scholarships, internships, and year-round academic and professional development support.[26] Elsewhere in the company, the Global Supplier Diversity Program aims to expand subcontracting opportunities to small business concerns, including HBCUs and other minority institutions, and participates in DoD's Mentor-Protégé agreement to assist small businesses in competing for prime contracts and subcontracts.[27] Northrup Grumman, S&K Electronics (a company located on the Flathead Reservation and owned by the confederated Salish and Kootenai tribes), and Salish Kootenai College have partnered through this program to offer training and certifications to bolster S&K Electronics' ability to manage processes, equipment, and technology.[28]

Regional partnerships. MSI partnerships with regional businesses provide additional opportunities to promote student success. For example, West LA College and the South Bay Workforce Investment Board have developed the Aero-Flex Pre-Apprenticeship Program, an employer-driven engineering framework.[29] Partnering employers have the flexibility to customize the curriculum, receive funding to support training and recruitment, and have access to a pool of talented job seekers. The program consists of work readiness training, industry-specific skills training, and on-the-job learning. Students receive an industry-recognized stackable credential, and the opportunity to complete college, enter into an apprenticeship, or continue to employment. Membership with the Society of Manufacturing Engineers (SME) is also included, providing access to SME mentor programs and scholarships.

As another example, STEM Core is a partnership model implemented at 14 community colleges in California to prepare students for STEM jobs. The program at Mission College offers accelerated mathematics and engineering courses combined with other academic resources and provides opportunities to compete for paid summer internships at Silicon Valley companies. Mission College also supports the MESA Community College Program (MESA CCP) (part the MESA Undergraduate Program described in Box 5-9), which supports STEM students' transition from community college to four-year institutions.[30] One of

---

[26] For more information, see http://www.nsbe.org/NGFIPP/home/about-the-program.aspx, accessed September 2018.

[27] For more information, see http://www.northropgrumman.com/suppliers/Pages/GSDP.aspx, accessed October 2018.

[28] For more information, see https://news.northropgrumman.com/news/releases/releases-20171205, accessed October 2018.

[29] For more information, see https://docs.wixstatic.com/ugd/b8c0dc_10e2bae72a9441c19ab6af87 a6858571.pdf, accessed October 2018.

[30] For more information, see http://mesa.ucop.edu/program/mesa-community-college-program/, accessed October 2018.

BOX 5-9
The Math Engineering Science Achievement
(MESA) Program[a]

The MESA program began in California in the 1970s to provide educationally and economically disadvantaged students and their families with skills and resources to achieve success in school, career, life, and STEM-related disciplines. In California, 40 community colleges participate in the MESA Community College Program. (MESA also has programs for middle and high schools, as well as a program for four-year engineering schools.) Outside of California, the MESA model has been replicated in 11 states, who together identify as a network called MESA USA.

The Community College Program provides academic enrichment, advising, and other resources with the goal to excel academically and transfer to four-year institutions with science, engineering, or math-based majors. Industry support helps students gain real-world experience and build connections. To date, no publicly available, national evaluation has been conducted, but MSI stakeholders anecdotally suggest that MESA has been successful in helping educationally disadvantaged students to become engineers, scientists, and other math-based professionals.

Independently, several institutions have evaluated the outcomes of their MESA programs. For example, at Santa Rosa Junior College (SRJC), MESA-participating students outperformed nonparticipants on measures related to course completion, retention, and GPA. As of fall 2017, 22 percent of all enrolled MESA students transferred to a four-year college or university during the 2016-2017 academic year (personal communication with administrators at Santa Rosa Junior College). Of those students, 96 percent persisted in a STEM major. Also in the 2016-2017 academic year, MESA transfer students demonstrated a 93 percent six-year completion rate, as compared to a 53 percent six-year completion rate for non-MESA SRJC students and a 48 percent six-year completion rate for all California community college students. Demonstrating similar metrics of success, during the committee's site visit, Mission College reported a 100 percent transfer success rate for MESA participants from fall 2015 through fall 2017.

---

[a] See http://www.mesausa.org/.

---

panies such as Oracle, the Southern California Gas Company, PG&E, Symantec, and Cisco.[31]

Local and community partnerships. In areas of the country where MSIs have few national industry partners nearby, local communities and industries play an important role in providing career-related experiences to students. One such example involves the UTRGV-Texas Manufacturing Assistance Center's Lean

---

[31] For more information, see https://mesa.ucop.edu/partner-sponsors/industry-partners/, accessed October 2018.

Sigma Academy, in which students work on projects with local industries and obtain an industry-recognized certification.[32] Another example is the South Texas College's Texas Regional STEM Degree Accelerator initiative, which aligns student curriculum, engagement and learning activities, and faculty instruction with regional STEM workforce needs.[33] These types of initiatives help to establish an active and mutually beneficial partnership between institutions and local STEM employers, as well as to provide unique opportunities for service learning and community engagement projects.

MSI-Government-Industry Partnerships

Small Business Innovation Research (SBIR) and Small Business Technology Transfer (STTR) programs are examples of U.S. public-private partnerships. SBIR and STTR were established to provide federal research and development funding to small business or nonprofit research institutions. Awarded contracts (or subcontracts) to MSIs could stimulate the long-term growth of the institutions' current STEM portfolios.

SBIR and STTR programs have a mutual objective to foster and encourage participation by minority and disadvantaged persons in technological innovation (NASEM 2015b). However, based on the 2015 U.S. Small Business Administration's SBIR/STTR annual report, only 8 percent of total SBIR obligations were awarded to Women-Owned Small Business Concerns, 3.5 percent to Socially or Economically Disadvantaged-Owned Small Business Concerns, and 2 percent to Historically Underrepresented Business-Certified Small Business Concerns (U.S. Small Business Administration 2015). These data suggest that strategic efforts are needed to help identify and address the programmatic challenges that may be uniquely specific to these populations. (See Box 5-10 for additional discussion.)

Non-MSI and MSI Partnerships

Partnerships between MSIs and between MSIs and non-MSIs enable institutions to pool their resources, share knowledge, and build community (Esters et al. 2016). The prevalence of these partnerships has increased in recent years in part due to funding from federal agencies, national foundations, and other funders eager to see more cross-institutional partnerships. For example, the Lumina Foundation recently sponsored a project titled "Building Student Success Knowledge Infrastructures Collaboratively" led by a partnership between Prairie View

---

[32] For more information, see https://www.utrgv.edu/tmac/services/more-services/index.htm, accessed October 2018.

[33] For more information, see https://www.southtexascollege.edu/grants/trsda/, accessed October 2018.

BOX 5-10
SBIR and STTR Awards[a]

The Small Business Innovation Research (SBIR) program, one of the largest examples of a U.S. public-private partnership, was authorized by Congress in the Small Business Innovation Development Act of 1982. Participation can spur a cyclic process for the growth of an MSI's larger STEM portfolio. Obtaining SBIR/STTR funding contributes to the development of innovation, expands the number of faculty and students involved in cutting-edge research, and fosters credibility for a given MSI's larger capabilities. It should be noted, however, that competition for funding is great.

Small Business Innovation Research Awards

The SBIR program has four primary objectives: (1) stimulate technical innovation, (2) use small businesses to meet federal research and development needs, (3) *foster and encourage participation by minority and disadvantaged persons in technological innovation*, and (4) increase private-sector commercialization of innovations derived from federal research and development (R&D). Congress requires federal agencies with R&D budgets in excess of $100 million to set aside 3.2 percent of their funds for SBIR programs. Given the program's objectives to support minorities in research and its significant funding capacity, MSIs are an underutilized resource of talent to contribute to the success of this program and to the innovations produced through it.

Small Business Technology Transfer Awards

The STTR program, an integral component of SBIR, is another promising practice for the MSI community. The STTR requires small business recipients to collaborate formally with nonprofit research institutions. The five largest federal research agencies participate in the STTR program are DoD, DOE, NASA, NIH, and NSF.

Participating Agencies

At the time of this report, 11 federal agencies participate in the SBIR program: Department of Agriculture, Department of Commerce, DoD, Department of Education, DOE, Department of Health and Human Services, Department of Homeland Security, Department of Transportation, Environmental Protection Agency, NASA, and NSF. Likewise, at the time of this report, 5 federal agencies participate in the STTR program: DoD, DOE, NASA, NIH, and NSF.

SOURCES: NASEM (2015c, 2016).
[a] See https://www.sbir.gov/about/.

A&M and the University of Texas-El Paso.[34] The Association of Public and Land Grant Universities, VentureWell, the U.S. Patent and Trademark Office, and the

---

[34] For more information, see https://hbculifestyle.com/collaborating-black-colleges/, accessed October 2018.

United Negro College Fund have come together to sponsor an initiative called the HBCU Collaborative. The collaborative is a cohort of 15 HBCUs participating in a multiyear project to encourage the creation of more government and industry partnerships to foster innovation, commercialization, and entrepreneurship.[35] The NIH-funded BUILD program also is set up to facilitate collaboration and partnerships among research-intensive and pipeline institutions. (See Box 5-8 for additional details on this program.) Characteristic of sustainable partnerships more generally, both types of institutions should see benefit for themselves and their students in order for the collaborations to thrive.

Nonprofit and Disciplinary/Professional Society Partnerships

Nonprofit organizations and professional, scientific, or honor societies can serve as advocates for MSIs and their students in a number of capacities, including their ability to connect them with local, regional, and national employers. Partnerships between advocacy organizations, MSIs, and the STEM workforce help to establish new scholarships, cooperative educational opportunities, and/or employment after graduation. At the very least, these partnerships may help to encourage students' continued participation in STEM fields. Examples include efforts of the NSBE, as described previously, and Advancing Minorities Interest in Engineering, a nonprofit organization invested in helping establish and expand alliances with government, industry, and academic partners to support programs that advance minorities' interest in engineering.[36]

The Hispanic Association of Colleges and Universities (HACU) is an example of a membership organization that represents colleges and universities committed to improving access to and the quality of postsecondary educational opportunities for Hispanic students.[37] HACU serves as an advocate for HSIs and their stakeholders on regional-, state-, and federal-level issues, conducts public policy analyses and research on matters that impact higher educational success for Hispanic students, hosts technical assistance workshops on available federal grant and capacity-building opportunities, and offers numerous internships, scholarships, college support programs, and career development opportunities for HSI students.

The American Indian College Fund (AICF) aims to boost Native American college completion rates through scholarships, research, and advocacy.[38] Scholarship recipients are encouraged to remain connected to the fund and to each other through the Circle of Scholars alumni program. AICF also recognizes the need to communicate with funders and policy makers by strengthening data collection

---

[35] For more information, see http://www.aplu.org/projects-and-initiatives/access-and-diversity/hbcu-innovation-commercialization-and-entrepreneurship/index.html, accessed October 2018.

[36] For more information, see https://www.amiepartnerships.org/, accessed October 2018.

[37] For more information, see https://www.hacu.net/hacu/HACU_101.asp, accessed October 2018.

[38] For more information, see https://collegefund.org/about-us/, accessed October 2018.

and analysis on American Indian student progress, including their fields of study, graduation rates, and representation at different colleges and universities.

The SDSU Research Foundation (SDSURF) illustrates another example of a university-nonprofit partnership. SDSURF is a nonprofit, auxiliary organization dedicated to assisting and advancing the research mission of SDSU through the administration of grants and contracts. As a tax-exempt organization, SDSURF has additional flexibility to raise and manage private funds that can be invested in a more diversified, and less restricted, manner. SDSURF supports the educational, research, and community service objectives of SDSU by developing faculty researchers, procuring new research opportunities, and engaging students in research projects, with the ultimate goal of increasing the overall research project portfolio.[39]

Private foundations represent another area of engagement for MSIs. Administrators from several of the committee's site visits spoke about building strategic relationships with organizations that see the value of diversifying the future workforce and who are launching initiatives to help achieve this goal, including the American Indian Policy Institute, the Carnegie Foundation, the United Negro College Fund, and the Thurgood Marshall College Fund, to name a few.

CHAPTER SUMMARY

The committee commissioned a literature search, conducted site visits, and sought other input to determine evidence-based strategies that support STEM students of color at MSIs. However, this proved a challenge, with self-reported data, surveys, and case studies the most frequently found when any evaluations took place at all. A lack of programmatic evaluations may be a consequence of several factors, including insufficient programmatic funds, overall lack of resources, personnel, and capacity, and the overall challenge to evaluate long-standing national programs as a collective. Funders and policy makers understandably seek this evidence when making resource and other decisions, leading the committee to conclude that building this knowledge base is a priority that merits a recommendation. (See Chapter 6 for the committee's recommendations to public and private funders to support the evaluation of MSIs and the effective strategies and promising programs they use to support their students.)

The evidence that does exist led the committee to identify *intentionality* as an important element of MSI success: ensuring that programs, practices, and policies are tailored to recognize and address student needs with cultural awareness. Students of color, particularly those in STEM fields, benefit from strategies grounded in intentionality and that enhance mission-driven leadership, promote institutional responsiveness, offer a culturally supportive campus climate, pro-

---

[39] For more information, see https://www.foundation.sdsu.edu/about_index.html, accessed October 2018.

vide easily accessible academic and student supports, offer sustained mentorship and sponsorship, create authentic research experiences, and seek opportunities through partnerships with the public, private, and nonprofit sectors. The committee's recommendations to support current and bolster future efforts to implement these strategies are presented in Chapter 6.

REFERENCES

Aikens, Melissa L., Melissa M. Robertson, Sona Sadselia, Keiana Watkins, Mara Evans, Christopher R. Runyon, Lillian T. Eby, and Erin L. Dolan. 2017. "Race and gender differences in undergraduate research mentoring structures and research outcomes." *CBE Life Sciences Education* 16 (2). doi: 10.1187/cbe.16-07-0211.

AIR (American Institutes for Research). 2012. Broadening Participation in STEM: A Call to Action. Available at: https://www.air.org/sites/default/files/downloads/report/Broadening_Participation_in_STEM_Feb14_2013_0.pdf. Accessed September 2018.

Alexander, Baine B., Julie Foertsch, and Susan Daffinrud. 1998. The Spend a Summer with a Scientist Program: An Evaluation of Program Outcomes and the Essential Elements for Success. Madison, WI: University of Madison-Wisconsin, LEAD Center.

Alexander, Baine B., Julie Foertsch, Susan Daffinrud, and Richard Tapia. 2000. "The Spend a Summer with a Scientist (SaS) Program at Rice University: A study of program outcomes and essential elements, 1991-1997." *CUR Quarterly* 20 (3):127-133.

Allen, Walter R., Joseph O. Jewell, Kimberly A. Griffin, and De'Sha S. Wolf. 2007. "Historically Black colleges and universities: Honoring the past, engaging the present, touching the future." *The Journal of Negro Education* 76 (3):263-280.

Alvarez, Stephanie and José Luis Martínez. 2014. "La palabra, conciencia y voz: Tato Laviera and The Cosecha Voices Project at The University of Texas-Pan American." New York: CUNY: Center for Puerto Rican Studies: 204-236.

Barlow, Amy E. L., and Merna Villarejo. 2004. "Making a difference for minorities: Evaluation of an educational enrichment program." *Journal of Research in Science Teaching* 41 (9):861-881.

Bauer, Karen W., and Joan S. Bennett. 2003. "Alumni perceptions used to assess undergraduate research experience." *The Journal of Higher Education* 74 (2):210-230.

Blake, Daniel. 2018. "Motivations and paths to becoming faculty at Minority Serving Institutions." *Education Sciences* 8 (1):30.

Bowles, Tyler J., and Jason Jones. 2004. "The effect of supplemental instruction on retention: A bivariate probit model." *Journal of College Student Retention: Research, Theory & Practice* 5 (4):431-437.

Bowles, Tyler J., Adam C. McCoy, and Scott C. Bates. 2008. "The effect of supplemental instruction on timely graduation." *College Student Journal* 42 (30):853.

Brock, Thomas. 2010. "Young adults and higher education: Barriers and breakthroughs to success." *The Future of Children* 20 (1):109-132.

Brown Jr., Edward E. 2011. "A multicontextual model for broadening participation in STEM related disciplines." *Online Submission* 8 (3):323-332.

Burge, Legand, Marlon Mejias, KaMar Galloway, Kinnis Gosha, and Jean Muhammad. 2017. Holistic Development of Underrepresented Students through Academic: Industry Partnerships. Paper presented at the Proceedings of the 2017 ACM SIGCSE Technical Symposium on Computer Science Education, Seattle, Washington.

Byars-Winston, Angela, Belinda Gutierrez, Sharon Topp, and Molly Carnes. 2011. "Integrating theory and practice to increase scientific workforce diversity: A framework for career development in graduate research training." *CBE Life Sciences Education* 10 (4):357-67. doi: 10.1187/cbe.10-12-0145.

Byars-Winston, Angela M., Janet Branchaw, Christine Pfund, Patrice Leverett, and Joseph New-ton. 2015. "Culturally diverse undergraduate researchers' academic outcomes and perceptions of their research mentoring relationships." *International Journal of Science Education* 37 (15):2533-2554. doi: 10.1080/09500693.2015.1085133.

Cahalan, Margaret and Laura Perna. 2015. Indicators of Higher Education Equity in the United States: 45 Year Trend Report, Washington, DC: Pell Institute for the Study of Higher Education, and Alliance for Higher Education and Graduate School of Education (GSE), PennAHEAD. Available: http://pellinstitute.org/downloads/publications-Indicators_of_Higher_Education_ Equity_in_the_US_2017_Historical_Trend_Report.pdf. Accessed October 2018.

Carlone, Heidi B., and Angela Johnson. 2007. "Understanding the science experiences of successful women of color: Science identity as an analytic lens." *Journal of Research in Science Teaching* 44 (8):1187-1218.

Carmichael, Mary C., Candace St. Clair, Andrea M. Edwards, Peter Barrett, Harris McFerrin, Ian Davenport, Mohamed Awad, Anup Kundu, and Shubha Kale Ireland. 2016. "Increasing URM undergraduate student success through assessment-driven interventions: A multiyear study using freshman-level general biology as a model system." *CBE Life Sciences Education* 15 (3). doi: 10.1187/cbe.16-01-0078.

Carpi, Anthony and Yana Mikhailova. 2003. "The Visionlearning project." *Journal of College Science Teaching* 33 (1):12.

Carpi, Anthony and Nathan. H. Lents. 2013. "Research by undergraduates helps underfinanced col-leges as well as students." *Chronicle of Higher Education* 60 (9): B30-B31.

Carpi, Anthony, Darcy M. Ronan, Heather M. Falconer, Heather H. Boyd, and Nathan H. Lents. 2013. "Development and implementation of targeted STEM retention strategies at a Hispanic-serving institution." *Journal of Hispanic Higher Education* 12 (3):280-299.

Carpi, Anthony, Darcy M. Ronan, Heather M. Falconer, and Nathan H. Lents. 2017. "Cultivating minority scientists: Undergraduate research increases self-efficacy and career ambitions for underrepresented students in STEM." *Journal of Research in Science Teaching* 54 (2):169-194.

Carrino, Stephanie Sedberry and William J. Gerace. 2016. "Why STEM learning communities work: The development of psychosocial learning factors through social interaction." *Learning Com-munities Research and Practice* 4(1), Article 3. Available at: https://washingtoncenter.evergreen. edu/lcrpjournal/vol4/iss1/3. Accessed October 2018.

Chaplot, Priyadarshini, Kathy Booth, and Rob Johnstone. 2013. Building a culture of inquiry: Using a Cycle of Exploring Research and Data to Improve Student Success. Berkeley, CA: The Research and Planning Group for California Community Colleges. Available at: www. rpgroup. org/sites/ default/files/CbD-Building. pdf. Accessed October 2018.

Chemers, Martin M., Eileen L. Zurbriggen, Moin Syed, Barbara K. Goza, and Steve Bearman. 2011. "The role of efficacy and identity in science career commitment among underrepresented minor-ity students." *Journal of Social Issues* 67 (3):469-491.

Choy, Susan P. 2002. Access & Persistence: Findings from 10 Years of Longitudinal Research on Students. ERIC Digest. Washington, DC: ERIC Clearinghouse on Higher Education.

Chun, Heejung, Merranda Romero Marin, Jonathan P. Schwartz, Andy Pham, and Sara M. Castro-Olivo. 2016. "Psychosociocultural structural model of college success among Latina/o students in Hispanic-Serving Institutions." *Journal of Diversity in Higher Education* 9 (4):385-400. doi: 10.1037/a0039881.

Clewell, Beatriz Chu (2005). Final Report on the Evaluation of the National Science Foundation Louis Stokes Alliances for Minority Participation Program. Washington, DC: The Urban Institute.

Cole, Elizabeth R., Kim A. Case, Desdamona Rios, and Nicola Curtin. 2011. "Understanding what students bring to the classroom: Moderators of the effects of diversity courses on student at-titudes." *Cultural Diversity and Ethnic Minority Psychology* 17 (4):397.

Commodore, Felecia, Marybeth Gasman, and Clifton F. Conrad. 2018. "WE OVER ME: Servant leadership, teamwork, and the success of Paul Quinn College." In Models of Success: How Historically Black Colleges and Universities Survive the Economic Recession, edited by Shametrice Davis, Walter M. Kimbrough. Charlotte, NC: Information Age Publishing, Inc.

Congos, Dennis H. 2002. "How supplemental instruction stacks up against Arthur Chickering's 7 principles for good practice in undergraduate education." Research and Teaching in Developmental Education 19 (1):75-83.

Conrad, Clifton and Marybeth Gasman. 2015. Educating a Diverse Nation. Cambridge, MA: Harvard University Press.

Crawford, Isaiah, Yolanda Suarez-Balcazar, Jill Reich, Anne Figert, and Philip Nyden. 1996. "The use of research participation for mentoring prospective minority graduate students." Teaching Sociology 24 (3): 256-263.

Crockett, Elahé T. 2014. "A research education program model to prepare a highly qualified workforce in biomedical and health-related research and increase diversity." BMC Medical Education 14:202. doi: 10.1186/1472-6920-14-202.

Cuellar, Marcela. 2014. "The impact of Hispanic-Serving Institutions (HSIs), emerging HSIs, and non-HSIs on Latina/o academic self-concept." The Review of Higher Education 37 (4):499-530.

Daniels, Heather, Sara E. Grineski, Timothy W. Collins, Danielle X. Morales, Osvaldo Morera, and Lourdes Echegoyen. 2016. "Factors influencing student gains from undergraduate research experiences at a Hispanic-Serving Institution." CBE Life Sciences Education 15 (3). doi: 10.1187/cbe.15-07-0163.

Dowd, Alicia C., and Estela Mara Bensimon. 2015. Engaging the "race question": Accountability and equity in U.S. higher education. New York: Teachers College Press.

Drew, Jennifer C., Monika W. Oli, Kelly C. Rice, Alexandria N. Ardissone, Sebastian Galindo-Gonzalez, Pablo R. Sacasa, Heather J. Belmont, Allen F. Wysocki, Mark Rieger, and Eric W. Triplett. 2015. "Development of a distance education program by a Land-Grant University augments the 2-year to 4-year STEM pipeline and increases diversity in STEM." PLoS One 10 (4):e0119548. doi:10.1371/journal.pone.0119548.

Drew, Jennifer C., Sebastian Galindo-Gonzalez, Alexandria N. Ardissone, and Eric W. Triplett. 2016. "Broadening participation of women and underrepresented minorities in STEM through a hybrid online transfer program." CBE Life Sciences Education 15 (3). doi: 10.1187/cbe.16-01-0065.

Eagan Jr., M. Kevin, Sylvia Hurtado, Mitchell J. Chang, Gina A. Garcia, Felisha A. Herrera, and Juan C. Garibay. 2013. "Making a difference in science education: The impact of undergraduate research programs." American Education Research Journal 50 (4):683-713. doi: 10.3102/0002831213482038.

Eby, Lillian T., Jean E. Rhodes, and Tammy D. Allen. 2007. "Definition and evolution of mentoring." The Blackwell handbook of mentoring: A multiple perspectives approach (pp. 7-20). Malden, MA: Blackwell Publishing.

Engle, Jennifer and Colleen O'Brien. 2007. "Demography Is Not Destiny: Increasing the Graduation Rates of Low-Income College Students at Large Public Universities." Pell Institute for the Study of Opportunity in Higher Education.

Espinosa, Lorelle L. 2011. "Pipelines and pathways: Women of color in undergraduate STEM majors and the college experiences that contribute to persistence." Harvard Educational Review 81 (2):209-240. doi: 10.17763/haer.81.2.92315ww157656k3u.

Espinosa, Lorelle L., Jennifer R. Crandall, and Malika Tukibayeva. 2014. Rankings, Institutional Behavior, and College and University Choice: Framing the National Dialogue on Obama's Ratings Plan. Washington, DC: American Council on Education.

Esters, Levon T., Amanda Washington, Marybeth Gasman, Felecia Commodore, Briana O'Neal, Sydney Freeman, Courtney Carter, and Chris D. Jimenez. 2016. Effective Leadership: A Toolkit for the 21st-Century Historically Black College and University President. University of Pennsylvania's Center for Minority-Serving Institutions. Available: https://cmsi.gse.upenn.edu/sites/default/files/MSI_LdrshpRprt_R3.pdf. Accessed October 2018.

Farquharson, Edward, Clemencia Torres de Mästle, E. R. Yescombe, and Javier Encinas. 2011. How to Engage with the Private Sector in Public-Private Partnerships in Emerging Markets. Washington, DC: World Bank. Available: https://ppiaf.org/documents/16. Accessed October 2018.

Felder, Richard M., and Rebecca Brent. 2016. Teaching and Learning STEM: A Practical Guide. Hoboken, NJ: John Wiley and Sons.

Flores, Stella. M., and Toby. J. Park. 2013. "Race, ethnicity, and college success: Examining the continued significance of the Minority-Serving Institution." *Educational Researcher* 42 (3):115-128. doi: 10.3102/0013189x13478978.

Freeman, Kassie. 2005. African Americans and College Choice: The Influence of Family and School. Albany, NY: SUNY Press.

Fullilove, Robert E., and Philip Uri Treisman. 1990. "Mathematics achievement among African American undergraduates at the University of California, Berkeley: An evaluation of the mathematics workshop program." *The Journal of Negro Education* 59 (3):463-478.

Gainen, Joanne. 1995. "Barriers to success in quantitative gatekeeper courses." *New Directions for Teaching and Learning* 1995 (61):5-14.

Gallup, Inc. 2018. "Measuring what matters: Examining the success of Achieving the Dream Network college associates in world and life." Washington, DC. Available at: http://www.achievingthedream.org/resource/17278/measuring-what-matters-examining-the-success-of-achieving-the-dream-network-college-graduates-in-work-and-life. Accessed September 2018.

Garcia, Gina A., and Otgonjargal Okhidoi. 2015. "Culturally relevant practices that 'serve' students at a Hispanic Serving Institution." *Innovative Higher Education* 40 (4):345-357.

García, Ofelia, Susana Ibarra Johnson, and Kate Seltzer. 2017. The Translanguaging Classroom: Leveraging Student Bilingualism for Learning. Philadelphia, PA: Caslon.

Gasiewski, Josephine A., M. Kevin Eagan, Gina A. Garcia, Sylvia Hurtado, and Mitchell J. Chang. 2012. "From gatekeeping to engagement: A multicontextual, mixed method study of student academic engagement in itroductory STEM courses." *Research in Higher Education* 53 (2):229-261. doi: 10.1007/s11162-011-9247-y.

Gasman, Marybeth, and Clifton F. Conrad. 2013. Minority Serving Institutions: Educating All Students. Philadelphia, PA: Penn Center for Minority Serving Institutions, Graduate School of Education, University of Pennsylvania.

Gasman, Marybeth, and Thai-Huy Nguyen. 2016. Historically Black Colleges and Universities as Leaders in STEM. University of Pennsylvania's Center for Minority-Serving Institutions. Available at: https://cmsi.gse.upenn.edu/sites/default/files/MSI_HemsleyReport_final_0.pdf. Accessed September 2018.

Gasman, Marybeth, Thai-Huy Nguyen, Clifton F. Conrad, Todd Lundberg, and Felecia Commodore. 2017. "Black male success in STEM: A case study of Morehouse College." *Journal of Diversity in Higher Education* 10 (2):181-200. doi: 10.1037/dhe0000013.

Ghee, Medeva, Micere Keels, Deborah Collins, Cynthia Neal-Spence, and Earnestine Baker. 2016. "Fine-tuning summer research programs to promote underrepresented students' persistence in the STEM pathway." *CBE Life Sciences Education* 15 (3):ar28. doi: 10.1187/cbe.16-01-0046.

Godreau, Isar, Jannette Gavillán-Suárez, Mariluz Franco-Ortiz, José M Calderón-Squiabro, Vionex Marti, and Jessica Gaspar-Concepción. 2015. "Growing faculty research for students' success: Best practices of a research institute at a Minority-Serving Undergraduate Institution." *Journal of Research Administration* 46 (2):55.

Google. 2018. Google Diversity Annual Report. Available: https://static.googleusercontent.com/media/diversity.google/en//static/pdf/Google_Diversity_annual_report_2018.pdf. Accessed October 2018.

Gregerman, Sandra R., Jennifer S. Lerner, William von Hippel, John Jonides, and Biren A. Nagda. 1998. "Undergraduate student-faculty research partnerships affect student retention." *The Review of Higher Education* 22 (1):55-72.

Griffin, Kimberly A., David Perez, Annie P. E. Holmes, and Claude E. P. Mayo. 2010. "Investing in the future: The importance of faculty mentoring in the development of students of color in STEM." *New Directions for Institutional Research* 2010:(148):95-103.

Gupta, Nayanee, Brian J. Sergi, Emma D. Tran, Rashida Nek, and Susannah V. Howieson. 2014. Research collaborations between universities and Department of Defense laboratories. IDA Science and Technology Policy Institute, Washington.

Habrowski, F. A., III and K.I. Maton. 2009. Change Institutional Culture, and You Change Who Goes into Science. *Academe* 95(3):11-15. May-Jun 2009.

Haeger, Heather and Carla Fresquez. 2016. "Mentoring for inclusion: The impact of mentoring on undergraduate researchers in the sciences." *CBE Life Sciences Education* 15(3). doi: 10.1187/cbe.16-01-0016.

Hanover Research. 2014. Early Alert Systems in Higher Education. Available at: https://www.hanoverresearch.com/wp-content/uploads/2017/08/Early-Alert-Systems-in-Higher-Education.pdf. Accessed September 2018.

Harrington, Melissa A., Andrew Lloyd, Tomasz Smolinski, and Mazen Shahin. 2016. "Closing the gap: First year success in college mathematics at an HBCU." *Journal of the Scholarship of Teaching and Learning* 16 (5):92-106.

Hathaway, Russel S., Biren A. Nagda, and Sandra R. Gregerman. 2002. "The relationship of undergraduate research participation to graduate and professional education pursuit: An empirical study." *Journal of College Student Development* 43 (5):614-631.

Hewlett, Sylvia A. 2013. Forget a Mentor, Find a Sponsor. Boston, MA: Harvard Business School Publishing.

Hodge-Clark, Kristen. 2017. Strengthening HBCU Governance and Leadership. Association of Governing Boards of Universities and Colleges. Available at: https://www.agb.org/sites/default/files/report_2017_strengthening_hbcu.pdf. Accessed September 2018.

Horn, Laura J., and C. Dennis Carroll. 1996. Nontraditional Undergraduates: Trends in Enrollment from 1986 to 1992 and Persistence and Attainment among 1989-90 Beginning Postsecondary Students. Postsecondary Education Descriptive Analysis Reports. Statistical Analysis Report: ERIC.

Hubbard, Steven M., and Frances K. Stage. 2009. "Attitudes, perceptions, and preferences of faculty at hispanic serving and predominantly Black institutions." *Journal of Higher Education* 80 (3):270-+. doi: DOI 10.1353/jhe.0.0049.

Hubbard, Steven M., and Frances K. Stage. 2010. "Identifying comprehensive public institutions that develop minority scientists." *New Directions for Institutional Research* 2010 (148):53-62.

Hunter, AnneBarrie, Sandra L. Laursen, and Elaine Seymour. 2007. "Becoming a scientist: The role of undergraduate research in students' cognitive, personal, and professional development." *Science Education* 91 (1):36-74.

Hurtado, Sylvia, Nolan L. Cabrera, Monica H. Lin, Lucy Arellano, and Lorelle L. Espinosa. 2009. "Diversifying science: Underrepresented student experiences in structured research programs." *Research in Higher Education* 50 (2):189-214. doi: 10.1007/s11162-008-9114-7.

Hurtado, Sylvia, M. Kevin Eagan, Minh C. Tran, Christopher B. Newman, Mitchell J. Chang, and Paolo Velasco. 2011. "'We do science here': Underrepresented students' interactions with faculty in different college contexts." *Journal of Social Issues* 67 (3):553-579.

Hurtado, Sylvia, Adriana Ruiz Alvarado, and Chelsea Guillermo-Wann. 2015. "Thinking about race: The salience of racial identity at two-and four-year colleges and the climate for diversity." *The Journal of Higher Education* 86 (1):127-155.

Hurtado, Sylvia, Damani White-Lewis, and Keith Norris. 2017. "Advancing inclusive science and systemic change: The convergence of national aims and institutional goals in implementing and assessing biomedical science training." *BMC Proceedings* 11 (12):17. doi 10.1186/s12919-0086-5.

Jones, Brett D., Marie C. Paretti, Serge F. Hein, and Tamara W. Knott. 2010. "An analysis of motivation constructs with first-year engineering students: Relationships among expectancies, values, achievement, and career plans." *Journal of Engineering Education* 99 (4):319-336.

Kezar, Adrianna and Elizabeth Holcombe. 2016. "Institutional transformation in STEM: Insights from change research and the Keck-PKAL project." In G. C. Weaver, W. D. Burgess, A. L. Childress, and L. Slakey (Eds.), Transforming Institutions: Undergraduate STEM Education for the 21st Century (pp. 67–74). West Lafayette: Purdue University Press.

Kim, Mikyong Minsun. 2002. "Historically Black vs. White institutions: Academic development among Black students." *The Review of Higher Education* 25 (4):385-407.

Kim, Mikyong Minsun, and Clifton F. Conrad. 2006. "The impact of Historically Black Colleges and Universities on the academic success of African-American students." *Research in Higher Education* 47 (4):399-427. doi: 10.1007/s11162-005-9001-4.

Kim, Young K., and Linda J. Sax. 2018. "The effect of positive faculty support on mathematical self-concept for male and female students in STEM majors." *Research in Higher Education* 50 (8):1074-1104.

LaVallie, Audrey, Eakalak Khan, and G. Padmanabham. 2013. Impact of a Research Experience Program on North Dakota Tribal College STEM Student Retention. Presented at the 2013 ASEE North Midwest Section Conference, Oct. 17-18, 2013, Fargo, ND. (Presented by A. LaVallie) Available at: http://whavenlabs.com/ASEEConference/html/papers/ASEE-NMWSC2013-0004.pdf. Accessed October 2018.

Locks, Angela M., Sylvia Hurtado, Nicholas A. Bowman, and Leticia Oseguera. 2008. "Extending notions of campus climate and diversity to students' transition to college." *The Review of Higher Education* 31 (3):257-285.

Lopatto, David. 2004. "Survey of undergraduate research experiences (SURE): First findings." *Cell Biology Education* 3 (4):270-277.

Lopatto, David. 2007. "Undergraduate research experiences support science career decisions and active learning." *CBE Life Sciences Education* 6 (4):297-306. doi: 10.1187/cbe.07-06-0039.

Maton, Kenneth I and Freeman A Hrabowski III. 2004. "Increasing the number of African American PhDs in the sciences and engineering a strengths-based approach." *American Psychologist* 59 (6):547.

Maton, Kenneth I., Freeman A. Hrabowski III, and Carol L. Schmitt. 2000. "African American college students excelling in the sciences: College and postcollege outcomes in the Meyerhoff Scholars Program." *Journal of Research in Science Teaching. The Official Journal of the National Association for Research in Science Teaching* 37 (7):629-654.

Maton, Kenneth I., Shauna A. Pollard, Tatiana V. McDougall Weise, and Freeman A. Hrabowski III. 2012. "Meyerhoff Scholars Program: A strengths-based, institution-wide approach to increasing diversity in science, technology, engineering, and mathematics." *Mount Sinai Journal of Medicine* 79 (5):610-23. doi: 10.1002/msj.21341.

Maton, K. I., Beason, T. S., Godsay, S., Sto Domingo, M. R., Bailey, T. C., Sun, S., & Hrabowski, F. A. 2016. Outcomes and Processes in the Meyerhoff Scholars Program: STEM PhD Completion, Sense of Community, Perceived Program Benefit, Science Identity, and Research Self-Efficacy. *CBE Life Sciences Education*, 15(3), p ii.

May, Gary S., and Daryl E. Chubin. 2003. "A retrospective on undergraduate engineering success for underrepresented minority students." *Journal of Engineering Education* 92 (1):27-39. doi: 10.1002/j.2168-9830.2003.tb00735.x.

McDonough, Patricia M., Anthony Lising Antonio, and James W. Trent. 1997. "Black students, Black colleges: An African American college choice model." *Journal for a Just and Caring Education* 3 (1):9-36.

Meling, Vanessa Bogran, Lori Kupczynski, Marie-Anne Mundy, and Mary E. Green. 2012. "The role of supplemental instruction in success and retention in math courses at a Hispanic-Serving Institution." *Business Education Innovation Journal* 4 (2).

Meling, Vanessa B., Marie-Anne Mundy, Lori Kupczynski, and Mary E. Green. 2013. "Supplemental instruction and academic success and retention in science courses at a Hispanic-serving institution." *World Journal of Education* 3 (3):11.

Merisotis, Jamie P., and Arnold M. Kee. 2006. "A model of success: The Model Institutions for Excellence Program's decade of leadership in STEM education." *Journal of Hispanic Higher Education* 5 (3):288-308.

Merriweather, Samuel Paul, Harriet A. Lamm, Shannon D. Walton, Karen L. Butler-Purry, Judy Kelley, Krystal E. Thomasson, John David Rausch Jr., Frank Pezold, and Kendall T. Harris. 2017. "TAMUS LSAMP Project: 25 Years of Success-Finding and Implementing Best Practices for URM STEM Students." 2017 ASEE Annual Conference & Exposition. Available at: sing url: https://www.asee.org/public/conferences/78/papers/18491/view. Accessed October 2018.

Mosina, N. 2014. "Using Wiki-Based Discussion Forums in Calculus:E-Pathway Toward Improving Students," Retention and Learning in STEM Gateway Courses. ISEC 2014. 4th IEEE Integral STEM Education Conference.

Murphy, Terrence E., Monica Gaughan, Robert Hume, and S. Gordon Moore Jr. 2010. "College graduation rates for minority students in a selective technical university: Will participation in a summer Bridge Program Contribute to Success?" *Education Evaluation and Policy Analysis* 32 (1):70-83. doi: 10.3102/0162373709360064.

Museus, Samuel D., Robert T. Palmer, Ryan J. Davis, and Dina Maramba. 2011. "Factors that influence success among racial and ethnic minority college students in the STEM circuit." *ASHE Higher Education Report* 36 (6):53-84.

Museus, Samuel D., and Uma M. Jayakumar. 2011. Creating Campus Cultures: Fostering Success Among Racially Diverse Student Populations. New York, NY: Routledge.

NAS, NAE, and IOM (National Academy of Sciences, National Academy of Engineering, and The Institute of Medicine). 2011. Expanding Underrepresented Minority Participation: America's Science and Technology Talent at the Crossroads. Washington, DC: The National Academies Press https://doi.org/10.17225/12984.

NASEM (National Academies of Sciences, Engineering, and Medicine). 2015a. Integrating Discovery-Based Research into the Undergraduate Curriculum: Report of a Convocation. Washington, DC: The National Academies Press. https://doi.org//10.17226/21851.

NASEM. 2015b. Innovation, Diversity, and the SBIR/STTR Programs: Summary of a Workshop. Washington, DC: The National Academies Press. https:// doi.org//10.17226/21738.

NASEM. 2015c. SBIR at the National Science Foundation. Washington, DC: The National Academies Press. https://doi.org/10.17226/18944.

NASEM. 2016. STTR: An Assessment of the Small Business Technology Transfer Program. Washington DC: The National Academies Press. https://doi.org/10.17226/21826.

NASEM. 2017a. Supporting Students' College Success: The Role of Assessment of Intrapersonal and Interpersonal Competencies. Washington, DC: The National Academies Press. https://doi.org/10.17226/24697.

NASEM. 2017b. Undergraduate Research Experiences for STEM Students: Successes, Challenges, and Opportunities. Washington, DC: The National Academies Press. https://doi.or 10.17225/24622.

NASEM. 2018. The Integration of the Humanities and Arts with Sciences, Engineering, and Medicine in Higher Education. Washington, DC. The National Academies Press. https://doi.org/10.17226/24988.

Nation's Report Card. 2018a. NAEP Mathematics Report Card. Percentage at or above Proficient in NAEP Mathematics at Grade 12, by Select Student Groups: 2015. Available: https://www.nationsreportcard.gov/reading_math_g12_2015/#mathematics?grade=12. Accessed October 2018.

Nation's Report Card. 2018b. 2015 Science Assesssment. Average Scores For Twelfth-Grade Students Assessed in NAEP Science, by Selected Student Groups: 2009 and 2015. Available at: https://www.nationsreportcard.gov/science_2015/#groups?grade=12. Accessed October 2018.

Nation's Report Card. 2018c. 2014 Technology & Engineering Literacy. Achievement Levels and Scale Scores by Student Groups. Available at: https://www.nationsreportcard.gov/tel_2014/#results/overall. Accessed October 2018.

Nguyen, Thai-Huy Peter. 2015. "Exploring Historically Black College and Universities' Ethos of Racial Uplift: Stem Students' Challenges and Institutions' Practices for Cultivating Learning and Persistence in STEM." Ph.D. Dissertation. Unviersity, Pennsylvania. Available at: https://repository.upenn.edu/cgi/viewcontent.cgi?article=2915&context=edissertations. Accessed October 2018.

NRC (National Research Council). 2014. Review of Army Research Laboratory Programs for Historically Black Colleges and Universities and Minority Institutions: Washington, DC: National Academies Press. https://doi.org/10.17225/18963.

Núñez, A.-M. 2014. Counting what counts for Latinas/os and Hispanic-Serving Institutions: A federal ratings system and postsecondary access, affordability, and success. Policy brief presented to the President's Advisory Commission on Educational Excellence for Hispanics, New York, NY.

Orfield, Gary, Jongyeong Ee, and Ryan Coughlin. 2017. "New Jersey's segregated schools: Trends and paths forward." Available at: https://escholarship.org/uc/item/5x78n1bd. Accessed October 2018.

Palmer, Robert T., Dina C. Maramba, and Marybeth Gasman. 2015. Fostering Success of Ethnic and Racial Minorities in STEM. New York: Routledge.

Palmer, Robert, Dina Maramba, Andrew Arroyo, Taryn Allen, Tiffany Fountaine Boykin, eds. 2018. Effective Leadership at Minority-Serving Institutions. New York: Routledge.

Parker, Tara L. 2012. The Role of Minority-Serving Institutions in Redefining and Improving Developmental Education. Atlanta: Southern Education Foundation.

Parthenon-EY Education. 2017. Public-Private Partnerships in Higher Education: What Is Right for Your Institution? Ernst & Young. Available at: https://www.ey.com/Publication/vwLUAssets/publi-private-partnerships-in-higher-education/$File/public-private-partnerships-in-higher-education.pdf. Accessed October 2018.

PCAST (President's Council of Advisors on Science and Technology). 2012. Report to the President. Engage to Excel: Producing One Million Additional College Graduates with Degrees in Science, Technology, Engineering, and Mathematics. Executive Office of the President. Available at: https://obamawhitehouse.archives.gov/sites/default/files/microsites/ostp/pcast-engage-to-excel-final_2-25-12.pdf. Accessed October 2018.

Perkmann, Markus, Valentina Tartari, Maureen McKelvey, Erkko Autio, Anders Broström, Pablo D'Este, Riccardo Fini, et al. 2013. "Academic engagement and commercialisation: A review of the literature on university–industry relations." *Research Policy* 42 (2):423-442.

Perna, Laura, Valerie Lundy-Wagner, Noah D. Drezner, Marybeth Gasman, Susan Yoon, Enakshi Bose, and Shannon Gary. 2009. "The contribution of HBCUs to the preparation of African American women for STEM careers: A case study." *Research in Higher Education* 50(1):1-23.

Pickens, Jeffrey. 2010. "Challenges of implementing the NIH extramural associate research development award (EARDA) at a minority-serving university." *Journal of Research Administration* 41 (3):69-76.

QEM (Quality Education for Minorties Network). 2012. Promising Practices in STEM Education and Research at Institutions Supported through the National Science Foundation (NSF)'s Tribal Colleges and Universities Program (TCUP). Washington, DC: Quality Education For Minorities Network. Available at: https://qemnetwork.squarespace.com/s/TCUP-Promising-Practices-Final.pdf. Accessed October 2018.

Rochat, Angela. 2015. Fostering Empowerment: Supporting Student Success at Native American Serving, Non-Tribal Institutions. Center for Minority Serving Institutions, University of Pennsylvania. Available at: https://cmsi.gse.upenn.edu/sites/default/files/MSI_AIANrprt_R3.pdf. Accessed October 2018.

Rubel, Laurie 2017. "Equity-directed instructional practices: Beyond the dominant perspective." *Journal of Urban Mathematics Education* 10(2):66–105.

Russell, Susan H, Mary P Hancock, and James McCullough. 2007. "Benefits of undergraduate research experiences." *Science* 316 (5824):548-549.

Ryder, Jim, John Leach, and Rosalind Driver. 1999. "Undergraduate science students' images of science." *Journal of Research in Science Teaching: The Official Journal of the National Association for Research in Science Teaching* 36 (2):201-219.

Santiago, Deborah A. 2007. "Voces (Voices): A Profile of Today's Latino College Students." Excelencia in Education (NJ1).

Schexnider, Alvin J. 2013. Saving Black Colleges: Leading Change in a Complex Organization. New York: Palgrave Macmillan.

Seymour, Elaine, and Nancy M. Hewitt. 1997. Talking about Leaving. Boulder, CO. Westview Press.

Seymour, Elaine, Anne-Barrie Hunter, Sandra L. Laursen, and Tracee DeAntoni. 2004. "Establishing the benefits of research experiences for undergraduates in the sciences: First findings from a three-year study." *Science Education* 88 (4):493-534.

Slade, John, Dedra Eatmon, Katrina Staley, and Karrie G. Dixon. 2015. "Getting into the pipeline: Summer bridge as a pathway to college success." *The Journal of Negro Education* 84 (2):125-138.

Slovacek, Simeon, Jonathan Whittinghill, Laura Flenoury, and David Wiseman. 2012. "Promoting minority success in the sciences: The minority opportunities in research programs at CSULA." *Journal of Research in Science Teaching* 49 (2):199-217. doi: 10.1002/tea.20451.

Stanton-Salazar, Ricardo. 1997. "A social capital framework for understanding the socialization of racial minority children and youths." *Harvard Educational Review* 67 (1):1-41.

Strayhorn, Terrell L. 2011. "Bridging the pipeline: Increasing underrepresented students' preparation for college through a summer bridge program." *American Behavioral Scientist* 55 (2):142-159.

Summers, Michael F. and Freeman A. Hrabowski. 2006. "Preparing minority scientists and engineers." *Science* 311 (5769):1870-1871. doi: 10.1126/science.1125257.

Tagg, John. 2003. The Learning Paradigm College. Bolton, MA: Anker Publishing Company.

Tachine, Amanda, Nolan L. Cabrera, and Elza Yellow Bird. 2017. "Home away from home: Native American students' sense of belonging during their first year in college." *The Journal of Higher Education* 88(5), 785-807.

Taniguchi, Hiromi and Gayle Kaufman. 2005. "Degree completion among nontraditional college students." *Social Science Quarterly* 86 (4):912-927.

Thao, Mao, Frances Lawrenz, Mary Brakke, Jamie Sherman, and Martin Matute. 2016. "Insights into implementing research collaborations between research-intensive universities and minority-serving institutions." *Natural Sciences Education* 45 (1).

Thiry, Heather, Sandra L. Laursen, and Anne-Barrie Hunter. 2011. "What experiences help students become scientists? A comparative study of research and other sources of personal and professional gains for STEM undergraduates." *The Journal of Higher Education* 82 (4):357-388.

Tinto, Vincent. 1993. Leaving College: Rethinking the Causes and Cures of Student Attrition. Chicago: University of Chicago Press.

Toldson, Ivory A. 2013. "Historically Black Colleges and Universities can promote leadership and excellence in STEM (Editor's Commentary). *The Journal of Negro Education* 82 (4): 359-367.

Toven-Lindsey, Brit, Marc Levis-Fitzgerald, Paul H. Barber, and Tama Hasson. 2015. "Increasing persistence in undergraduate science majors: A model for institutional support of underrepresented students." *CBE Life Sciences Education* 14 (2). doi: 10.1187/cbe.14-05-0082.

Tsui, Lisa. 2007. "Effective strategies to increase diversity in STEM fields: A review of the research literature." *The Journal of Negro Education* 76 (4):555-581.

Twigg, Carol A. 2005. Increasing Success for Underserved Students. Sarotoga Springs, NY: National Center for Academic Transformation.

U.S. Small Business Administration. 2015. SBIR/STTR 2015 Annual Report, Available at: https://www.sbir.gov/sites/default/files/FY15_SBIR-STTR_Annual_Report.pdf. Accessed September 2018.

Ushomirsky, Natasha, and David Williams. 2015. Funding Gaps 2015: Too Many States Still Spend Less on Educating Students Who Need the Most. Education Trust.

Ward, Carol, Kacey Widdison Jones, Ryan Coles, Loren Rich, Stan Knapp, and Robert Madsen. 2014. "Mentored research in a tribal college setting: The Northern Cheyenne case." *Journal of Research in Rural Education* (Online) 29 (3):1.

Washington, Nicki A., Legand Burge, Marlon Mejias, Ketly Jean-Pierre, and Qi'Anne Knox. 2015. "Improving Undergraduate Student Performance in Computer Science at Historically Black Colleges and Universities (HBCUs) through Industry Partnerships." Proceedings of the 46th ACM Technical Symposium on Computer Science Education. Association for Computing Machinery. pp. 203-206.

Whittaker, Joseph A. and Beronda L. Montgomery. 2012. "Cultivating diversity and competency in STEM: Challenges and remedies for removing virtual barriers to constructing diverse higher education communities of success." *Journal of Undergraduate Neuroscience Education* 11 (1):A44-51.

Widmar, Gary E. 1994. "Supplemental instruction: From small beginnings to a national program." *New Directions for Teaching and Learning* 1994 (60):3-10.

Wieman, Carl. 2017. Improving How Universities Teach Science: Lessons from the Science Education Initiative. Cambridge, MA: Harvard University Press.

Wilcox, Kim F., and Carol Koehler. 1996. "Supplemental Instruction: Critical Thinking and Academic Assistance." Metropolitan Universities: An International Forum.

Williams Pichon, Henrietta. 2016. "Descubriendo mi lugar: Understanding sense of belonging and community of black STEM-H students enrolled at a Hispanic serving institution." *Journal for Multicultural Education* 10 (2):135-151.

Wilson-Kennedy, Zakiya S., Margaret I. Kanipes, and Goldie S. Byrd. 2018. "Transforming STEM education through collaborative leadership at Historically Black Colleges and Universities." *CBE—Life Sciences Education* 17 (3), es13.

6

A Shift in Priorities to Support the Future STEM Workforce: Recommendations for an Impactful Change

Minority Serving Institutions (MSIs) provide a gateway to postsecondary education for millions of students of color—a population that is an increasingly critical portion of the U.S. workforce. Two-year and four-year MSIs educate nearly 30 percent of all undergraduates in the United States, yet they are often overlooked and underutilized in efforts by stakeholders to foster new programs and systems that support stronger science, technology, engineering, and mathematics (STEM) education, research and development, technology, and innovation. Our committee was charged with addressing this urgent national issue. In light of the demographics of the nation, as well as the growing complexity of STEM workforce needs in the United States and across the globe, we concluded that the nation's more than 700 MSIs are poised to bolster a well-trained, diverse, and domestic STEM-capable workforce.

As context, we provided an overview of the various types of MSIs, describing their commonalities and unique characteristics, as well as the diverse student bodies that they serve. Compared to non-MSIs, their students are more likely to be not only students of color, but also lower income and the first in their families to attend college. Many students are balancing school with jobs and family responsibilities and have different needs than historically "traditional" students. In spite of the limited resources of these students and the institutions themselves, MSIs have been successful in providing multifaceted return on investment for students, communities, and the STEM workforce. With targeted funding, attention, and support, they can contribute much more.

We have provided key findings throughout this report and showcased effective programs, practices, and strategies that bolster the success of students of color at MSIs. In reviewing the literature, in our site visits, in committee presentations, and in our own experience, we realized that many of these initiatives, such as mentoring or undergraduate research opportunities, can and should benefit *all* students. MSIs and their stakeholders can maximize the benefits when they root these initiatives in what we have defined as *intentionality*: a purposeful, culturally mindful method of engagement that targets and tailors the design, implementation, and evaluation of an effort to effectively meet the needs of its intended population of students. **Intentionality is a critical component of the seven strategies that we identified as promoting the academic success and career preparation of students at MSIs—mission-driven leadership, institutional responsiveness, a supportive campus environment, academic supports, sustained mentorship, authentic research opportunities, and meaningful public-private partnerships.**

Although there is some evidence of *what works* at MSIs, there is a lack of rigorous research on this critical topic. The need for more research and program evaluations to inform decision making is reflected in our recommendations. So, too, is our recognition that efforts to scale up promising initiatives or to promote systemic change will not be effectively realized without *intentional* and targeted funding and policy support from stakeholders of higher education and the STEM workforce, including federal and state policy makers, government agencies, business and industry, nongovernmental organizations, and professional and scientific associations. **In the recommendations outlined below, the committee challenges stakeholders to initiate a substantial, and potentially uncomfortable, shift in their thinking.** We challenge the nation's public and private investors to capitalize on the unique strengths and attributes of MSIs, and to invest in programs and strategies that equip them with the necessary resources, faculty talent, and vital infrastructure to flourish.

The committee also recognizes that this challenge to the nation carries implications for MSIs. As we urge the nation to turn to these institutions as high-priority resources for STEM talent, MSIs must continue to pursue high levels of excellence, quality, and rigor. In the recommendations below, the committee asks MSIs to take bold and innovative measures to ensure that they fully capitalize on untapped resources, and to take a critical, holistic look at their current resources and academic offerings to prioritize those that contribute most directly to students' workforce readiness in high-demand fields, as well as to their sociocultural development and preparation for active citizenship in their communities, on a national and global stage.

In that spirit, we have organized our 10 recommendations under the broad areas of *Leadership, Public and Private Partnerships, Financial Investments, Institutional Research Capacity,* and *Performance Measures.* **We ask all partners involved in this shared enterprise to approach these recommendations with a heightened sense of urgency and an ever-present focus on intentionality.** With a committed joint effort among stakeholders, MSIs and their students can bolster the nation's achievements in STEM and catapult its standing in the current global economy.

RECOMMENDATIONS

I. Cultivate a Culture of Success through Strong Leadership

Recommendation 1: MSIs have a unique opportunity—and responsibility—to design and implement policies and practices that are intentional in focus when it comes to educating and graduating students of color and those from low-income and first-generation backgrounds. Many MSIs, especially those with rich histories of serving students of color, are already demonstrating such intentionality. Others, including "emerging" MSIs, are new to this journey and are in need of culture change to serve a diverse student body.

To best support the success of their students, particularly those in STEM fields, the leadership of MSIs, including governing boards, presidents, deans, and provosts, should develop appropriate policies, infrastructure, and practices that together create a culture of intentionality upon which evidence-based, outcomes-driven programs and strategies to support student success are created and sustained.

Recommended strategies include establishing or improving

- Dynamic, multilevel, mission-driven policies that affect and guide leadership priorities—including policies that reflect a deep understanding of the relationships between investments in STEM teaching and research and the development of the next generation of STEM workers;
- Institutional responsiveness to student needs—particularly the skills and experiences needed by students entering a rapidly evolving labor market in science, engineering, computer science, and the health professions;
- Campus climates that create and support a sense of belonging for students;
- Tailored academic initiatives and social support services that promote positive learning outcomes and facilitate MSI student retention and success;
- Effective mentorship and sponsorship of students so they have access and support to pursue graduate education and careers in industry, government, academia, and the nonprofit sector;
- Undergraduate research experiences with state-of-the art equipment and facilities under the tutelage of faculty and employers who are familiar with the types of research skills needed for graduates to thrive in the STEM workplace; and

- Mutually beneficial public- and private-sector partnerships that give MSI students access to research, training, and work experiences that are rigorous and relevant.

To support the continued success, growth potential, and adaptability of these strategies, **MSIs should determine, through rigorous evaluations, the impact of promising programmatic or institutional initiatives on outcomes of success for students, faculty, and institutions, as well as their local and regional communities.** The outcomes of these evaluations may highlight marketable return on investments for current and future funders of MSIs, and reveal high-priority areas for improvement. To assist with this effort, MSIs may need to seek out partnerships with academic, government, or private industry stakeholders.

Recommendation 2: To cultivate a pipeline of forward-looking, mission-driven MSI leaders, MSIs and their stakeholders, including professional associations and university-based leadership programs, should prioritize and invest in succession planning and professional development training programs for current and future leaders of these institutions, including presidents, provosts, deans, directors, governing board members, and faculty.

Training should be evidence based, sustained, and embedded in the context and culture of the institution. The knowledge and skills obtained through these trainings should address the unique challenges and opportunities for MSIs and their student populations, and provide the skills for leadership to navigate challenging fiscal climates and other internal and external pressures.

Areas of professional development should include

- Principles and fiduciary responsibilities of institutional governance and shared leadership;
- Strategic planning and implementation to set institutional priorities that reflect the need to invest in programs that best meet the needs of students entering a rapidly evolving labor market;
- Effective principles and practices of mentorship and succession planning;
- Equity-minded leadership and cultural competency;
- Fundraising, particularly the need to position MSIs to effectively compete for STEM-focused federal grants and contracts;
- Use of data and evidence to inform and communicate institutional policy and practice, and to invest in institutional research capacity, so leaders understand their institutions' true strengths and competitive advantage, especially in STEM fields;
- Strategies and practices for establishing strong, sustainable partnerships with non-MSIs and with local, regional, and national employers;

- Effective marketing and communication of MSIs' value and contributions to local communities, the STEM workforce, and the national economy.

II. Establish New and Expand Current
Public- and Private-Sector Partnerships

Recommendation 3: Leadership from within MSIs, non-MSIs, government agencies, tribal nations, state agencies, private and corporate foundations, and professional, higher education, and scientific associations should prioritize efforts to establish new or expand current mutually beneficial and sustainable partnerships. These partnerships should support education, research, and workforce training for the nation's current and future STEM workforce.

MSIs should consider the following concrete, actionable steps:

- Prioritize partnership opportunities that leverage the institution's core assets, such as a diverse student body, committed faculty, student support infrastructure, and culture of intentionality.
- Identify potential partners' needs and effectively communicate how the institution is strategically positioned to help address these needs.
- Articulate clearly defined goals for partnerships that are aligned with institutional mission and supported by administration, faculty, and staff. A primary emphasis should be on giving MSI students access to high-quality research, mentoring, internships, and apprenticeships, on par with the nation's top-tier universities such that MSI students secure experiences in classrooms and laboratories that give them competitive pathways to graduate education and careers in STEM.
- Secure a mix of partnerships with different STEM-focused efforts at the federal, state, and regional levels, including with other institutions of higher education, local and regional employers, and tribal nations. There is potential for these partnerships to provide funding and incentives for new programs that anchor economic development efforts (e.g., business incubators, training centers, and entrepreneurial development programs) in MSI departments.
- Establish a separate program management system focused on the creation of mutually beneficial partnerships, rooted in continuous improvement methods, with designated, full-time staff to evaluate and progressively enhance those partnerships.

We also call on the business sector—which often speaks about a commitment to equity and diversity and to a highly skilled STEM workforce—to create new and expand current local, regional, and national partnerships with MSIs. Efforts should include the following:

- Create formal partnerships with MSIs. They may take the form of financial support, research capacity building, visiting faculty appointments, professional development opportunities, or other innovative initiatives that serve the interests of both the business and the MSI.
- Create work-based learning opportunities for MSI students and faculty that provide access to state-of-the-art research and laboratory experiences that reflect real-world research activities. Such internships or apprenticeships should provide hands-on, experiential learning opportunities—either on-site or on-campus but with direct involvement of business and industry leaders to provide instruction and mentorship.
- Create regional "MSI-Business-STEM Consortiums," composed of leaders from key industrial sectors such as technology, health, finance, aerospace, and others to mobilize long-term, sustainable support for greater investments in MSIs and their students. This is an opportunity for the business community, which often gives voice to diversity and inclusion, to make a tangible and real commitment to diversity, inclusion, and economic prosperity by investing in MSIs.

Non-MSIs and nongovernmental organizations, including nonprofit organizations, private foundations, and professional, higher education, and scientific associations, should collaborate with MSIs to accomplish the following:

- Fund and organize regional workshops that connect MSI leadership and research faculty with managers and grants officers from government research agencies to better understand current and future priorities in research and development, obtain best practices in proposal writing for each agency, and gain opportunities for engagement;
- Fund and organize regional consortia to provide MSIs, particularly those that are the most resource challenged, with a national platform to promote their value to the STEM workforce and national economy, and to highlight their current efforts to develop the next generation of STEM talent;
- Develop new and expand current initiatives to connect MSI STEM students with innovative research, training, apprenticeship, and workforce opportunities; and
- Create cross-sector collaborations that provide intentional and seamless STEM pathways for students who begin their education at a two-year MSI.

III. Create New and Expand Current Financial Investments

The recommendations below are directed to funding agencies and higher education stakeholders (Recommendations 4-7) and Congress (Recommendations 8 and 9).

Recommendation 4: Public and private funding agencies should continue to develop and expand grant competition programs that serve the nation's MSIs (e.g., the National Science Foundation's Hispanic Serving Institutions Program, National Institutes of Health's Research Infrastructure in Minority Institutions). **Such agencies include but are not limited to the Department of Education, Department of Energy, Department of Defense, National Aeronautics and Space Administration, National Science Foundation, National Institutes of Health, tribal nations, state agencies, private and corporate foundations, and local, regional, and national businesses.**

- Specific efforts should support the evidence-based strategies and promising programs outlined in this report and include the following:
  - Target new education, research, and capacity-building grants to MSIs that have a demonstrated commitment to enhanced research and teaching infrastructure. This includes funds to support new and modern laboratories, advanced classroom technologies, core facilities for interdisciplinary research, and work-based learning programs that encompass state-of-the-art science, engineering, and medical equipment and facilities.
  - Create or modify grant programs to implement incentives for non-MSIs to partner in mutually beneficial ways with MSIs on areas related to STEM education, research, and teaching, including the facilitation of student transfer (e.g., from two-year to four-year institutions), mentorship programs for junior faculty, and student access to graduate education.
  - Require that all newly issued grant awards have sufficient and designated funding to support rigorous evaluation of programmatic outcomes for the students, institution, and workforce. This evidence should be used to determine the scalability and sustainability of model programs.

Recommendation 5: While we recommend that stakeholders increase competitive funding for MSIs (see Recommendation 4), we also recognize that many MSIs are substantially underresourced, without the appropriate institutional research staff and grant, contract, and sponsored research offices to effectively compete for high-stakes dollars, including large, multiyear, multi-million-dollar federal grants and contracts to support STEM education and build long-term research capacity. **We recommend that public and private funding agen-**

cies (e.g., Department of Education, Department of Energy, Department of Defense, National Aeronautics and Space Administration, National Science Foundation, National Institutes of Health, state agencies, private and corporate foundations, and local, regional, and national businesses) reconsider the practicality of current competitive funding models for under-resourced MSIs.

In the face of MSIs' limited capacity, funding organizations should

- Offer "seed" or "planning" grants to MSIs that enable them to secure the resources and depth of knowledge needed to develop and/or expand their grant offices;
- Offer training programs and real-time guidance and collaboration to MSI grants officers and, even more importantly, to MSI faculty researchers so that they can master the complex grants and contracts processes and understand the requirements for an effective proposal or bid; and
- Reallocate existing funds to increase organizations' overall investments or issue new, innovative, noncompetitive, demonstration grants to MSIs to evaluate the outcomes of promising programs on campus, particularly those focused on advancing student success in STEM fields.

To build a culture of evidence and increase the institutional research infrastructure at MSIs, targeted areas of support should

- Strengthen institutional data systems that can more effectively monitor student performance, identify performance gaps and their causes, and promote data-informed solutions;
- Establish models of shared leadership whereby faculty and staff can more easily access and utilize data for decision making; and
- Recruit and hire designated, full-time staff trained in data analytics and institutional research practices.

Recommendation 6: Just as we recommend that MSI stakeholders increase investments in MSIs, we are cognizant of the current funding climate for competitive grants. Therefore, **we call upon MSI presidents and senior leadership to independently or in collaboration with local, regional, and national partners (e.g. other MSIs, non-MSIs, business, and industry) take aggressive, proactive steps to better position themselves to compete for public and private STEM research contracts and grants.**

Concerted efforts by MSIs interested in enhancing their competitiveness in STEM education should include the following actions:

- Establish partnership opportunities with other MSIs, non-MSIs, government agencies, or private industries that can provide access to or assist in the development of the necessary infrastructure to support research activities, such as core facilities or faculty oversight committees.
- Create strong, well-resourced offices of sponsored research that cultivate and maintain relationships with federal and private funders, and champion the unique added value of MSIs and their return on investment for students, communities, and the economy. To assist with this effort, MSIs may need to seek out formal or informal partnerships with academic, government, or private industry stakeholders.
- Advance efforts to seek out relevant funding agency officials and grants officers (e.g., National Institutes of Health, National Science Foundation) at conferences and professional meetings, and establish a stronger presence in Washington, DC, in order to cultivate the relationships that are often key for increasing competitiveness for grants and contracts.
- Support and incentivize professional development and training for MSI faculty and staff to acquire knowledge about the grants and acquisition processes within relevant funding agencies, and about current research on teaching and learning that will inform grant applications. This could take the form of faculty service and participation in intergovernmental personnel exchanges, such as appointments as program officers in federal research agencies, and support for faculty to attend conferences on effective teaching and learning.
- Provide educational enrichment opportunities for MSI governing boards and senior leadership to remain updated on the most effective budgetary allocation and monitoring processes to support high-level research endeavors and appropriate STEM teaching infrastructure.
- We urge university leaders to reevaluate the overall returns on investment for low-participation programs and majors on campuses, and where necessary and appropriate, reallocate certain resources to STEM disciplines and courses that support sociocultural development and preparation. These hard choices may help to advance institutional missions and more effectively train students to thrive in the local, regional, or national workforce.

Recommendation 7: To support informed decision making and strategic financial investments in MSIs, public and private funding agencies should issue new and expand current grant opportunities for evidence-based research related to MSIs. Such agencies include but are not limited to the Department of Education, National Science Foundation, National Institutes of Health, tribal nations, state agencies, private and corporate foundations, and local, regional, and national businesses.

In particular, funding agencies should solicit and support proposals that examine

- Institutional diversity within and across MSIs;
- Outcomes of success for MSIs and their students, broadly defined;
- MSIs' contributions to local, regional, and national workforces (i.e., comprehensive returns on investment);
- Unique challenges for MSIs and their students and strategies to address these challenges;
- Effective strategies to advance institutional missions; and
- Sociobehavioral and sociocultural research on the factors and conditions that moderate and mediate the implementation and efficacy of programmatic interventions at MSIs.

Recommendation 8: To more effectively measure MSIs' returns on investments, and to inform current and future public-private partnership initiatives, we urge Congress to prioritize actions to enhance clarity, transparency, and accountability for all federal investments in STEM education and research at MSIs. We recommend that short- and long-term efforts are taken.

For improvements in the short term, we recommend that Congress require all relevant federal agencies to

- Identify an MSI liaison, which would become the responsible organization or representative to coordinate activities, track investments, and report qualitative and quantitative progress toward increasing participation in STEM research and development programs;
- Produce an annual procurement forecast of opportunities including but not limited to grants, contracts, or subcontract opportunities, cooperative agreements, and other transactional agreements that will enable increased participation of MSIs in basic, applied, and advanced STEM research and development programs;
- Report on the level of participation of MSIs as prime recipients/contractors or subrecipients/subcontractors, including the type of procurement mechanisms (i.e., contracts, grants, cooperative agreements, and other transactional agreements) and the current investment totals that support STEM research and development programming;
- Categorize MSI investments and distinguish between type of investments (i.e., internships versus training grants versus basic/applied/advanced research actions);
- Track proposal submissions by MSIs (as lead investigators, principal investigators (PIs), or co-PIs) in federal contracts, grants, cooperative agreements, other transactional agreements, and Small Business Innovation Research (SBIR)/Small Business Technology Transfer (STTR) programs; and

- Participate in SBIR/STTR programs to report MSI level of participation, including metrics on level of pursuits.

For sustained, more systemic improvements, we recommend that Congress require federal agencies to produce an annual MSI STEM Research and Procurement Report that provides an account of specific investments and measurable outcomes on the institutions, faculty, students, and priorities of the national agencies. The report would distinguish between procurement vehicles (i.e., grants, contracts, cooperative agreements, GSA schedules, SBIR/STTR programs) and areas of investments (i.e., health, physical science, biological, engineering, IT/cybersecurity, homeland, aerospace/space, defense, transportation, agriculture, social sciences, natural resources and the environment, and energy). This report could serve as a critical resource for policy makers, government agencies, and MSIs to assess and benchmark the impact of national investments in underserved high-potential communities. The findings from this report may also encourage other stakeholders (e.g., major federal prime contractors, industry, and nonprofit organizations) to partner with MSIs in broader STEM research and development initiatives.

Recommendation 9: As it considers regular adjustments to federal higher education policies and programs—including, but not limited to, the reauthorization of the Higher Education Act—Congress should use the legislative process to incent greater investments in MSIs and the strategies outlined in this report to support their students. We suggest that leaders of congressional committees with oversight on higher education consider the following legislative actions:

- Significantly increase annual appropriations to support need-based aid and capacity-building funds for MSIs (e.g., Pell grant and Title III and V funding). This funding should include institutional endowment-building activities.
- Invest in new and expanded funding mechanisms that strengthen the STEM infrastructure on MSI campuses in the ways described above.
- Create and fund programs that encourage innovative teaching, learning, and laboratory experiences in STEM on MSI campuses, but that remain mindful to the guiding principle of intentionality. We further encourage the requirement that any such programs include a strong and rigorous evaluation component, and the resources required to support high-quality evaluation, to measure the impact of new initiatives on student learning and on career outcomes for STEM graduates.

IV. Improve the Assessment of MSI Performance and Accountability

Recommendation 10: In response to the growing diversity in student pathways to degree attainment, federal and state educational agencies (e.g., U.S. Department of Education and state higher education agencies and coordinating boards), state legislators, and other entities that utilize indicators of student success, including for accountability purposes, should reassess and refine current methods of measuring student outcomes to take into consideration institutional missions, faculty investment, student populations, student needs, and institutional resource constraints.

When using metrics for accountability purposes or designing performance funding models, we urge policy makers to

- Avoid an overreliance on graduation rates and other standardized metrics that fail to account for the varying educational pathways that many MSI students take. Alternatives include disaggregating success rates by enrollment intensity or expanding the time period by which students are tracked.
- Take into account diverse institutional missions, institutional resource constraints, student populations, and student needs. Whenever possible, analyses should disaggregate data on student demographics.
- Examine intermediary outcomes and institutional commitment to serving a diverse student body, such as developmental course completion, the availability of resources and opportunities that target underrepresented students, and the proportion of students of color enrolled relative to an institution's surrounding community.
- Reward institutions with a demonstrated ability to improve outcomes over time, instead of establishing performance thresholds that declare institutional "winners" and "losers."

We also urge MSI leaders and their stakeholders, including professional associations and university-based leadership program leaders, advocates, accreditation boards, and higher education researchers, to develop and support alternative metrics of success to best capture the achievements of MSIs and students (e.g., novel initiatives or partnerships to advance institutional mission, two-year institutions' transfer rates, student advancement in competencies, student income mobility, and postgraduate success).

Appendix A

Biographical Sketches for Committee Members and Staff

COMMITTEE MEMBERS

Lorelle L. Espinosa (*Co-Chair*) is the vice president for research at the American Council on Education (ACE), a national membership organization that mobilizes the higher education community to shape effective public policy and foster innovative, high-quality practice. She is responsible for developing and managing the organization's thought leadership portfolio and for ensuring a strong evidence base across ACE's myriad programs and services. Espinosa has served the higher education profession for 20 years, beginning in student affairs and undergraduate admissions at the University of California, Davis; Stanford University; and the Massachusetts Institute of Technology. Prior to ACE, she held senior roles at the Institute for Higher Education Policy and Abt Associates. Espinosa's scholarship spans a variety of issues, including race-conscious practices in selective college admissions, the role of Minority Serving Institutions in meeting 21st century educational and workforce goals, contributors to positive campus racial climate, and diversity and inclusion in the STEM disciplines. She has contributed opinion and scholarly works to peer-reviewed journals, academic volumes, and industry publications and websites, including the *Harvard Educational Review*, *Research in Higher Education*, the *Chronicle of Higher Education*, *Inside Higher Ed*, *Diverse Issues in Higher Education*, CNN.com, and HigherEdToday.org. Espinosa earned her Ph.D. in higher education and organizational change from the University of California, Los Angeles; her bachelor of arts from the University of California, Davis; and her associate of arts from Santa Barbara City College.

Kent McGuire (*Co-Chair*) is the program director of education at the William and Flora Hewlett Foundation. He leads the investments of deeper learning and open educational resources strategies, with a focus on helping all students succeed in college, work, and civic life. McGuire is a veteran of the national education movement for public education. Previously, he was the president and CEO of the Southern Education Foundation, an organization committed to advancing public education in the American South, with a focus on equity and excellence. Prior to that, he served as the dean of the College of Education at Temple University and was a tenured professor in the Department of Educational Leadership and Policy Studies. From 2001 to 2003, he was a senior vice president at the Manpower Demonstration Research Corporation, where he split his time between research projects on school reform and directing its department on education, children, and youth. He has also been an education program officer at the Pew Charitable Trusts and directed the education program at the Lilly Endowment. McGuire served as Assistant Secretary of the U.S. Department of Education from 1998 to 2001. He earned his Ph.D. in public administration from the University of Colorado, an M.A. from Columbia University Teacher's College, and a B.A. in economics from the University of Michigan. He serves on the boards of the Wallace Foundation, the Institute for Education Leadership, and the Panasonic Foundation.

Jim Bertin is the math instructor at Chief Dull Knife College, a tribally run community college that serves primarily Native students on the reservation in Billings, Montana. Bertin, a pillar of the mathematics and science community at Chief Dull Knife College, directs the Chief Dull Knife College rocket team for the NASA-supported First Nations Launch (FNL) competition. The FNL is an annual competition that offers Tribal Colleges and Universities the opportunity to demonstrate engineering and design skills through direct application in high-powered rocketry.

Anthony Carpi is associate provost and dean of research at John Jay College, CUNY. He is founder of the STEM mentoring program *PRISM*, and director of the college's Office of Student Research & Creativity. He has published extensively in the scientific and educational literature, most recently in the *Journal of Research in Science Teaching* on the impact of research experiences on the career decisions of underrepresented students in science. In 2011, he was awarded a Presidential Award for Excellence in Science, Math, and Engineering Mentoring by President Barack Obama for his work on diversifying the STEM pipeline. He is founder of the open educational STEM learning system Visionlearning (www.visionlearning.com), which provides high-quality science content to students and teachers. In his capacity as dean of research, he has overseen a doubling in the college's external grant portfolio and scholarly productivity. Carpi earned his M.S. and Ph.D. from Cornell University in environmental toxicology and obtained his B.S. in chemistry from Boston College.

Aprille J. Ericcson has held numerous positions during her 25+ year tenure with the National Aeronautics and Space Administration (NASA). In 2017, Ericsson assumed the position of new business lead for the NASA Goddard Space Flight Center (GSFC) Instrument Systems and Technology Division. Most recently, she served as the capture manager for a proposed Astrophysics mid-sized Class Explorer, called STAR-X. Prior to that proposal development, Ericsson served as the GSFC program manager for SBIR/STTR. Formerly, she served as the deputy to the chief technologist for the Applied Engineering and Technology Directorate. As an altitude control systems analyst, she developed practical control methods and analyzed structural dynamics for several space science missions. She served as a NASA HQs program executive for Earth Science, and a business executive for Space Science. As an instrument project manager she has led spaceflight instrument teams and proposal developments. Dr. Ericsson's graduate school research at Howard University was developing control methods for orbiting large space platforms such as ISS. She has served as an adjunct faculty member at several universities. Currently, she sits on technical academic boards at the National Academies, MIT, and previously at Howard University as a trustee. Ericsson has won numerous awards. The most prestigious are "The 2016 Washington Award" from the Western Society of Engineers and a 2018 "Tau Beta Pi Distinguished Alumnus" awarded by the oldest American Engineering Honor Society. Ericsson is the first female to receive a Ph.D. in mechanical engineering from Howard University and the first African-American civil servant female to receive a Ph.D. in engineering at NASA GSFC. She received her B.S. in aeronautical/astronautical engineering from MIT.

Lamont Hames is president and CEO of LMH Strategies, Inc., a Washington, DC-based leadership, management, and human systems consulting firm. He leads a team of practitioners that serve as professional advisors to clients by optimizing priorities within their organization's culture while delivering strategy, structure, and measurable outcomes-based solutions. Prior to founding LMH Strategies, Hames led business development strategy for small and medium-sized organizations within technology and higher education markets. As the former chief of staff for the NASA Office of Small Business Programs, Hames spearheaded policy and programs that emphasized inclusive participation of diverse businesses and higher education institutions in the federal marketplace. Initiatives such as its Mentor-Protégé program not only remain in place today but also have been emulated by other federal agencies and large commercial companies as a best practice. During his tenure, NASA was consistently recognized for its award-winning supplier diversity program. Hames entered public service as a presidential management fellow and worked on Capitol Hill with details on the House Small Business Committee and later with former U.S. Senator Carol Moseley-Braun (Illinois). He worked on legislation that resulted in the establishment of the woman-owned small business designation and advocating for higher education Minority Serving Institution participation in procurement, research, and development at federal agencies. Hames graduated with an M.S. in management information systems from Bowie State University in 1993.

Wesley L. Harris (NAE) is the Charles Stark Draper professor of aeronautics and astronautics and housemaster of New House Residence Hall at the Massachusetts Institute of Technology (MIT), where he was previously associate provost (2008-2013) and head of the Department of Aeronautics and Astronautics (2003-2008). Before joining MIT he was a NASA associate administrator, responsible for all programs, facilities, and personnel in aeronautics (1993-1995); vice president and chief administrative officer of the University of Tennessee Space Institute (1990-1993); and dean of the School of Engineering and professor of mechanical engineering at the University of Connecticut, Storrs (1985-1990). In his early career at MIT (1972-1985) he held several faculty and administrative positions, including professor of aeronautics and astronautics. He earned a B.S. (with honors) in aerospace engineering from the University of Virginia in 1964 and M.S. and Ph.D. degrees in aerospace and mechanical sciences from Princeton University in 1966 and 1968, respectively.

Eve J. Higginbotham (NAM) is the inaugural vice dean for inclusion and diversity of the Perelman School of Medicine at the University of Pennsylvania, a position she assumed on August 1, 2013. She is also a senior fellow at the Leonard Davis Institute for Health Economics and professor of ophthalmology at the University of Pennsylvania. She has been a member of the National Academy of Medicine (NAM) since 2000 and is now an elected member of the NAM Council, upon which she serves on the finance committee. She is the immediate past president of the AΩA Medical Honor Society. Notable prior leadership positions in academia include dean of the Morehouse School of Medicine in Atlanta, Georgia, senior vice president for Health Sciences at Howard University, and professor and chair of the Department of Ophthalmology and Visual Sciences at the University of Maryland in Baltimore, a position she held for 12 years. A graduate of MIT with undergraduate and graduate degrees in chemical engineering and Harvard Medical School, she completed her residency in ophthalmology at the Louisiana State University Eye Center and fellowship training in the subspecialty of glaucoma at the Massachusetts Eye and Ear Infirmary in Boston. Higginbotham is a current member of the Defense Health Board, advisory to the Secretary of Health Affairs of the Department of Defense; Board of Directors of Ascension of which she is secretary of the Board and a member of the Executive, Finance, and Audit Committees; member of the Board of the AΩA Medical Honor Society of which she leads the Leadership Development Committee; and member of the editorial board of the *American Journal of Ophthalmology*. She is a vice chair of the National Eye Institute-supported Ocular Hypertension Treatment Study, a randomized clinical trial, recently funded for a 20-year follow-up study of this unique cohort of patients. She is currently a member of the Association of Research in Vision and Ophthalmology, American Academy of Ophthalmology, American Clinical and Climatological Association, American Academy of Arts and Sciences, Harvard-MIT Health Sciences and Technology Advisory Board, and the Visiting Committee of the Institute of Medical Engineering and Science at MIT. Higginbotham is a former member of the Board of Overseers at Harvard University, former member of the MIT Corporation, and a former chair of the U.S. Food and Drug Administration Ophthalmic Devices Panel. She is the past president of the following organizations: the Maryland Society Eye Physicians, the Baltimore City Medical Society, and the Harvard Medical School Alumni Council. She formerly chaired her section of the National Academy of Medicine and is a former member of the NAM membership committee. Higginbotham, a practicing glaucoma specialist at the University of Pennsylvania, has authored more than 150 peer-reviewed articles and co-edited four ophthalmology textbooks. She continues to remain active in scholarship related to health policy, STEM, and patient care.

Spero M. Manson (NAM) is distinguished professor of public health and psychiatry, directs the Centers for American Indian and Alaska Native Health, occupies the Colorado Trust Chair in American Indian Health, and serves as associate dean of research in the Colorado School of Public Health at the University of Colorado Denver's Anschutz Medical Center. His programs include 10 national centers, which pursue research, program development, training, and collaboration with 250 Native communities, spanning rural, reservation, urban, and village settings across the country. Manson has acquired $250 million in sponsored research to support this work, and published more than 250 articles on the assessment, epidemiology, treatment, and prevention of physical, alcohol, drug, as well as mental health problems over the developmental life-span of Native people. His numerous awards include the American Public Health Association's prestigious Rema Lapouse Mental Health Epidemiology Award (1998), three special recognition awards from the Indian Health Service (1996, 2004, 2011), election to the Institute of Medicine (2002); two Distinguished Mentor Awards from the Gerontological Society of America (2006, 2007); the Association of American Medical Colleges' Nickens Award (2006); the George Foster Award for Excellence from the Society for Medical Anthropology (2006); the National Institutes of Health Health Disparities Award for Excellence (2008); and the Bronislaw Malinowski Award from the Society for Applied Anthropology (2019). Manson is widely acknowledged as one of the nation's leading authorities in regard to Indian and Native health. He earned his B.A. in anthropology from the University of Washington and his M.A. and Ph.D. in anthropology from the University of Minnesota. Dr. Manson is a citizen of the Pembina Chippewa tribe.

James T. Minor serves as assistant vice chancellor and senior strategist at the California State University (CSU), Office of the Chancellor. He was appointed to provide leadership and strategy to advance CSU's Graduation Initiative 2025 focused on dramatically increasing graduation rates while eliminating equity gaps between low-income and underserved students and their peers. Minor previously served as the Deputy Assistant Secretary in the Office of Postsecondary Education at the U.S. Department of Education. He was appointed by the Obama Administration to provide overall leadership and administration for federal programs designed to expand access to higher education, strengthen institutional capacity, and promote postsecondary innovation. Under his leadership, the Higher Education Program office was responsible for more than $7.5 billion in active programming across the nation and U.S. territories. He has served as director of Higher Education Programs at the Southern Education Foundation, faculty member at the Institute of Higher Education at the University of Georgia, associate professor of higher education policy at Michigan State University, and a research associate in the Pullias Center for Higher Education at the University of Southern California. His scholarly work has focused on academic governance, higher education policy, and improving institutional performance. He is also a recognized thought leader on Minority Serving Institutions, higher education policy development, and issues related to improving degree completion nationally. Minor's published articles have appeared in the *Review of Higher Education*, *Educational Researcher*, *Thought & Action*, *Academe*, *New Directions for Higher Education*, and *the American Educational Research Journal*. An author of many scholarly articles, reviews, national reports, and book chapters, he holds a B.A. from Jackson State University, an M.A. from the University of Nebraska, and a Ph.D. from the University of Wisconsin-Madison.

Leo S. Morales is chief diversity officer and professor in the School of Medicine and adjunct professor in the School of Public Health, University of Washington. He directs the Center for Health Equity, Diversity and Inclusion in the School of Medicine and co-directs the Latino Health Center in the School of Public Health. Morales conducts population research on health equity for Latino communities. He received his medical and public health degrees from the University of Washington, and the doctorate in policy analysis from the Rand Graduate School.

Anne-Marie Núñez is an associate professor of educational studies at The Ohio State University and employs sociological approaches to examine three areas in higher education: social stratification and equity, institutional diversity, and inclusive organizational cultures. More specifically, she has studied the higher education trajectories of Latino, first-generation, English Learner, working, and migrant students. In addition, her research has addressed the contributions of Hispanic-Serving Institutions (HSIs) to the U.S. higher education enterprise. More recently, she has extended her work to develop inclusive organizational cultures, with the aim of broadening participation among diverse students in science fields, including those in HSIs. Her publications have appeared in a wide range of general and specialized outlets, including top-tier journals in education such as *Educational Researcher*, *American Educational Research Journal*, and *Harvard Educational Review*. Her work has been generously funded by the National Science Foundation, Spencer Foundation, and Association for Institutional Research, among others. Her co-edited book *Hispanic-Serving Institutions: Advancing Research and Transformative Practice*, the first book to focus on HSIs as organizations, won a 2016 International Latino Book Award. In 2016, she was also recognized as an outstanding teacher, through the White House Initiative in Educational Excellence for Hispanics #LatinosTeach project. Beyond academia, her work has influenced federal policy efforts addressing students of color, Minority Serving Institutions, and the sciences, and her expertise has been featured in diverse outlets, such as *The New York Times* and the National Public Radio's show *Morning Edition*. She holds an A.B. in social studies from Harvard University, M.A. in administration, policy analysis, and evaluation from Stanford University, and an M.A. and Ph.D. in higher education and organizational change from University of California Los Angeles.

Clifton Poodry is a senior science education fellow at the Howard Hughes Medical Institutes (HHMI). Prior to joining HHMI as a senior fellow, Clifton A. Poodry was the director of the Training, Workforce Development and Diversity Division at the National Institute for General Medical Sciences (NIGMS), National Institutes of Health (NIH). He was responsible for developing and implementing NIGMS's policies and plans for research training programs and capacity-building programs that reflect NIGMS's long-standing commitment to research training and the development of a highly capable, diverse biomedical and behavioral research workforce. Poodry was a professor of biology at the University of California, Santa Cruz, where he also served in several administrative capacities. As a professor, Poodry was involved with NIH-sponsored Minority Biomedical Research Support and Minority Access to Research Careers (MARC) programs and as a director of an HHMI Undergraduate Biological Sciences program. As a program director for Developmental Biology at the National Science Foundation, Poodry developed the minority supplement initiative that was copied widely at National Science Foundation and later at NIH. Poodry is a native of the Tonawanda Seneca Indian Reservation in western New York. He earned both a B.A. and an M.A. in biology at the State University of New York at Buffalo, and received a Ph.D. in biology from Case Western Reserve University.

William Spriggs is a professor in, and former chair of, the Department of Economics at Howard University and serves as chief economist to the AFL-CIO. In his role with the AFL-CIO he chairs the Economic Policy Working Group for the Trade Union Advisory Committee to the Organization for Economic Cooperation and Development, and serves on the board of the National Bureau of Economic

Research. He is currently on the Advisory Board to the Minneapolis Federal Reserve Bank Opportunity & Inclusive Growth Institute, and on the editorial boards for *Public Administration Review* and the *Journal of the Center for Policy Analysis and Research* (of the Congressional Black Caucus Foundation). He previously served on the joint National Academy of Sciences and National Academy of Public Administration's Committee on the Fiscal Future for the United States. He was the 2016 recipient of the National Academy of Social Insurance's Robert M. Ball Award for Outstanding Achievements in Social Insurance and the 2014 NAACP Benjamin L. Hooks' Keeper of the Flame Award. From 2009 to 2012, Spriggs served as Assistant Secretary for the Office of Policy at the United States Department of Labor, having been appointed by President Barack Obama and confirmed by the U.S. Senate. At the time of his appointment, he also served as chairman of the Healthcare Trust for UAW Retirees of the Ford Motor Company and as chairman of the UAW Retirees of the Dana Corporation Health and Welfare Trust; vice chair of the Congressional Black Caucus Political Education and Leadership Institute; and on the joint National Academy of Sciences and National Academy of Public Administration's Committee on the Fiscal Future for the United States; and, as senior fellow of the Community Service Society of New York; and on the boards of the National Employment Law Project and very briefly for the Eastern Economic Association. His previous work experience includes roles leading economic policy development and research as a senior fellow and economist at the Economic Policy Institute; executive director for the Institute for Opportunity and Equality of the National Urban League; senior advisor for the Office of Government Contracting and Minority Business Development for the U.S. Small Business Administration; senior advisor and economist for the Economics and Statistics Administration of the U.S. Department of Commerce; economist for the Democratic staff of the Joint Economic Committee of Congress; and staff director for the independent, federal National Commission for Employment Policy. He is a former president of the National Economics Association, the organization of America's professional Black economists. He also taught for six years at Norfolk State University and for two years at North Carolina A&T State University. He is a member of the National Academy of Social Insurance and the National Academy of Public Administration. Spriggs graduated with a B.A. from Williams College in 1977. He received his Ph.D. in economics from the University of Wisconsin-Madison in 1984.

Victor K. Tam is currently the dean of science, technology, engineering, and mathematics (STEM) at Santa Rosa Junior College (SRJC), a two-year community college in Northern California. His professional career has been focused in community college education. He started as an assistant professor of chemistry in 2007 at Foothill College, and oversaw a STEM internship program placing community college students into research experiences at four-year institutions. In 2014, he transitioned to the position of dean of physical sciences, mathematics, and engineering. Part of his work included facilitation of a STEM Summer Camp for middle and high school students to increase interest in STEM fields. Tam assumed his current position at SRJC in 2016, and is currently working on the design of a new STEM building for the 100 year-old institution. He has served as co-PI on two different NSF S-STEM grants to address student retention and success rates, as well as career preparation for STEM majors. Tam holds a B.S. in chemistry from the University of California, Berkeley, and a M.S. and Ph.D. in chemistry from the University of California, San Diego.

Maria Cristina Villalobos holds the Myles and Sylvia Aaronson professorship in the School of Mathematical and Statistical Sciences (SMSS) at the University of Texas Rio Grande Valley (UTRGV) and is the founding director of the Center of Excellence in STEM Education, which focuses on strengthening STEM academic programs and providing resources for the academic and professional development of faculty and students, especially increasing the numbers of underrepresented students attaining STEM graduate degrees. Villalobos served as interim director of SMSS from 2015 to 2017 transitioning the school through the first two years of UTRGV. Her research areas include optimization, optimal control, and STEM education. In addition, she has been recognized at the national level for student mentoring and STEM leadership with the 2013 Distinguished Undergraduate Institution Mentor Award from the Society for the Advancement of Chicanos/ Hispanics and Native Americans in Science (SACNAS) and a 2012 HENAAC Luminary Award from the Great Minds in STEM. She is also a recipient of the 2013 University of Texas Regents' Outstanding Teaching Award and the 2016 American Association of Hispanics in Higher Education Service/Teaching Award. She also served on the SACNAS Board of Directors (2015-2017). Villalobos is a Ford Foundation fellow and Alfred P. Sloan scholar. Villalobos was born and raised in the Rio Grande Valley of Texas, is a first-generation college graduate, and received her bachelor's degree in mathematics from the University of Texas-Austin and her Ph.D. in computational and applied mathematics from Rice University in 2000.

Dorothy Cowser Yancy is president emerita of Shaw University and Johnson C. Smith University (JCSU). She retired from Shaw University on December 31, 2013, and holds the title of president emerita at both Johnson C. Smith University and Shaw University. She has been awarded Honorary Doctorates from Virginia State University, JCSU, and Shaw University. She earned certificates in management development from Harvard University and is listed as an arbitrator with the Federal Mediation and Conciliation Services, the National Mediation Board, and the American Arbitration Association. She is also a special magistrate with the Florida Public Employee Relations Commission and a senior consultant for Academic Search, Inc. She also serves as a consultant on governance, the presidency and other higher education topics. At Shaw University from 2009 to 2010, she was able to stabilize the financial state of the university, which was listed in the Toxic Asset Group of BankAmerica, by securing a $31 million federal loan. She restructured and refinanced the university's debt, balanced the budget, raised the composite financial index score to a positive number and recruited one of the largest freshmen classes in the history of the university. She retired September 2010. She arrived back at Shaw September 1, 2011, after the campus was torn apart by the April 16, 2011, tornado. By April 16, 2012, the devastation had been abated and all buildings were back in use. Yancy has earned the respect of the higher education community throughout her career. She served as a professor of history, technology and society and in the School of Management at the Georgia Institute of Technology (Atlanta) from 1972 to 1994. At Georgia Tech, she was the first African-American to be promoted and tenured as a full professor. Previously, she taught at several institutions including Albany State University, Hampton University, Evanston Township High School, and Barat College, where she was the director of the Afro-American Studies Program. Yancy was the first American to lecture at the Academy of Public Administration and Social Studies of the Small Hural in Ulan Bator, Mongolia in 1991. She has published more than 40 articles and labor arbitration cases in academic journals. She has served on many boards including the Board of Directors of Bank America of the Carolinas; Charlotte Chamber of Commerce; National Association of Independent Colleges and Universities; Council of Independent Colleges; and the Charlotte Urban League. Currently, she serves as a member of the Board of Trustees of Morehouse College and Communities in School, Atlanta, and as an individual member of the United Negro College Fund. She has received numerous awards and accolades. In 2002 she was inducted into the most prestigious honor society in the nation, the Delta of Georgia Chapter of Phi Beta Kappa, and in February 2011 she was recognized by Dominion in the "Strong Men and Women: Excellence in Leadership" series. She received the Honorary Alumni Award by the Georgia Tech Alumni Association in 2011, and in 2013 she was the recipient of the Dr. Dorothy I. Height Leadership Award from the International Salute to the Life and Legacy of Martin Luther King, Jr., Washington, DC. Dr. Yancy holds a bachelor of arts degree in history and social science from Johnson C. Smith University, a master of arts degree in history from the University of Massachusetts, Amherst, and a Ph.D. in political science from Atlanta University. She has been awarded honorary doctorates from Virginia State University, Shaw University, and JCSU.

Lance Shipman Young serves as associate professor and chair of the Department of Chemistry at Morehouse College. He has served as a visiting scientist at the Fred Hutchinson Cancer Research Center in Seattle, Washington, and as Lewis-Sigler Institute Fellow at Princeton University. Young has long been an advocate for curriculum reform geared toward more successful engagement of students in both the classroom and in the laboratory and has spearheaded several funded initiatives aimed at the total development of undergraduates in STEM.

He has served as an educational consultant for institutions seeking science education reform at the undergraduate level, including Clark Atlanta University, the University of the Virgin Islands, and North Carolina Central University, and he has extensive experience in training, development, and implementation related to Peer Led Team Learning (PLTL). Young has published several papers in the area of protein biochemistry and structural biology and, since joining the faculty at Morehouse in 2003, has mentored numerous undergraduates in his research laboratory—with the majority successfully pursuing terminal degrees in graduate and professional programs upon graduation. A graduate of Morehouse, he completed Ph.D. study at Texas A&M University and served as a FIRST postdoctoral fellow at Emory University School of Medicine.

STUDY STAFF

Leigh Miles Jackson, Ph.D., serves as the study director for the Board on Higher Education and Workforce's consensus study, *Closing the Equity Gap: Securing Our STEM Education and Workforce Readiness Infrastructure in the Nation's Minority-Serving Institutions.* Previously, Jackson worked in the Health and Medicine Division with the Board on Population Health and Public Health Practice and directed the report *The Health Effects of Cannabis and Cannabinoids: The Current State of Evidence and Recommendations for Research.* She also worked in the Division of Behavioral and Social Sciences and Education with the Board on Children, Youth, and Families and directed the report *Advancing the Power of Economic Evidence to Inform Investments in Children, Youth, and Families.* Prior to joining the National Academies, she was a developmental psychopathology and neurogenomics research fellow at Vanderbilt University, where she investigated the role of chronic sleep disturbance and specific epigenetic modifications on the health outcomes of adolescents. Jackson has a bachelor's degree in chemistry from Wake Forest University and a Ph.D. in molecular and systems pharmacology from Emory University.

Barbara Natalizio, Ph.D., was a program officer with the Board on Higher Education and Workforce at the National Academies of Science, Engineering, and Medicine. Prior to joining the Academies, she was an American Association for the Advancement of Science Science and Technology Policy Fellow serving in the Directorate for Education and Human Resources, Division of Graduate Education, at the National Science Foundation. There, she gained a comprehensive awareness of and appreciation for effective evaluation, assessment, and policy that enables her continued support of higher education reform and STEM workforce development at the national level. Dr. Natalizio received her bachelor's degree in biochemistry and history from Montclair State University and her Ph.D. in molecular genetics and microbiology from Duke University.

Irene Ngun is an associate program officer with the Board on Higher Education and Workforce at the National Academies of Sciences, Engineering, and Medicine. She also serves as associate program officer for the Committee on Women in Science, Engineering, and Medicine, a standing committee of the National Academies. Before joining the National Academies she was a congressional intern for the U.S. House Committee on Science, Space, and Technology (Democratic Office) and served briefly in the office of Congresswoman Eddie Bernice Johnson of Texas (D-33). Ngun received her M.A. from Yonsei Graduate School of International Studies (Seoul, South Korea), where she developed her interest in science policy. She received her B.A. from Goshen College in biochemistry and molecular biology and global economics.

Austen Applegate is a research associate with the Board on Higher Education and Workforce and the Committee on Women in Science, Engineering, and Medicine at the National Academies of Sciences, Engineering, and Medicine. Prior to joining the National Academies, he worked in a number of professional fields including international development, clinical research, and education. Applegate holds a B.A. from Guilford College in psychology and sociology. It was during this time he developed his interest in social science research and policy through his coursework in behavioral medicine, clinical assessment, public health, health policy, qualitative and quantitative research methodology, race and gender disparities, and social science history.

Thomas Rudin is the director of the Board on Higher Education and Workforce at the National Academies of Sciences, Engineering, and Medicine—a position he assumed in mid-August 2014. Prior to joining the Academies, Rudin served as senior vice president for career readiness and senior vice president for advocacy, government relations and development at the College Board from 2006 to 2014. He was also vice president for government relations from 2004 to 2006 and executive director of grants planning and management from 1996 to 2004 at the College Board. Before joining the College Board, Rudin was a policy analyst at the National Institutes of Health. In 1991, Rudin taught courses in U.S. public policy, human rights, and organizational management as a visiting instructor at the Middle East Technical University in Ankara, Turkey. In the early 1980s, he directed the work of the Governor's Task Force on Science and Technology for North Carolina Governor James B. Hunt, Jr., where he was involved in several new state initiatives, such as the North Carolina Biotechnology Center and the North Carolina School of Science and Mathematics. He received a bachelor of arts degree from Purdue University, and he holds master's degrees in public administration and in social work from the University of North Carolina at Chapel Hill.

BIOGRAPHICAL SKETCHES FOR CONSULTANTS

Andrés Castro Samayoa is assistant professor of higher education at the Lynch School of Education at Boston College and assistant director for assessment and senior research associate at the Penn Center for Minority Serving Institutions. Born in El Salvador, Samayoa's work seeks to improve educational experiences for students of color—specifically centering the work of Minority Serving Institutions in the postsecondary sector. His research projects focus on two inter-related lines of inquiry: one of them draws on sociohistorical perspectives on how federal policy making affects MSIs. Second, he focuses on contemporary approaches to cultivating a more equitable ethoracial representation in K-12 and postsecondary education, with a specific focus in the humanities and social sciences at Hispanic Serving Institutions. He has co-edited two books on Minority Serving Institutions: *A Primer on Minority Serving Institutions* (Routledge, in press) and *Educational Challenges at Minority Serving Institutions* (Routledge, 2017). His collaborative research has been published in *Educational Sciences, Journal of Latinos & Education, American Educational Research Journal,* and *Teachers College Record.* His work has been supported by the Andrew W. Mellon Foundation, the W.K. Kellogg Foundation, and CLAGS: The Center for LGBTQ Studies in New York City. Samayoa received his doctorate from the University of Pennsylvania's Graduate School of Education. Prior to his time at PennGSE, he completed an M.Phil. as a Gates Scholar at Cambridge University and a B.A. at Harvard University.

Marybeth Gasman is the Judy & Howard Berkowitz Professor in the Graduate School of Education at the University of Pennsylvania. Her areas of expertise include the history of American higher education, Minority Serving Institutions (with an emphasis on Historically Black Colleges and Universities), racism and diversity, fundraising and philanthropy, and higher education leadership. Gasman is the founding director of the Penn Center for Minority Serving Institutions (MSIs), which works to amplify the contributions, strengthen, and support MSIs and those scholars interested in them. She holds secondary appointments in History, Africana Studies, and the School of Social Policy and Practice. Gasman is the author or editor of 25 books, including *Educating a Diverse Nation* (Harvard University Press, 2015 with Clif Conrad), *Envisioning Black Colleges* (Johns Hopkins University Press, 2007), and *Academics Going Public* (Routledge Press, 2016). Her newest book, *Making Black Scientists* (with Thai-Huy Nguyen), is forthcoming with Harvard University Press. She has written more than 250 peer-reviewed articles, scholarly essays, and book chapters. Gasman has penned more than 450 opinion articles for the nation's newspapers and magazines and is ranked by *Education Week* as one of the 10 most influential education scholars in the nation. She has raised more than $22 million in grant funding to support her research and that of her students, mentees, and MSI partners. She serves on the board of trustees of The College Board as well as Paul Quinn College, a small, urban, Historically Black College in Dallas, Texas. She considers her proudest accomplishment to be receiving the University of Pennsylvania's Provost Award for Distinguished Ph.D. Teaching and Mentoring, serving as the dissertation chair for more than 80 doctoral students since 2003.

DeShawn Preston is a program manager for institutional effectiveness at Morehouse School of Medicine. Previously he served as SEF's Higher Education Research Fellow. He earned a Ph.D. in higher educational leadership at Clemson University, and his research agenda focuses on African American students in graduate and professional programs. He also received a policy certificate for the Strum Thurmond School of Policy. During his time at Clemson he served graduate assistantship in the Charles H. Houston Center for the Study of the Black Experience in Education. Preston also serves as a young scholar on the editorial board for the *Journal of Negro Education*. His research focuses on a number of issues pertaining to students of color in higher education. He has worked on several projects dealing with minorities students in STEM, the impact of developmental education on Black students. In addition to research, Preston considers himself to be an advocate for Historically Black Colleges and Universities. Prior to joining SEF, Preston worked as a summer intern for the White House Initiative for HBCUs. During his tenure, he was instrumental in preparing for the national 2015 HBCU conference and authored a number of blog posts on strategies for how HBCUs can optimize their use of funding opportunities offered by the federal government. He has also served as a Graduate Research Fellow for the United Negro College Fund's Frederick D. Patterson Research Institute. He holds a M.A. in American history from Howard University and a B.A. in history from Oakwood University.

Matthew Soldner currently serves as commissioner of the National Center for Education Evaluation and Regional Assistance (NCEE). Soldner was most recently a principal researcher at American Institutes for Research and is focused on postsecondary education. Soldner's expertise is the analysis and translation of federal, state, and/or institutional data to products and tools that can inform the work of postsecondary policymakers, institutional leaders, and students and their families. Areas of expertise include transitions from high school or the workforce to college; undergraduate persistence and attainment outcomes; college financing and federal student aid programs; early labor market outcomes; career and technical education (CTE) at the postsecondary level; postbaccalaureate training; and methodological issues related to the design, execution, and evaluation of sample surveys. Prior to joining AIR, Soldner was a senior technical advisor for the Department of Education's National Center for Education Statistics, providing methodological and analytic guidance on studies such as the National Postsecondary Study Aid Study, the Beginning Postsecondary Students Longitudinal Study, the Baccalaureate and Beyond Longitudinal Study, and the Integrated

Postsecondary Education Data System. His work has been presented at national conferences and published as book chapters and in journals such as the *Journal of Higher Education*, *Research in Higher Education*, and the *Journal of College Student Development*. Soldner holds a Ph.D. from the University of Maryland, College Park.

Morgan Taylor is a senior policy research analyst for the American Council on Education, where she manages research projects and analyzes quantitative and qualitative data on issues such as diversity, equity, and inclusion; Minority Serving Institutions; and institutional leadership. She also lends her expertise to matters related to higher education policy and governance. Prior to joining ACE, Taylor served as a research analyst at Excelencia in Education, where she used higher education policy, data analysis, and evidence-based institutional practices to develop reports and infographics on issues affecting Latinos in higher education. Through this work, Taylor interpreted quantitative research and data into policy, with the intention of adding a human connection to data. Taylor holds an M.P.P. in public policy from The George Washington University and a B.A. from Grand Valley State University.

Paula Whitacre is a writer and editor. She has worked with many divisions at the National Academies as an independent consultant, including Policy and Global Affairs, Behavioral and Social Sciences and Education, and Agriculture and Natural Resources. She also has provided her expertise to many other organizations involved in education, the environment, health, and international development. She is the author of *A Civil Life in an Uncivil Time* (Potomac Books, 2017) and of articles on aspects of U.S. social history. She has bachelor's and master's degrees in international studies from Johns Hopkins University.

Appendix B

Public Session Agendas

COMMITTEE MEETING

April 10, 2017

Meeting Location
The National Academies' Keck Center
Room 201
500 5th Street, NW
Washington, DC 20001

Open Session Agenda

1:00 p.m. Welcome, Introductions, and Opening Remarks
Kent McGuire, Committee Chair

1:10 p.m. • Introductory Remarks
    ◦ **Kenneth Wright**
       Policy Advisor
       Office of Science and Technology Policy
       Executive Office of the President
    ◦ **Ja'Ron K. Smith**
       Director of Urban Affairs and Revitalization Policy
       Domestic Policy Council
       Executive Office of the President

- Remarks from Sponsor Organizations
  - **Elizabeth Boylan**
    Program Director, Programs on STEM Higher Education
    Alfred P. Sloan Foundation
  - **Mary K. Blanusa**
    Program Officer, Education
    The Leona M. and Harry B. Helmsley Charitable Trust
  - **Carol S. Jimenez**
    Acting Director, Deputy Director
    Office of Minority Health
    U.S. Department of Health and Human Services

- Question and Answer Session with Committee and Sponsors
- Public Comment Period

COMMITTEE MEETING

July 17, 2017

Meeting Location
American Council on Education
One Dupont Circle NW
Washington, DC 20036
202-939-9300

9:30 a.m.   **Welcome and Introduction to Study**
Mr. Tom Rudin, Director, Board on Higher Education and
    Workforce, National Academies of Sciences, Engineering,
    and Medicine
Dr. Lorelle L. Espinosa, Committee Co-Chair
Dr. Kent McGuire, Committee Co-Chair

9:40 a.m.   **Introductory Remarks**
*The Value of Diversity in Higher Education and the
    21st Century Workforce*
Dr. Earl Lewis, President, The Andrew W. Mellon Foundation

10:00 a.m.   **PANEL 1: Current Challenges and Opportunities for MSIs**
Speakers:

- Dr. Robert Terry Palmer, Associate Professor, Howard
  University

- Chancellor Judy Miner, Chancellor, Foothill-De Anza Community College District
- Dr. Julie Park, Assistant Professor, University of Maryland, College Park
- Dr. Lee Bitsoi, Chief Diversity Officer, Stony Brook University

Moderator: Dr. Cecilia Rios Aguilar, Associate Professor, Director of the Higher Educational Research Institute, UCLA

11:00 a.m.   Q/A with audience

11:30 p.m.   Break for Lunch
(Catered lunch for committee and guest speakers)

12:30 p.m.   **PANEL 2: Innovative Programs and Strategies on MSI Campuses**

Speakers:

- Dr. Herb Schroeder, Founder, Vice Provost, Alaska Native Science and Engineering Program
- Ms. Rachael Brown, Associate Professor, STEM Accelerator Grant Professional Development Coach, South Texas College
- Dr. Wil Del Pilar, Vice President of Higher Education Policy and Practice, The Education Trust

Moderator: Dr. Anthony Carpi, Committee member

1:15 p.m.   Q/A with audience

1:45 p.m.   **PANEL 3: Partnerships with Business, Industry, Government Agencies**

Speakers:

- Mr. Derek McGowan, Program Manager, Higher Education Institutions, Global Diversity and Inclusion, Lockheed Martin
- Mr. Melvin Greer, Grant Managing Director and Senior Research Fellow, *Greer Institute* for Leadership and Innovation
- Dr. Tien Pham, Senior Campaign Scientist, Information Sciences, U.S. Army Research Laboratory
- Mr. Johnny C. Taylor, Jr., President and CEO, Thurgood Marshall Fund

Moderator: • Dr. Chad Womack, National Director, STEM Initiatives and
                  the Fund II Foundation UNCF STEM Scholars Program

2:45 p.m.   Q/A with audience

3:15 p.m.   Break

3:30 p.m.   **PANEL 4: Ensuring the Success of Minorities at MSIs
               Through Effective Public Policy**
Speakers:

               • Ms. Lezli Baskerville, President and CEO, National
                 Association for Equal Opportunity in Higher Education
               • Mr. Neil Horikoshi, President & Executive Director,
                 Asian & Pacific
               • Islander American Scholarship Fund
               • Mr. Jim Hermes, Associate Vice President of
                 Government Relations, American Association of
                 Community Colleges
               • Dr. John Moder, Senior Vice President/Chief Operating
                 Office, Hispanic Association of Colleges and Universities
               • Ms. Carrie L. Billy, President & CEO, American Indian
                 Higher Education Consortium

Moderator: Mr. Tom Rudin, Director, Board on Higher Education and
               Workforce, National Academies of Sciences, Engineering, and
               Medicine

4:30 p.m.   Q/A with audience

Appendix C

Site Visit Overview

Serving as a significant component of the committee's information-gathering efforts, from September 2017 through November 2017, a subset of committee members conducted informational site visits at nine Minority Serving Institutions (MSIs) that implement promising models, policies, practices, and/or strategies to help propel more students toward degree attainment in science, technology, engineering, and mathematics (STEM) fields and toward strong preparation for success in STEM careers. Participating MSIs were selected from a list of nominated institutions culled from discussions with key stakeholders of the study's report. Nominations were accepted from the University of Pennsylvania's Center on Minority Serving Institutions and from MSI association groups (e.g., United Negro College Fund, Hispanic Association of Colleges and Universities, American Indian Higher Education Consortium, Asian & Pacific Islander American Scholarship Fund). While it would have been valuable to visit more schools, time and financial resources required tough decisions on which institutions to visit. In the selection of sites, the committee made a conscious effort to include a diversity of perspectives represented across the different classifications of MSIs, size of institution, setting (rural, urban, etc.), and region.

Institution	Designation	Governance	Type	Location
Dillard University	HBCU	Private	Four-year	New Orleans, LA
Mission College	AANAPISI	Public	Two-year	Santa Clara, CA
Morgan State University	HBCU	Public	Four-year	Baltimore, MD
North Carolina A&T State University	HBCU	Public	Four-year	Greensboro, NC
Salish Kootenai College	TCU	Public	Four-year	Pablo, MT
San Diego State University	HSI	Public	Four-year	San Diego, CA
University of Texas Rio Grande Valley	HSI	Public	Four-year	Pharr, TX
West Los Angeles College	HSI	Public	Two-year	Culver City, CA
Xavier University	HBCU	Private	Four-year	New Orleans, LA

At each site visit, candid discussions were held with presidents, deans, provosts, faculty and staff, students, recent alumni, and community and industry partners. As a result of the open and candid discussion held during these site visits, the committee was able to collect unique data, both qualitative and quantitative in nature, on illustrative examples of long-standing models and approaches to support racial and ethnic minorities in STEM, as well as to identify examples of promising and innovative efforts that address the changing STEM landscape and future workforce needs. These data helped to inform several of the research conclusions and recommendations within this report.

Group Interview Agendas

Agenda: Morgan State University

September 11, 2017

8:15 AM	Coffee/Welcome/Brief Introductions
8:30 AM	Presentation from President of Morgan State University
9:00 AM	Discussion with Administration

9:45 AM	Meet with Faculty/Staff
10:30 AM	Tour of STEM Lab
11:00 AM	Tour of School of Computer, Mathematical, and Computer Sciences
11:15 AM	LUNCH
12:00 PM	Meet with Faculty/Staff
1:00 PM	Meet with Students and Alumni
2:30 PM	Committee Debrief

Agenda: West Los Angeles College

November 13, 2017

10:45 AM	Welcome/Introductions
11:00 AM	Committee meets with Administrators
12:30 AM	LUNCH with Faculty/Staff
1:45 AM	BREAK
2:00 PM	Meeting with Community/Industry Partners
3:15 PM	Committee meets with Students and Alumni
4:30 PM	Adjourn

Agenda: San Diego State University

September 22, 2017

8:30 AM	Coffee/Welcome/Brief Introductions
9:00 AM	Meet with Administrators
10:30 AM	BREAK
11:00 AM	Lab Tour
11:45 PM	Lunch
1:00 PM	Meet with Faculty/Staff
2:15 PM	BREAK
2:30 PM	Meet with Students and Alumni
3:45 PM	Adjourn

Agenda: Dillard University

October 10, 2017

10:15 AM	Coffee Mixer Welcome/Overview of Institution
10:30 AM	Committee meets Administrators
12:00 PM	Lunch with Faculty
1:45 PM	Meeting with Community Partners, Laboratory, STEM Facility Tour
2:30 PM	Break
2:45 PM	Meet with Students and Alumni
4:00 PM	Adjourn

Agenda: Xavier University

October 11, 2017

8:00 AM	Coffee Mixer Welcome/Brief introduction
9:00 AM	Committee meets with Administrators
9:45 AM	Brief Tour
10:15 AM	Meeting with Faculty and Staff
11:00 AM	Break
11:15 AM	Meet with Faculty and Staff
12:00 PM	Lunch Meet with Recent Alumni
1:00 PM	Break
1:30 PM	Meet with Students
2:15 PM	Meet with Faculty/Staff
3:00 PM	Adjourn

Agenda: University of Texas Rio Grande Valley

October 23, 2017

8:00 AM	Welcome/Overview of Institution
9:00 AM	Tour of Campus
10:30 AM	Meet with Administrators
11:45 AM	Break
12:00 PM	Lunch with Faculty and Staff
1:00 PM	Meet with Community Partners
2:00 PM	Break
2:15 PM	Meet with Students and Alumni
3:15	Meet with Department Chairs
4:00PM	Adjourn

Agenda: North Carolina A&T State University

November 6, 2017

10:15 AM	STEM Lab Facilities Tour
11:00 AM	Break
11:15 AM	Meet with Students
12:00 PM	Lunch with Administrators
1:00 PM	Meet with Interim Provost
1:45 PM	Break
2:00 PM	Meet with Faculty and Staff
3:00PM	Adjourn

Agenda: Mission College

November 8, 2017

9:00 AM	Coffee Mixer
9:15 AM	Committee meets Executive Cabinet
9:45 AM	STEM Leadership Team
10:45 AM	BREAK
11:00 AM	STEM Learning Center & Cisco Lab Tour
11:30 AM	Lunch (meet w/ Faculty & Staff)
12:30 PM	BREAK
12:45 PM	STEM Leadership Team
1:45 PM	Committee meets with 6-7 students/early post-docs/recent alumni
2:45 PM	Wrap-up / Adjourn

Agenda: Salish Kootenai College

November 13, 2017

8:45 AM	Welcome/Introductions
9:00 AM	Meet with Administrators
11:00 AM	Meet with STEM Faculty
12:00 PM	Lunch Meet with STEM Students
1:00 PM	Tour of Campus
2:00 PM	Meet with Other STEM Faculty
3:00 PM	Meet with "STEM Academy" Students

Sample of Site Visit Discussion Questions

<u>To Administration, Faculty, and Staff</u>

- What are some of your institution's long-standing and emergent or promising practices as it concerns outreach, recruitment, and retention of underrepresented minority students into STEM programs at your institution?
- What are some of your long-standing and/or recent best practices for facilitating the transition of underrepresented minority graduates of STEM programs at MSIs to appropriate next phases in their career trajectories?
- Where are some of the greatest challenges in sustaining and/or scaling up your successful programs or practices?
- How does the administration define "success"? How does your MSI recognize and celebrate success?
- What are some of the institutional policies that help to facilitate success for students in STEM courses?
- What are some policies that may serve as barriers to success, and how has your institution addressed those barriers?
- How are faculty members at your institution supported in their efforts to improve their teaching and enhance their research portfolio?
- How does your institution strengthen the knowledge base and experiential learning opportunities of your students (and faculty)? How might those practices be adopted or adapted by other MSIs and by all institutions?
- Can you describe efforts toward pedagogy that are helping students succeed in STEM?
- What resources would matter in enrolling more students, or if retaining the students is the objective, what resources would you need?

<u>To Students and Recent Alumni</u>

- How would you describe the culture and climate for STEM students at your MSI? Are you aware of any steps your MSI has taken to enhance the culture and climate—in STEM departments and campus-wide?
- From your perspective, how would you define "student success"?
- Do you feel that your MSI has made sufficient efforts to celebrate and honor quality and excellence among students? Do you feel that your institution sufficiently recognizes your successes?
- Does your institution promote collaboration among other STEM students? Do you, as a STEM student, sometimes feel isolated in your efforts or pathway to progress?
- Do you feel supported and appropriately mentored within this program? Has your MSI recently created new support systems and structures for the well-being of their students?

- Has your MSI developed effective and sustainable means for enabling STEM graduates to move to graduate training? To employment?

To Industry/Community Partners:

- How do you support MSIs?
- Do you find that students graduating from MSIs have the necessary skill sets to excel in your work environment? If yes, how so? If not, do you teach them?

Appendix D

Reference Links to Illustrative Examples of Promising Programs at MSIs That Support Students in STEM

Achieving the Dream (ATD)	http://www.achievingthedream.org/
Aero-Flex Pre-Apprenticeship program	https://www.sbwib.org/aero-flex
Alaska Native Science and Engineering Program (ANSEP)	http://www.ansep.net/
Aztec Mentoring Program (AMP)	https://amp.sdsu.edu/about
B3 Bilingual Program-University of Texas, Rio Grande Valley	https://www.utrgv.edu/strategic-plan/other-areas-of-focus/bilingual-bicultural-and-biliterate/index.htm
Black Scholars @ West LA College	http://www.wlac.edu/Academic/Cohort-Programs.aspx
Bridges@SDSU	http://www.scibridge.sdsu.edu/aboutBridges.html
Building Infrastructure Leading to Diversity (BUILD)	https://www.nigms.nih.gov/training/dpc/pages/build.aspx

Building on Inclusive Excellence (BIE) Hiring Program—San Diego State University	https://fa.sdsu.edu/tenure/hiring
California Guided Pathways Project	https://www.caguidedpathways.org/
Cooperative Research and Development Agreement (CRADA)	https://www.ott.nih.gov/policy/cradas
Department of Commerce's Minority Business Development Agency	https://www.mbda.gov/page/2018-mbda-broad-agency-announcement
Early Alert System—Salish Kootenai College	https://www.hanoverresearch.com/wp-content/uploads/2017/08/Early-Alert-Systems-in-Higher-Education.pdf https://www.skc.edu/student-success/
Embedded Tutoring Program—Mission College	http://missioncollege.edu/depts/academic-support/embedded_tutoring.html
ENGAGE 2BE—NC A&T State University	https://www.ncat.edu/coe/departments/caee/files/engage2be.html
Extreme Science Internships (ESI)—Morgan State University	https://www.morgan.edu/school_of_computer_mathematical_and_natural_sciences/student_programs/internships_and_fellowships/extreme_science_internships.html
Freshman Academic Success Track (FAST)—San Diego State University	http://studentaffairs.sdsu.edu/nspp/FAST/
Fund for the Improvement of Post-Secondary Education (FIPSE)	https://www2.ed.gov/about/offices/list/ope/fipse/index.html
General Services Administration-HBCU Initiative	https://osbp.nasa.gov/docs/event-presentations/2018_02/speaker/1345_GSA-and-DON_Networking-Federal-Agencies-panel-TAGGED.pdf

Global Supply Chain Diversity Program— Northrop Grumman	https://www.northropgrumman.com/suppliers/Pages/GSDP.aspx
HBCU Innovation and Entrepreneurship Collaborative	http://www.aplu.org/projects-and-initiatives/access-and-diversity/hbcu-innovation-commercialization-and-entrepreneurship/index.html
Historically Black Colleges and Universities Undergraduate Program (HBCU-UP)	https://www.nsf.gov/funding/pgm_summ.jsp?pims_id=5481
Improving Undergraduate STEM Education: Hispanic-Serving Institutions (HSI Program)	https://www.nsf.gov/funding/pgm_summ.jsp?pims_id=505512&org=NSF&more=Y
Initiative for Maximizing Student Development (IMSD)	https://www.nigms.nih.gov/Training/IMSD/Pages/default.aspx
Louis Stokes Alliances for Minority Participation (LSAMP)	https://www.nsf.gov/funding/pgm_summ.jsp?pims_id=13646
Mathematics Emporium Model (MEM)—NCT A&T State University	http://www.thencat.org/R2R/AcadPrac/CM/MathEmpFAQ.htm
Mathematics, Engineering, and Science Achievement Program (MESA/MESA CCP)	http://www.mesausa.org/
Maximizing Access to Research Careers Program (MARC)	https://www.nigms.nih.gov/Training/MARC/Pages/USTARAwards.aspx
MC²IT Innovation in Education—Mission College	http://missioncollege.edu/community/mc2it/

Minority Science and Engineering Improvement Program (MSEIP)	https://www2.ed.gov/programs/iduesmsi/index.html
MSI STEM Research and Development Consortium (MSRDC)	https://www.msrdconsortium.org/
MUREP Institutional Research Opportunities (MIRO)	https://www.nasa.gov/offices/education/programs/national/murep/home/index.html
MUREP STEM Engagement Portfolio (MSE)	https://www.nasa.gov/offices/education/programs/national/murep/home/index.html
MUREP Sustainability and Innovation Collaborative (MUSIC)	https://www.nasa.gov/offices/education/programs/national/murep/home/index.html
NASA Minority University Research and Education Activity (MUREP)	https://www.nasa.gov/offices/education/programs/national/murep/home/index.html
National Society of Black Engineers (NSBE) Integrated Pipeline Program	https://www.nsbe.org/NGIP.aspx#.W323Is5KhQI
NOAA Partnership Program with Minority-Serving Institutions (EPP/MSI)	http://www.noaa.gov/office-education/epp-msi/undergraduate-scholarship
Peer Mentoring Program XULA/PreMed Office at Xavier University	https://www.xavier.edu/peermentor/
Pre-Freshman Accelerated Curriculum in Engineering Program (PACE)—Morgan State University	https://www.atmocenter.org/pace/
Program for Research Initiatives in Science and Math (PRISM)—John Jay College, CUNY	http://prismatjjay.org/

Project LEARN (Leading & Energizing African American Students for Research and Knowledge)—West LA College	http://www.wlac.edu/ProjectLEARN/index.aspx
PUENTE Community College Program—Mission College	http://missioncollege.org/depts/puente/index.html
Research Centers in Minority Institutions (RCMI)—NIH	https://www.nimhd.nih.gov/programs/extramural/coe/rcmi.html
Research Initiative for Scientific Enhancement (RISE)	https://www.nigms.nih.gov/Training/RISE/
STEM CORE—Mission College	http://missioncollege.edu/student_services/stem/STEM_Core.html
Summer Undergraduate Research Fellowships (SURF)	https://www.nist.gov/summer-undergraduate-research-fellowship-surf
Texas Regional STEM Degree Accelerator South Texas College	https://www.southtexascollege.edu/grants/trsda/
The Center for Academic Success and Achievement (CASA) Academy Summer Bridge Program—Morgan State University	https://www.morgan.edu/enrollment_management_and_student_success/center_for_academic_success_and_achievement/casa_academy_summer_bridge_program.html
The Department of Defense Mentor-Protégé Program (MPP)	https://business.defense.gov/Programs/Mentor-Protege-Program/
The Student Mentoring and Research Training (SMART) program— University of Texas Rio Grande Valley	https://www.utrgv.edu/engaged/smart/index.htm

Train the Trainer: Preparing Mentoring and Advisors at Xavier University of Louisiana (P-Max)—Xavier University	http://www.xula.edu/build/evaluation.html
TRIO Programs	https://www2.ed.gov/about/offices/list/ope/trio/index.html
Troops to Engineers (T2E)—San Diego State University	https://www.engineering.sdsu.edu/admissions/troops_to_eng.aspx
Undergraduate Student Training in Academic Research (U-STAR)	https://www.nigms.nih.gov/Training/MARC/Pages/USTARAwards.aspx
Vision Project—free, open education STEM learning module	https://www.visionlearning.com/en/
Year-Up Los Angeles—West LA College	http://www.wlac.edu/yearup/index.aspx

Appendix E

Commissioned Literature Review

ANALYSIS OF RESEARCH PERTAINING TO UNDER
REPRESENTED MINORITIES (URMS), MINORITY
SERVING INSTITUTIONS (MSIS) AND STEM

Marybeth Gasman, University of Pennsylvania
Andrés Castro Samayoa, Boston College
Alice Ginsberg, University of Pennsylvania
Penn Center for Minority Serving Institutions

Prepared for
National Academy of Sciences Ad Hoc Committee

*Closing the Equity Gap: Securing Our STEM Education and Workforce
Readiness Infrastructure in the Nation's Minority Serving Institutions*

August 6, 2017; revised September 3, 2017; revised November 2, 2017

Search #1:
Literature Collection Strategy for Research on Under Represented Minorities (URMs) and STEM

A total of 78 articles, reports, journal articles, book chapters, dissertations, and proceedings were identified as relevant for examination in this review of the literature focused on STEM education and underrepresented minorities (URMs). The committee-directed criteria for examination in this review was as follows:

- Manuscript had to be in publication no later than 2006 (and up through 2017) and indexed in either EBSCO, ERIC, Google Scholar, ProQuest Dissertations, and/or PubMed.
- The substantive focus of the manuscript had to focus on specific practices, policies, and/or programs that were focused on supporting students' success in STEM fields.
- Reports that primarily offered an overview of enrollment/completion/ persistence and/or other broad-level aggregate data by racial/ethnic groups in STEM were excluded from inclusion.

Search terms:
"underrepresented minority" and STEM (false positives reduced by using full phrasing)

URM and STEM
"underrepresented minority" and "science, technology, engineering, and mathematics"
"underrepresented minority" and "promising practices"
"students of color" and "science, technology, engineering, and mathematics"
"Meyerhoff" and "science, technology, engineering, and mathematics"

Common Findings in Research Studies Pertaining to MSIs Across the studies, we identified three recurring themes:

- The importance of undergraduate research experience in STEM
- Peer support groups improve students' persistence
- Curricular structures affect students' persistence in STEM

Overall Assessment of Research Pertaining to URMs and STEM

A preponderance of research focused on URMs and STEM is framed through self-reported data collected via surveys. These studies explore various domains of students' experiences: from their participation in undergraduate research experiences, to their relationship with faculty. There are other studies that focus on case studies, either single institution programs or programs supported through federal funds.

Note, also, that there were findings that were excluded but are nonetheless worth mentioning. For example, there is evidence of randomized controlled trials exploring the effectiveness of mentoring in undergraduate education. However, these were not focused on STEM and were thus ineligible. Similarly, we noted previous efforts from the National Academies of Sciences, Engineering, and Medicine to examine literature in the field focused on underrepresented minorities (e.g. an assessment of National Institutes of Health Minority research and training programs). However, these were excluded as they were published beyond the 10-year window of time of publication.

Search #2:
Literature Collection Strategy for Research on Minority Serving Institutions and Student Success and Best Practices

A total of 30 articles, reports, journal articles, book chapters, dissertations, and proceedings were identified as relevant for examination in this review of the literature focused on Minority Serving Institutions and student success and best practices. The committee-directed criteria for examination in this review were as follows:

- Manuscript had to be in publication no later than 2006 (and up through 2017) and indexed in either EBSCO, ERIC, Google Scholar, ProQuest Dissertations, Scopus, and/or Web of Science (WOS).
- The substantive focus of the manuscript had to be on specific practices, policies, and/or programs that were focused on supporting students' success.
- Reports that primarily offered an overview of enrollment/completion/ persistence and/or other broad-level aggregate data by racial/ethnic groups were excluded from inclusion.

Search terms:
"Minority Serving Institutions" and "race" and "ethnicity"
"Minority Serving Institutions" and "student success"
"Historically Black Colleges and Universities" or "HBCUs" and "student success"
"Hispanic Serving Institutions" or "HSI" and "student success"
"Tribal Colleges and Universities" or "TCU" and "student success"
"Asian American and Native American Pacific Islander Serving Institutions" or
      "AANAPISIs" and "student success"
"Historically Black Colleges and Universities" or "HBCUs" and best practices
"Hispanic Serving Institutions" or "HSI" and best practices
"Tribal Colleges and Universities" or "TCU" and best practices
"Minority Serving Institutions" and "best practices"
"Asian American and Native American Pacific Islander Serving Institutions" or
      "AANAPISIs" and "student success"
"Minority Serving Institutions" and "RISE" (no results as RISE is not a logged
      search term)
"Historically Black Colleges and Universities" and "RISE (no results as RISE
      is not indexed)

"Hispanic Serving Institutions" and "RISE" no results as RISE is not indexed)

Common Findings in Research Studies Pertaining to MSIs Across the studies, we identified four recurring themes:

- The MSI environment and its link to academic and student success
- The role of MSIs in promoting college completion
- The importance of culturally relevant approaches to learning
- The role of MSIs in promoting developmental education

Overall Assessment of Research Pertaining to MSIs

The committee's standards for inclusion include quasi-experimental design, experimental design, multisite case studies, or rich and deep single-site case studies. The majority of literature on MSIs is focused on understanding the sector and its contributions to higher education. Other areas of exploration are student success, student identity, learning, and developmental education. The majority of MSI research uses a case study methodology and is multisite in nature. A small number of research studies use propensity score matching and is mainly focused on degree attainment.

What are the common or distinct challenges faced by MSI students? What are best practices at the various MSI types?

Regardless of MSI type and the racial and ethnic group of students, similar findings surface across the various studies. These include: the need for students to embrace their full identities, the power of culturally relevant assignments in retention efforts, the importance of collaboration over competition, and the vital nature of peer support and peer-to-peer mentoring.

Search #3:
Literature Collection Strategy for Research on Minority Serving Institutions and STEM

A total of 64 articles, reports, journal articles, book chapters, dissertations, and proceedings were identified as relevant for examination in this review of the literature focused on STEM Education and Minority Serving Institutions. The committee-determined criteria for examination in this review were as follows:

- Manuscript had to be in publication no later than 2006 (and up through 2017) and indexed in either EBSCO, ERIC, Google Scholar, ProQuest Dissertations, Scopus, and/or Web of Science (WOS).

- Minority Serving Institutions overall or by individual sector had to be explicitly identified within the author(s)' discussion. The study did not need to only focus on MSIs for inclusion, as a study could also be comparative in nature.
- The substantive focus of the manuscript had to focus on specific practices, policies, and/or programs that were focused on supporting students' success in STEM fields.
- Reports that primarily offered an overview of enrollment/completion/ persistence and/or other broad-level aggregate data by racial/ethnic groups in STEM were excluded from inclusion.

Search terms:
"Minority Serving Institutions" and "STEM"
"Historically Black Colleges and Universities" or "HBCUs" and "STEM"
"Hispanic Serving Institutions" or "HIS" and "STEM"
"Tribal Colleges and Universities" or "TCU" and "STEM"
"Asian American and Native American Pacific Islander Serving Institutions" or "AANAPISIs" and "STEM"
"RISE" (no results, as RISE is not an indexed term in database)

Common Findings in Research Studies Pertaining to MSIs and STEM:
Across the studies, we identified six recurring themes:

- The importance of sustained and personalized faculty and peer mentoring throughout the undergraduate and graduate experience
- Opportunities to do hands-on and culturally relevant research
- Early recruitment of students and the importance of summer bridge programs
- Opportunities to engage in summer institutes and other STEM-related extracurricular community activities
- More sequenced and comprehensive courses, with special attention to Gateway courses
- Improving career counseling and helping students with the transition to graduate school and into the STEM workforce

Overall Assessment of Research Pertaining to MSIs and STEM

The committee's standards for inclusion include: quasi-experimental design, experimental design, multisite case studies, or rich and deep single-site case studies. Very few studies meet this standard, limiting the research quality and generalizability. The majority of studies are multisite case studies.

What are the common and distinct challenges faced by students in STEM at the various MSI types?

Whereas Hispanic Serving Institutions (HSIs) and Asian American and Native American Pacific Islander Serving Institutions (AANAPISIs) tend to have more developed infrastructure and research facilities, Historically Black Colleges and Universities (HBCUs) and Tribal Colleges and Universities (TCUs) need additional resources in order to attract students and provide opportunities in STEM.

HBCUs and TCUs have more low-income students and more Pell grant-eligible students than HSIs and AANAPISIs; however, all MSI types have more low-income and Pell grant-eligible students than the national average. Due to the large numbers of low-income students at all MSI types, students face common challenges that influence retention and degree attainment.

Students in STEM at TCUs and HSIs face greater resistance from families when they want to move to another state for graduate STEM programs.

Additional Significant Findings Pertaining to MSIs and STEM

These findings surfaced in some of the research studies but were not as prevalent as those mentioned above. In addition, there was little research to support these findings beyond one case study at one MSI.

- The importance of the "welcoming" and communal nature of MSIs, which encourages students to support each other and increases student confidence.
- MSIs should look for "diamonds in the rough" (e.g., students who are not STEM superstars but have strong potential).
- The importance of family support for STEM majors and higher education overall.
- Hiring more minority STEM faculty is essential to student success.
- Students need more opportunities to present their research at conferences.

The following is the bibliography showing results from the commissioned literature review. Search limits were quasi-experimental design, experimental design, multisite case studies, or rich and deep single-site case studies. Additional studies that pertain to URMs and STEM were also considered by the committee but are not listed below.

1. Carpi, A., Ronan, D. M., Falconer, H. M., Boyd, H. H., and Lents, N. H. (2013). Development and implementation of targeted STEM retention strategies at a Hispanic-serving institution. *Journal of Hispanic Higher Education*, *12*(3), 280-299.
2. Carpi, A., Ronan, D. M., Falconer, H. M., and Lents, N. H. (2017). Cultivating minority scientists: Undergraduate research increases self-efficacy and career ambitions for underrepresented students in STEM. *Journal of Research in Science Teaching*, *54*(2), 169-194.

3. Chun, H., Marin, M., Schwartz, J., Pham, A., and S. Castro-Olivo, (2016). Psychosociocultural structural model of college success among Latina/o students in Hispanic-serving Institutions. *Journal of Diversity in Higher Education*, 9(4), 385-400.

4. Conrad, C., and Gasman, M. (2015). *Educating a diverse nation: Lessons from Minority Serving Institutions*. Cambridge, MA: Harvard University Press.

5. Corwin, L. A., Graham, M. J., and Dolan, E. L. (2015). Modeling Course-Based Undergraduate Research Experiences: An Agenda for Future Research and Evaluation. *CBE Life Sciences Education*, 14(1). https://doi.org/10.1187/cbe.14-10-0167

6. Crisp, G., Nora, A., and Taggart, A. (2009). Student characteristics, pre-college, college, and environmental factors as predictors of majoring in and earning a STEM degree: An analysis of students attending a Hispanic serving institution. *American Educational Research Journal*, 46(4), 924-942.

7. Drew, J. C., Galindo-Gonzalez, S., Ardissone, A. N., and Triplett, E. W. (2016). Broadening Participation of Women and Underrepresented Minorities in STEM through a Hybrid Online Transfer Program. *CBE Life Sciences Education*, 15(3). https://doi.org/10.1187/cbe.16-01-0065

8. Eagan, M. K., Hurtado, S., Chang, M. J., García, G. A., Herrera, F. A., and Garibay, J. C. (2013). Making a Difference in Science Education: The Impact of Undergraduate Research Programs. *American Educational Research Journal*, 50(4), 683–713. https://doi.org/10.3102/0002831213482038

9. Flores, S. and Park, T. (2013). Race, ethnicity, and college success: Examining the continued significance of the Minority-Serving Institution. *Educational Researcher*, 42(3), 115-128.

10. Flores, St. and Park, T. (2015). The effect of enrolling in a Minority-Serving Institution for Black and Hispanic students in Texas, *Research in Higher Education*, 56(3), 247-276.

11. Gasman, M. and Nguyen, T. (2016) *HBCUs as Leaders in STEM*. Philadelphia, PA: Penn Center for Minority Serving Institutions.

12. Gasman, M., Nguyen, T. H., Conrad, C. F., Lundberg, T., and Commodore, F. (2017). Black male success in STEM: A case study of Morehouse College. *Journal of Diversity in Higher Education*, 10(2), 181.

13. García, G. and Okhidoi, O. (2015). Culturally relevant practices that "serve" students at a Hispanic Serving Institution, *Innovative Higher Education*, 40(4), 345-357.

14. Gasiewski, J., Eagan, M.K., García, G., Hurtado, S., and M. Chang (2011). From gatekeeping to engagement: A multicontextual mixed method study of student academic engagement in introductory STEM courses. *Research in Higher Education*, 53(2), 229-261.

15. Hubbard, S. M., and Stage, F. K. (2010). Identifying comprehensive public institutions that develop minority scientists. *New Directions for Institutional Research*, 148, 53-62.

16. Hurtado, S., Eagan, M.K., Tran, M., Newman, C., Chang, M., and P. Velasco (2011). "We do science here": Underrepresented students' interactions with faculty in different college contexts. *Journal of Social Issues*, 67(3), 553-579.

17. Kim, M. and Conrad, C. (2006). The impact of Historically Black Colleges and Universities on the academic success of African American students. *Research in Higher Education*, 47(4), 399-427.

18. Nguyen, T. (2015). Exploring Historically Black College and Universities' Ethos of Racial Uplift: STEM Students' Challenges and Institutions' Practices for Cultivating Learning and Persistence in STEM.

19. Parker, T. (2012). *The role of Minority-Serving Institutions in redefining and improving developmental education*. Atlanta, GA: Southern Education Foundation.

20. Perna, L., Lundy-Wagner, V., Drezner, N. D., Gasman, M., Yoon, S., Bose, E., and Gary, S. (2009). The contribution of HBCUs to the preparation of African American women for STEM careers: A case study. *Research in Higher Education*, 50(1), 1-23.

21. Schultz, P. W., Hernandez, P. R., Woodcock, A., Estrada, M., Chance, R. C., Aguilar, M., and Serpe, R. T. (2011). Patching the Pipeline: Reducing Educational Disparities in the Sciences Through Minority Training Programs. *Educational Evaluation and Policy Analysis*, *33*(1). https://doi.org/10.3102/0162373710392371.

22. Slovacek, S., Whittinghill, J., Flenoury, L., and Wiseman, D. (2012). Promoting minority success in the sciences: The minority opportunities in research programs at CSULA. Journal of Research in Science Teaching 49, no. 2 (2012): 199-217.

23. Stassun, K., Burger, A. and Lange, E. (*2010*) The Fisk-Vanderbilt Masters-to-PhD Bridge Program: A model for broadening participation of underrepresented groups in the physical sciences through effective partnerships with Minority-Serving Institutions. *Journal of Geoscience Education*: May 2010, 58(3), 135-144.

24. Teranishi, R., Martin, M., Pazich, L., Alcantar, C., and T. Nguyen, (2014). *Measuring the impact of MSI-funded programs on student success: Findings from the evaluation of Asian American and Native American Pacific Islander-Serving Institutions*. Los Angeles, CA: National Commission on Asian American and Pacific Islander Research in Education.

25. Thao, M., Lawrenz, F., Brakke, M., Sherman, J., and M. Matute, (2016). Insights into implementing research collaborations between research-intensive universities and Minority-Serving Institutions, *Natural Sciences Education*, 45(1), 1-12.

26. Toven-Lindsey, B., Levis-Fitzgerald, M., Barber, P. H., and Hasson, T. (2015). Increasing Persistence in Undergraduate Science Majors: A Model for Institutional Support of Underrepresented Students. *CBE Life Sciences Education*, *14*(2). https://doi.org/10.1187/cbe.14-05-0082.

27. Woodcock, A., Hernandez, P. R., and Schultz, P. W. (2016). Diversifying Science: Intervention Programs Moderate the Effect of Stereotype Threat on Motivation and Career Choice. *Social Psychological and Personality Science*, *7*(2), 184–192. https://doi.org/10.1177/1948550615608401.

Appendix F

Supplemental Data

TABLE F-1 Distributions of Minority Serving Institutions by Sector

	HBCU	TCU	AANAPISI	HSI	PBI	ANNH	NASNTI	Non-MSI
Public Four-Year	40	1	36	78	8	7	9	436
Private Nonprofit Four-Year	41	0	24	86	24	4	2	1,101
Public Two-Year	11	25	54	181	56	14	12	711
Private Nonprofit Two-Year	7	8	6	32	17	3	4	167
Total	**99**	**34**	**120**	**377**	**105**	**28**	**27**	**2,415**

NOTES:

1. Integrated Postsecondary Education Data System (IPEDS) data, collection year 2015, were used to create the list of institutions throughout this report for analysis run by the American Council on Education. Data in this report reflect Title IV participating, degree-granting, public and private, nonprofit, two-year and four-year institutions that offered undergraduate degrees. College Scorecard 2015-2016 data were used to flag institutions that were eligible to apply for federal MSI funding in that given fiscal year through Title III and Title V of the Higher Education Opportunity Act of 2008. Out of 3,129 total institutions, 714 were eligible for MSI designation. Of these institutions, 76 were eligible for more than one MSI designation.

2. Institutions were classified into a sector based on the institutional category variable and control variable in IPEDS. Within institutional category, all institutions categorized as degree-granting, primarily baccalaureate or above institutions were classified as four-year institutions, and all institutions categorized as degree-granting, not primarily baccalaureate or above and degree-granting, associate's and degree-granting, associate's and certificates institutions were classified as two-year institutions. The control variable was used to classify institutions as public or private nonprofit.

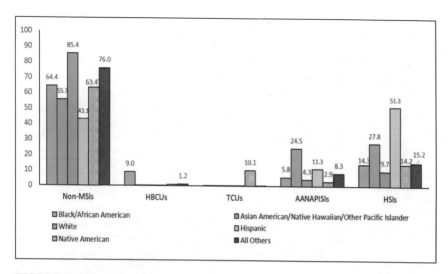

FIGURE F-1 Total share of enrollment by race/ethnicity at MSI types, 2016 data.
SOURCE: IPEDS 2016 Completions and Institutional Characteristics data. Analysis by the American Institutes for Research for this report.
NOTE: IPEDS data, collection year 2015, were used to create the list of institutions throughout this report for analysis run by the American Council on Education. Data in this report reflect Title IV participating, degree-granting, public and private, nonprofit, two-year and four-year institutions that offered undergraduate degrees. College Scorecard 2015-2016 data were used to flag institutions that were eligible to apply for federal MSI funding in that given fiscal year through Title III and Title V of the Higher Education Opportunity Act of 2008. Out of 3,129 total institutions, 714 were eligible for MSI designation. Of these institutions, 76 were eligible for more than one MSI designation.

TABLE F-2 Raw Data Used in Calculations for Figure 3-4

	Total Number of Students Enrolled	Total Number of Students Enrolled in STEM Fields	Total Number of Students Enrolled in Non-STEM Fields
HBCU	81,903	35,751	46,152
AANAPISI	25,0417	121,237	129,180
HSI	475,574	205,917	269,657
Non-MSI	2,980,105	1,191,208	1,788,897

SOURCE: IPEDS 2016 Fall Enrollment and Institutional Characteristics data. Analysis by the American Institutes for Research for this report.

NOTES:

1. IPEDS data, collection year 2015, were used to create the list of institutions throughout this report for analysis run by the American Council on Education. Data in this report reflect Title IV participating, degree-granting, public and private, nonprofit, two-year and four-year institutions that offered undergraduate degrees. College Scorecard 2015-2016 data were used to flag institutions that were eligible to apply for federal MSI funding in that given fiscal year through Title III and Title V of the Higher Education Opportunity Act of 2008. Out of 3,129 total institutions, 714 were eligible for MSI designation. Of these institutions, 76 were eligible for more than one MSI designation.

2. Total completions includes the following credentials: prebaccalaureate certificates, associate degrees, bachelor's degrees, postbaccalaureate certificates, master's degrees, and doctoral degrees.

3. For completions, the racial category "other" is defined as the combination of "nonresident," "race unknown," and "two or more races." Race reporting varies across years in the IPEDS, so information pertaining to Pacific Islanders is not available for all years and would be combined with counts for Asian American students.

4. For the completions data, all Classification of Instructional Programs (CIP) codes were converted to current CIP codes using available crosswalks, before applying the classifications based on the NSF taxonomy. The following CIP code conversion required for some IPEDS data files prior to 2004 was added to the crosswalk to convert 1990s to 2000s CIP codes: 8.0199, 8.0299, 8.0899, 8.1299 to 52.19. For the completions data, counts were collapsed across majornum 1 and 2. Completion degree type codes changed slightly in 2010 and later versions of the data, so slightly different groupings were used. For completions data prior to 2010: "3"=Associate, "5"=Bachelor, "7"=Master, "9"=Doctor, "10"=Doctor, "1"=Pre-BA Certificate, "2"=Pre-BA Certificate, "4"=Pre-BA Certificate, "6"=Post-BA Certificate, "8"=Post-BA Certificate, and "11"=Post-BA Certificate. For completions data from 2010 and later: "3"=Associate, "5"=Bachelor, "7"=Master, "17"=Doctor, "18"=Doctor, "19"=Doctor, "1"=Pre-BA Certificate, "2"=Pre-BA Certificate, "4"=Pre-BA Certificate, "6"=Post-BA Certificate, and "8"=Post-BA Certificate.

5. For all but a few runs, data were not filtered using the First Look Report criteria. The First Look Report uses provisional IPEDS data, and therefore totals may be slightly different from those reported in other federal reports, though these differences will be minor.

TABLE F-3 Raw Data Used in Calculations for Figure 4-7

	Total Number of Completions	Total Number of Completions in STEM Fields	Total Number of Completions in Non-STEM Fields
HBCU	55,922	13,117	42,805
AANAPISI	304,346	90,540	213,806
HSI	724,728	158,721	566,007
Non-MSI	4,008,443	867,663	3,140,780

SOURCE: IPEDS 2016 Fall Enrollment and Institutional Characteristics data. Analysis by the American Institutes for Research for this report.

NOTE:

1. IPEDS data, collection year 2015, were used to create the list of institutions throughout this report for analysis run by the American Council on Education. Data in this report reflect Title IV participating, degree-granting, public and private, nonprofit, two-year and four-year institutions that offered undergraduate degrees. College Scorecard 2015-2016 data were used to flag institutions that were eligible to apply for federal MSI funding in that given fiscal year through Title III and Title V of the Higher Education Opportunity Act of 2008. Out of 3,129 total institutions, 714 were eligible for MSI designation. Of these institutions, 76 were eligible for more than one MSI designation.

2. Total completions includes the following credentials: pre-baccalaureate certificates, associate degrees, bachelor's degrees, post-baccalaureate certificates, master's degrees, and doctoral degrees.

3. For completions, the racial category "other" is defined as the combination of "nonresident," "race unknown," and "two or more races." Race reporting varies across years in the IPEDS, so information pertaining to Pacific Islanders is not available for all years and would be combined with counts for Asian American students.

4. Classification of CIP codes into Science and Engineering categories was based on the fields of study classification found in the National Science Foundation's (NSF's) "Science and Engineering Degrees: 1966–2012," appendix B, with additions made to cover CIP codes found in the IPEDS completions data that were not included in the NSF taxonomy. For the completions data, all CIP codes were converted to current CIP codes using available crosswalks, before applying the classifications based on the NSF taxonomy. The following CIP code conversion required for some IPEDS data files prior to 2004 was added to the crosswalk to convert 1990s to 2000s CIP codes: 8.0199, 8.0299, 8.0899, 8.1299 to 52.19. For the completions data, counts were collapsed across majornum 1 and 2. Completion degree type codes changed slightly in 2010 and later versions of the data, so slightly different groupings were used. For completions data prior to 2010: "3"=Associate, "5"=Bachelor, "7"=Master, "9"=Doctor, "10"=Doctor,"1"=Pre-BA Certificate, "2"=Pre-BA Certificate, "4"=Pre-BA Certificate,"6"=Post-BA Certificate, "8"=Post-BA Certificate, and "11"=Post-BA Certificate. For completions data from 2010 and later: "3"=Associate, "5"=Bachelor, "7"=Master, "17"=Doctor, "18"=Doctor, "19"=Doctor, "1"=Pre-BA Certificate, "2"=Pre-BA Certificate, "4"=Pre-BA Certificate, "6"=Post-BA Certificate, and "8"=Post-BA Certificate.

5. For all but a few runs, data were not filtered using the First Look Report criteria. The First Look Report uses provisional IPEDS data, and therefore totals may be slightly different from those reported in other federal reports, though these differences will be minor.

TABLE F-4 Raw Data Used in Calculations for Figure 4-8

	Total Number of STEM Bachelor's Degrees Earned by African American Students
Non-HBCUs	54,918
HBCUs	8,554

	Total Number of STEM Bachelor's Degrees Earned by Asian American Students
Non-AANAPISIs	66,192
AANAPISIs	12,455

	Total Number of STEM Bachelor's Degrees Earned by Hispanic Students
Non-HSIs	89,733
HSIs	36,368

SOURCE: IPEDS 2016 Completions and Institutional Characteristics data. Analysis by the American Institutes for Research for the current report.

NOTES:

1. IPEDS data, collection year 2015, were used to create the list of institutions throughout this report for analysis run by the American Council on Education. Data in this report reflect Title IV participating, degree-granting, public and private, nonprofit, two-year and four-year institutions that offered undergraduate degrees. College Scorecard 2015-2016 data were used to flag institutions that were eligible to apply for federal MSI funding in that given fiscal year through Title III and Title V of the Higher Education Opportunity Act of 2008. Out of 3,129 total institutions, 714 were eligible for MSI designation. Of these institutions, 76 were eligible for more than one MSI designation.

2. Total completions includes the following credentials: prebaccalaureate certificates, associate degrees, bachelor's degrees, postbaccalaureate certificates, master's degrees, and doctoral degrees.

3. For completions, the racial category "other" is defined as the combination of "nonresident," "race unknown," and "two or more races." Race reporting varies across years in the IPEDS, so information pertaining to Pacific Islanders is not available for all years and would be combined with counts for Asian American students.

4. Classification of CIP codes into Science and Engineering categories was based on the fields of study classification found in the NSF's "Science and Engineering Degrees: 1966–2012," appendix B, with additions made to cover CIP codes found in the IPEDS completions data that were not included in the NSF taxonomy. For the completions data, all CIP codes were converted to current CIP codes using available crosswalks, before applying the classifications based on the NSF taxonomy. The following CIP code conversion required for some IPEDS data files prior to 2004 was added to the crosswalk to convert 1990s to 2000s CIP codes: 8.0199, 8.0299, 8.0899, 8.1299 to 52.19. For the completions data, counts were collapsed across majornum 1 and 2. Completion degree type codes changed slightly in 2010 and later versions of the data, so slightly different groupings were used. For completions data prior to 2010: "3"=Associate, "5"=Bachelor, "7"=Master, "9"=Doctor, "10"=Doctor, "1"=Pre-BA Certificate, "2"=Pre-BA Certificate, "4"=Pre-BA Certificate, "6"=Post-BA Certificate, "8"=Post-BA Certificate, and "11"=Post-BA Certificate. For completions data from 2010 and later: "3"=Associate, "5"=Bachelor, "7"=Master, "17"=Doctor,"18"=Doctor, "19"=Doctor, "1"=Pre-BA Certificate, "2"=Pre-BA Certificate, "4"=Pre-BA Certificate, "6"=Post-BA Certificate, and "8"=Post-BA Certificate.

5. For all but a few runs, data were not filtered using the First Look Report criteria. The First Look Report uses provisional IPEDS data and therefore totals may be slightly different than those reported in other federal reports, though these differences will be minor.